Multimedia Sports Journalism

Multimedia Sports Journalism

A Practitioner's Guide for the Digital Age

EDWARD KIAN
Oklahoma State University

BRADLEY SCHULTZ
University of Mississippi

GALEN CLAVIO
Indiana University

MARY LOU SHEFFER
University of Southern Mississippi

New York   Oxford
OXFORD UNIVERSITY PRESS

Oxford University Press is a department of the University of Oxford. It furthers the University's objective of excellence in research, scholarship, and education by publishing worldwide. Oxford is a registered trade mark of Oxford University Press in the UK and certain other countries.

Published in the United States of America by Oxford University Press
198 Madison Avenue, New York, NY 10016, United States of America.

For titles covered by Section 112 of the US Higher Education Opportunity Act, please visit www.oup.com/us/he for the latest information about pricing and alternate formats.

CIP data is on file at the Library of Congress
ISBN: 978-0-19-063563-3

1 2 3   20 19 18
Printed by LSC Communications, Inc.
Printed in the United States of America

BRIEF CONTENTS

CONTENTS

CHAPTER 11 Sports Show Production   191

PREFACE

Sports media professionals of all types throughout the United States were in shock when industry leader and global conglomerate ESPN laid off around 100 employees over a week in the spring of 2017 (Perez, 2017). The list of those losing their jobs included well-known names representing all types of media, such as SportsCenter television anchors Jade McCarthy and Sara Walsh, television reporter Britt McHenry and talk-show host Jay Crawford. There were well-known former athletes who appeared regularly on ESPN television and radio broadcasts such as Jerome Bettis, Trent Dilfer and Danny Kannell. Also included were sport-specific insiders and top reporters with a print focus for ESPN Internet such as Andy Katz and Dana O'Neil (men's college basketball), Brett McMurphy (college football), Jayson Stark (Major League Baseball), Marc Stein (National Basketball Association), Ed Werder (National Football League) and NBA draft expert Chad Ford (Harris, 2017).

Since its launch in 1979, ESPN had emerged as the industry standard and it was the most-desired workplace for sports journalists of all types due to its dominance in all realms of sports media and television rights deals with almost every major sports league or association in the world. For example, Jemele Hill is now one of ESPN's most prominent talk-show shots and television analysts. But her background was as a sports reporter and later as a columnist in newspapers. She began her tenure with ESPN working more as a columnist for ESPN Internet and reporter for *ESPN The Magazine* before branching out to have her work and expertise appear throughout ESPN's various multimedia platforms (Kian & Zimmerman, 2012). Most of ESPN's better-known reporters with print backgrounds and broadcast talent also regularly crossed over on various platforms, and all were expected to be active and engaged on social media.

However, ESPN's rise was largely attributable to its desirability in cable and satellite television packages. As of 2017, ESPN, which is part of nearly every cable and satellite subscription package in the United States, received $7.21 per subscriber from each subscription, with consumers paying their television provider more than $9 per ESPN channel even if they never watched any of its stations (Gaines, 2017).

The increasing costs of cable and satellite television subscriptions coupled with a lack of à la carte options has led to some viewers — particularly Millennials — to become cord-cutters. Such viewers opt to give up their cable or satellite subscriptions, electing to possibly view television programing through other, cheaper options online and through social media. This has resulted in the ESPN television subscriber base falling from 99 to 88 million in recent years, with future declines expected to become more rapid (Sherman, 2017).

But what did the layoffs mean for the future of a sports media industry that had already experienced rapid change in the digital age? Consumers switched from reading daily newspapers and watching nightly local television newscasts for scores and highlights to being able to consumer 24-7 instant sports content via the Internet and social media, and from a plethora of a sports-only stations and shows on television and radio. In particular, what do the ESPN layoffs mean for aspiring sports media professionals?

"A necessary component of managing change involves constantly evaluating how we best utilize all of our resources, and that sometimes involves difficult decisions," ESPN president John Skipper wrote in a letter to employees in announcing layoffs. "Our content strategy — primarily illustrated in recent months by melding distinct, personality-driven SportsCenter TV editions and digital-only efforts with our biggest sub-brand — still needs to go further, faster . . . and as always, must be efficient and nimble. Dynamic change demands an increased focus on versatility and value, and as a result, we have been engaged in the challenging process of determining the talent — anchors, analysts, reporters, writers and those who handle play-by-play — necessary to meet those demands" (Bonesteel, 2017, ¶ 2).

In sum, ESPN, which has since hired several top sports media pros from other outlets, including NBA reporter extraordinaire Adrian Wojnarowski from Yahoo! Sports, seeks professionals who are versatile, can excel across various media platforms and who can adapt quickly in a constantly changing media landscape. This book focuses on teaching a variety of multimedia skills and on the ability to adapt in preparing for the next generation of sports media and sports communication professionals of all types.

THE BOOK

Multimedia Sports Journalism: A Practitioner's Guide for the Digital Age serves as the first practitioner guide/textbook covering all the major fields encompassing multimedia sports journalism and sports communication in the Internet era, including online sports journalism and the various types of social media most impactful in sports communication. In addition to their recognition as prolific sports journalism researchers, the quartet of authors for this text collectively worked in and continue to do projects professionally in every major realm of sports journalism, providing them with practical experiences, expertise, knowledge and industry contacts. This text focuses on the daily tasks and skills needed to best report, write, discuss, film and produce the major types of sports media content.

This is the first comprehensive, practitioner, skills- and industry-focused sports journalism textbook that accounts for the convergence of media in the Internet era. All of the key fields within the sports journalism profession are featured. More important, the varied skills needed for 21st-century practitioners in this field are highlighted throughout the text.

Areas of sports journalism discussed in detail include: (1) basic sports reporting, (2) television sports broadcasting and reporting, (3) sports radio and podcasting, (4) sports technical and video production, (5) sports show production, (6) sports writing and editing for newspapers, magazines and traditional online sports sites, (7) sports photo journalism, (8) sports public relations and collegiate sports information, and all major forms of both, (9) sports online journalism and (10) sports social media.

Each chapter includes profiles, anecdotes, quotes, tips and photographs from sports journalism industry professionals appropriate for the content discussed within that chapter. Instruction is augmented by "best practices" breakout boxes for producing various types of media content and interviews with top industry professionals in each chapter. Finally, all chapters conclude with a summary, review questions and suggested group activities. A glossary of key terms and sports-specific terminology provides a handy reference for students and young professionals at the end of the text.

Section 1 Introducing Key Topics in Multimedia Sports Journalism

Chapter 1, *Introduction to Multimedia Sports Journalism*, briefly covers the history of sports journalism, focusing largely on how different types of media have converged into the modern digital age now dominated by the Internet and social media. For example, a television broadcaster shoots video that is uploaded to the station's website, along with an accompanying article for the website. Topics such as the financial growth of major sports media companies like ESPN, convergence of different types of sports media in this era of corporate media consolidation, explosion in sports television rights deals and the downsizing of traditional sports journalism jobs to make room for more multimedia and multitaskers are detailed.

Chapter 2, *Ethical, Legal and Minority Issues*, covers several areas of importance, including the introduction of key legal concepts, laws and major court decisions that affect sports journalists and sports communication professionals. Real-life ethical dilemmas faced by sports journalists are broached, along with their decision-making processes and options. Foci are placed on the ethical challenges of 21st-century sports media convergence that the Internet and social media bring to sports journalism, particularly in crises communication coverage and responses. The history, statistical representation, social challenges, networking through professional organizations and career opportunities for minority groups and women in sports journalism are examined and merged with ethical concepts.

Chapter 3, *Preparing for Careers in Multimedia Sports Journalism*, focuses on the place and growth of sports journalism/communication/media in academia, and how students can best garner practical experiences/internships. It discusses professional sports journalism organizations and explains résumé preparation (with example CVs included along with tips for designing and adding content to individual online portfolios). It explains how to look for and apply for full-time jobs (with example cover letters) and provides tactics when actually interviewing for positions. Intertwined with these topics will be a discussion of what to expect in the future of sports journalism convergence in the digital age and how aspiring sports journalism professionals can best adapt to future changes. This focuses primarily on emergent technologies and audience adaptation.

Section 2 Practical Skills for Careers in Multimedia Sports Journalism

Chapter 4, *Basics of Sports Reporting*, is the first of the practitioner-based chapters. It focuses on the basics of reporting, storylines, interviews, using quotes and citing sources that should be followed regardless of the media type or specific outlet where a sports journalist works. Tips for keeping basic statistics for a variety of sporting contests are included and the rising popularity of advanced sports analytics is introduced. The need for impartiality and objectivity in all forms of sports communications (including in-house media relations and public relations departments for professional teams and university athletics departments) is emphasized throughout, so that students learn they cannot be fans who show bias covering games regardless of which area of media they work. The advantages and challenges of using social media for sports reporting in the digital age are also analyzed.

Chapter 5, *Sports Writing for Newspapers, Websites and Magazines*, is another practitioner-based chapter that introduces sports AP-style guidelines and instructs how to write various types of sports articles (e.g., game stories, features, notebooks, advances, columns, enterprise reporting, longform journalism). It also covers such basics as rules/tenets of sports writing, developing creative leads for articles, the inverted pyramid and tips for writing on deadline. Best practices are broached to address the challenges of writing in the Internet era for a newspaper published the next day or a magazine the next week, as well as writing blogs and separate, live content for the same print publication's website.

Chapter 6, *Social Media and Sports Journalism*, evaluates the manner in which journalists, teams and fans utilize social media to engage in the sports communication process. This chapter begins with an overview of major types of modern sports social media (e.g., Facebook, Twitter, Instagram, Snapchat) and also provides an overview of interactive content delivery platforms such as blogs and YouTube. The heart of the chapter provides a how-to guide and best practices for using these major social media avenues in multimedia sports journalism, including message construction, distribution and maximizing the effectiveness of each social medium by considering its inherent technological strengths and weaknesses. It concludes with an evaluation of the impact of the social media community on the journalism process and the roles that sports journalists of all types can play within a technologically mediated social environment such as Twitter or Facebook.

Chapter 7, *Sports Public Relations and Sports Information*, provides brief overviews of sports public relations and collegiate sports information, but focuses more on skills needed in the sports public relations profession, such as how to write a press release, communicative skills needed in interacting with media, key organizational stakeholders, and communicating directly to the public as well as strategies for responses in crises communication scenarios in a digital era dominated by social media. This chapter ties into the previous two in mentioning that most sports PR pros/SIDs started as sports journalists from traditional media and that the style and types of writing for sports PR/SID is 90 percent similar to newspaper sports writing. Increasingly though, more professional and collegiate media relations/sports information departments are producing more of their own multimedia content, which can then be distributed directly unfiltered to target audiences through their official team websites and social media platforms, a trend emphasized throughout the chapter.

Chapter 8, *Television Sports Broadcasting*, is a practitioner-based chapter that examines two important areas of the sportscasting world. The first part of this chapter looks at sports radio and focuses on best practices for broadcast preparation, play-by-play and color commentary on games, hosting sports talk call-in shows and interacting with journalists, athletes and other guests on-air. Part two focuses on online sportscasting. This section provides an evaluation of the similarities, differences and transition points between traditional radio sportscasts, online podcasts and online live sportscasts, with particular attention paid to the influences of technology and its impact on the sportscasting process. It also delves into emerging broadcast and narrowcast technologies in the online sportscasting spectrum, including YouTube and Google live broadcasts, the Periscope and Meerkat applications, and short-loop applications such as Vine and Instagram. Included are descriptions of technical setup and best practices for producing high-quality and dynamic online media.

Chapter 9, *Sports Radio and Online Sportscasting*, begins with a brief overview of broadcasting and its importance in the sports media landscape, especially in terms of economics and technology. It then shifts to practical strategies for specific roles within television sports broadcasting. The anchor is discussed in terms of writing ability, performance, audience interaction (e.g., social media) and personal branding. The reporter section describes the process of creating packages and walks the reader through from story creation to final product. The role of the play-by-play person is thoroughly explained, including the role of preparation, the duties before and during games, and the contrast between television and radio. The role of sideline reporting is discussed, including the current debate over sexual objectification and pandering. The chapter concludes with strategies for student success in these areas, emphasizing the value and need for internships, work in student media and industry networking.

Chapter 10, *Sports Video Production and Sports Photo Journalism*, focuses on video production for televised and/or live-streamed sporting events, including descriptions of the equipment, key positions and duties of personnel needed to produce a live sporting event. This tech-focused chapter includes tips on using video-editing software (e.g., Final Cut Pro, Avid). It also discusses best practices for shooting photography for various sports, shooting portrait shots and taking photographs and shooting video with a smart phone or other mobile device. Moreover, using photo-based social media apps such as Instagram are introduced.

Chapter 11, *Sports Show Production*, delves deeply into preparation for producing sports shows, with a focus on doing so for television. Much of this chapter is applicable to both television and radio show production, with major differences between the two media pointed out. Examples of run-down sheets and script writing are included.

REFERENCES

Bonesteel, M. (2017, April 26). ESPN's massive round of layoffs hit familiar faces, including Marc Stein, Andrew Brandt and Adam Caplan. *The Washington Post* online. Retrieved from https://www.washingtonpost.com/news/early-lead/wp/2017/04/26/espn-announces-layoffs-with-100-people-reportedly-affected/?utm_term=.a35ce44cbc8e

Gaines, C. (2017, March 7). Cable and satellite TV customers pay more than $9 per month for ESPN networks whether they watch it or not. *Business Insider*. Retrieved from http://www.businessinsider.com/cable-satellite-tv-sub-fees-espn-networks-2017-3

Harris, S. J. (2017, May 31). ESPN layoffs. Updated list of biggest names laid off. *Sporting News* online. Retrieved from http://www.sportingnews.com/other-sports/news/list-of-biggest-names-laid-off-at-espn-updates-ed-werder-john-buccigross/eyf1kwjj6gpt10erj8ke3n1tp

Kian, E. M., & Zimmerman, M. H. (2012). The medium of the future: Top sports writers discuss transitioning from newspapers to online journalism. *International Journal of Sport Communication, 5*, 285–304.

Sherman, E. (2017, April 27). The inside story of ESPN's layoffs–and where it goes from here. *Poynter*. Retrieved from http://www.poynter.org/2017/the-inside-story-of-espns-layoffs-and-where-it-goes-from-here/457630/

AUTHOR BIOS

Edward (Ted) M. Kian, Ph.D.

Edward (Ted) M. Kian, Ph.D., is Professor and the Welch-Bridgewater Endowed Chair of Sports Media in the School of Media and Strategic Communications at Oklahoma State University. Dr. Kian earned an undergraduate degree in journalism from the University of Georgia, a master's in sport management from the University of Texas at Austin and a Ph.D. in sport administration from Florida State University. Previously he was on the faculty at the University of Central Florida, where he was founding coordinator of the Sport Leadership & Coaching graduate program and held the rank of tenured Associate Professor of Sport Administration. Dr. Kian's research focuses on sport media, specifically examining portrayals of gender and LGBTQ in content, social media and Web 2.0, attitudes and experiences of sport media members and marketing of sport. He has authored more than 90 journal articles, conference papers, books and book chapters, with his work appearing in top journals from a variety of academic disciplines, such as *International Journal of Sport Communication, International Review for the Sociology of Sport, Journal of Applied Sport Management, Journal of Broadcasting & Electronic Media, Journal of Homosexuality, Journal of Sports Media, Public Relations Review, Sociology of Sport Journal* and *Women in Sport and Physical Activity Journal*. Dr. Kian is a coauthor for the popular overview textbook *Strategic Sport Communication* (2016). He has reviewed more than 100 submissions for 29 different academic journals as an editorial board member or ad-hoc reviewer. Outlets such as "60 Minutes," *The New York Times, USA Today*, Fox Sports and the Nieman Journalism Lab at Harvard University have cited his research, journalism or expertise. Dr. Kian has 15 years of professional experience in sport communications, working in newspapers, magazines, media relations, Internet sites and radio, while authoring more than 2,000 popular-press articles. His positions included three years as a sportswriter and editor for the Los Angeles Newspapers Group, where he was among a team of Long Beach *Press-Telegram* reporters honored with an Associated Press Sports Editors national award for investigative journalism. He also worked full time for Gannett as a sportswriter for the *Pensacola News Journal*, served as editor and website manager for *Horns Illustrated* magazine, and was among the original contracted bloggers for AOL FanHouse.

Brad Schultz, Ph.D.

Brad Schultz, Ph.D., is a former professor of journalism in the School of Journalism & New Media at the University of Mississippi. He has spent more than 30 years in the practice and study of sports journalism, beginning with his work as a sports anchor, producer, reporter, writer and editor for commercial television. His research interests focus on how new technologies impact sports journalism, and he has authored or coauthored more than four dozen journal articles and conference presentations. Dr. Schultz has written or edited 10 books, most of them dealing with sports or broadcasting. He is the creator and founding editor of *The Journal of Sports Media*, a scholarly journal that publishes sports research. Dr. Schultz is also an active documentarian, having produced several sports-related programs that have appeared on public television. One of those won a national Aurora Award in 2011 for Best Sports Documentary. His other awards and honors include Best Sports Reporting from the Associated Press in both Texas and Oklahoma, and Best Newscast from the Cleveland Press Club. Dr. Schultz left academia in 2017 and is currently the pastor at Zion United Church of Christ in Shelbyville, Indiana.

Galen Clavio, Ph.D.

Galen Clavio, Ph.D., is an associate professor of sports communication in the Media School at Indiana University, and also serves as the director of the National Sports Journalism Center. Clavio has been at Indiana University since 2009, and previously worked in the Sport Management and Communication program in the School of Public Health. Prior to joining Indiana University, Clavio served as an assistant professor at the University of Miami. Dr. Clavio's research focuses on social media and its applications in sport, including the ways in which social media affects and moderates communication among and between sport organizations, sport media, and sport consumers. He has authored over 40 peer-reviewed journal articles, including works that have been published in such leading journals as *Communication and Sport*, the *International Journal of Sport Communication*, the *Journal of Sports Media*, the *Journal of Sport Management*, and *Sport Marketing Quarterly*. He has also made more than 60 presentations at national and international conferences, and has authored or coauthored several book chapters. He has served as an invited moderator for panels at the Sloan Sports Analytics Conference at MIT and the Sport Marketing Association yearly conference. Clavio has been cited or interviewed by a variety of major media outlets, including *The New York Times*, *The Chicago Tribune*, *USA Today*, the *International Business Times*, *The Sporting News*, CBS and Gizmodo. Clavio has created several applied courses for sports communication students, including classes focusing on sportscasting and play-by-play, blogging and social media, and applied social media techniques in sports media. Prior to entering academia, he served as a play-by-play broadcaster, a media relations director and sports director in the sports media industry, and continues to work as a podcaster and freelance sportscaster. Clavio earned his undergraduate degree in sport communication from Indiana University, a master's in athletic administration and sport management from Indiana University and a Ph.D. in sport management from Indiana University.

Mary Lou Sheffer, Ph.D.

Mary Lou Sheffer, Ph.D., joined the University of Southern Mississippi broadcast journalism faculty in 2008 and is the broadcast journalism sequence head. She holds a Ph.D. in mass communication and public policy from Louisiana State University, a Master's in telecommunication and a B.A. in radio/television, both from Southern Illinois University. Her research areas include sports media, media management and the influence of new technologies (especially social media) on established news mediums. She has published numerous book chapters and 24 top-tier, peer-reviewed journals outlets such as *The Sports Journal*, *Journal of Sports Media*, *Journal of Communication Studies*, *Newspaper Research Journal*, *Electronic News*, *Journal of Computer Mediated Communication*, *The International Journal of Media Management* and *Berkshire Encyclopedia of World Sport*. She has won numerous research awards through AEJMC, and is recognized as a preeminent scholar in sports and social media. Dr. Sheffer is an active member of AEJMC's Sports Interest Division and has served twice as its research chair and PF&R chair. She served on numerous conference panels and presented over 40 conference papers. Currently, Dr. Sheffer is the editor of the *Journal of Sports Media* and the coeditor of *Sports and Religion in the 21st Century* (Rowan & Littlefield, 2015). Dr. Sheffer has over 10 years professional experience in broadcasting that includes positions such as one-man-band, news/sports videographer, director (for newscast, sports shows, telethons and special events), mulitmedia journalist and PSA director. Dr. Sheffer is also a documentary videographer for several award-winning programs that aired on PBS. Most recently, she produced, shot and edited a half-hour documentary titled "WYD: A Pilgrimage of Mercy," which covered the Catholic Church's World Youth Day in Krakow, Poland. She is a native of Chicago, Illinois, and therefore an avid Cubs fan.

ACKNOWLEDGMENTS

The authorship team of Ted, Brad, Galen and Mary Lou express appreciation to the entire team at Oxford University Press, who have been affable, professional, insightful, helpful and understanding throughout this process. In particular, we are forever indebted to former Oxford assistant editor Paul Longo, who recruited us and was instrumental in the launch of this project; acquisitions editor Toni Magyar; and editorial assistant Alyssa Quinones. This book would not have been published without each of their amazing efforts.

We are also thankful to the dozens of external reviewers for their comments, critiques and suggestions from our initial proposal through feedback for each submitted chapter:

Travis R. Bell
University of South Florida
Linda Thorsen Bond, Ph.D.
Stephen F. Austin State University
Tommy Booras
Tennessee State University
Greg Bowers
University of Missouri
Michael D. Bruce
University of Alabama
Rick Brunson
University of Central Florida
John Carvalho
Auburn University
Robert Coloney
Sacred Heart University
Rory Faust
Northern Arizona University
David Grannis
California Lutheran University
Brendan O'Hallarn
Old Dominion University
Cailin Brown Leary
The College of Saint Rose
Mark Lodato
Arizona State University
Larry Londino
Montclair State University

Michael Martinez
University of Tennessee
Vicki Michaelis
University of Georgia
Anthony Moretti
Robert Morris University
Brianna Newland
University of Delaware
Maxey Parrish
Baylor University
Kimi Puntillo
St. John's University
Kevin Robbins
University of Texas at Austin
Amy F. Roquemore
Stephen F. Austen State University
Matthew S. Ruckman
University of West Florida
Ed Sherman
DePaul University
John Spinda
Clemson University
Andrew Stem
Valparaiso University
David Welch Suggs Jr., Ph.D.
University of Georgia

This book is practitioner-oriented, in part thanks to insight and knowledge from many sports media professionals representing all realms of the industry. This is so evident by their quotes and profiles throughout the text.

Thanks also goes out to our colleagues and administrators at our respective schools/departments and universities — the School of Media and Strategic Communications at Oklahoma State University, the School of Journalism & New Media at the University of Mississippi, the Media School at Indiana University and the School of Journalism and Mass Communication at the University of Southern Mississippi — who provided us with the time and structure to complete this project.

Finally, the following family members and individuals deserve special praise for their emotional support, time sacrifices, understanding and constant encouragement throughout this process: Dr. Kian wishes to thank Martie Kian, David Kian, Christy Kian, Hayden Kian and especially the late Dr. Mo Kian, who passed away during this project; Dr. Schultz is grateful for 15 years with the University of Mississippi, and thanks Dean Will Norton and Assistant Dean Charlie Mitchell for their help, support and advice over the years. He also gives thanks to his wife Darlene for her support as they start this new chapter in their lives. Dr. Clavio wishes to thank Laura Clavio, Katie Clavio and Eris Clavio; Dr. Sheffer wishes to thank the entire Sheffer family, Chuck Cook, Tim Finnigan, Jeff Haeger, Patrick Hartney, Charlotte McLoughlin and Tanner Watson.

CHAPTER 1

Introduction to Multimedia Sports Journalism

Photo 1.1 Michael Peters serves as sports editor of the *Tulsa World*, where he oversees a multimedia operation much different than the small Texas papers where he began his career. Photo courtesy of Michael Peters

Michael Peters remembers Fridays fondly from his first full-time job as a sports writer for the Bryan-College Station *Eagle* newspaper, a position he began shortly after graduating from Texas A&M in 1993. Following a hard week of tasks such as churning out articles each day, answering phones, compiling statistics, copy editing and helping with page layout, Fridays were essentially a laid-back reward for Peters and many of the other sports writers covering high school football in Texas. In fact, Peters would occasionally sleep in on Friday morning and often enjoyed a round of golf before cruising up to the high school football game he was slated to cover an hour or so before kickoff.

During the game, he would record and tally individual and team statistics by hand, and also keep a running play-by-play of what transpired on the field. After

Photo 1.2 Michael Peters, sports editor for the *Tulsa World*, speaks to a group of students at the Associated Press Sports Editors (APSE) 2016 Great Plains Regional meeting.
Photo courtesy of Michael Peters

the game, he would interview coaches and players, making sure to jot down the best quotes on his notepad. Then he would leave the stadium and return to the office to write his game story that would appear in the Saturday edition of the *Eagle*, often sticking around for another hour or so to help out in other areas, such as writing round-ups from other sports events and taking phone calls for scores and statistics. "High school football Friday nights were so much fun," Peters said. "It was the day of the week you only had one thing to focus on—the game you were covering."

Peters is now the sports editor at the *Tulsa World*, but times have changed. The reporters who cover preps under Peters's direction in high school football-crazed Oklahoma do not consider fall Fridays to be laid-back in this digitalized and multimedia age in which sports media professionals now work.

In contrast to the Fridays Peters once enjoyed, a typical game day for a high school sports reporter at the *Tulsa World* and many other major news outlets *now* generally entails:

- Writing an afternoon blog, feature and/or separate game preview for the online site of the newspaper, which is in addition to what the reporter wrote on Thursday that appeared in Friday's newspaper edition.
- Posting stats, nuggets, comments, updates (injuries, etc.) and predictions for Friday night games throughout the day on social media (e.g., Twitter, Facebook, etc.) to build interest, and possibly appearing on a local radio station and/or television partner before or during the game.

- Arriving even earlier to high school games, as reporters are often expected to write a pregame blog for the media outlet's website (e.g., injury updates), and maybe shoot video and/or take photos to be uploaded to the same site.
- Keeping individual stats and a running play-by-play during the game, just like Peters did. However, they are also expected to post on social media throughout each game, sometimes write blog posts at halftime or even at the end of every quarter, and possibly shoot video or photos during the game, too.
- Filing a game story (without quotes) for the website and possibly for the first (extended) edition of the newspaper, almost all of which now have much earlier deadlines than when Peters started in the business.
- Going down to the field or locker rooms to get quotes from players and coaches for game stories, postgame blogs and follow-up stories, just as they did in the past. But instead of just writing down quotes or using a cassette recorder, reporters now often use their phones to video-record these interviews, which are often uploaded to the paper's website.
- Shooting video reports from the games they covered, doing stand-ups on camera, and, increasingly, cutting up video to create highlight reels. These are duties more newspaper reporters are being asked to do more frequently. Podcasts are also often expected.

This equates to a lot of work for modern-era newspaper sports writers covering high school football, often starting early Friday afternoon and going past midnight, all the time constantly producing media content. The amount of multimedia content expected of sports journalists only increases as their beat responsibilities become more high profile and competitive in nature, such as covering a major-college athletics or a pro sports team (Pedersen, Laucella, Kian, & Geurin, 2016).

Additionally, the ability to produce multimedia content in a variety of forms has also become the norm for those working in all types of sports media, including television, radio, and team and league media relations (i.e., public relations) departments. The latter are increasingly producing more of their own media content in an attempt to bypass traditional media and instead to disseminate content directly to consumers (Stoldt, Noble, Ross, Richardson, & Bonsall, 2013). In the digital era, there are very few jobs in sports media that focus on just one medium and almost none of those jobs are entry-level positions. "Today, the emphasis is on multimedia reporting, or producing different versions of the same story for print, broadcast and the Web" (Schultz & Arke, 2015, p. 9).

Note: In this text, the terms sports media, sports journalism and sports communication will often be used interchangeably to describe this field. Regardless of terms used to describe it, the sports media profession today is very competitive. Versatility in multimedia skills and the ability to adapt to changing technologies are now skills that are necessary for someone entering and advancing in the field in this era of media convergence dominated by the Internet and social media (Kian & Murray, 2014).

Photo 1.3 ESPN's Jemele Hill emphasizes the importance of multimedia skills when she speaks to students, such as this group of Oklahoma State University Sports Media majors. Photo courtesy of Courtney Bey

"You either learn new skills and embrace the new technologies that develop or unfortunately you probably lose your job in this field," said Jemele Hill, a former newspaper reporter turned newspaper and online columnist, who now co-hosts the popular ESPN television talk show "His and Hers." "The technologies change, but the basics of reporting and telling a story still remain the same" (personal communication, 2016).

Sadly, many of the print reporters who failed to enhance their multimedia skills lost their jobs over the past two decades as the traditional newspaper industry lost readership due to the advent of the Internet and social media (Butler, Zimmerman, & Hutton, 2013). However, some traditional print reporters became more valuable to their companies and/or more marketable (e.g., many jumped to work for online sites in higher-paying jobs) because they increased their notoriety and the readership of their content through social media (Kian & Zimmerman, 2012).

"As fans increasingly rely on new media, you'll notice the best Web sites and the blogs where the reporting is the best are locations that offer new information, terrific stories and unique perspectives—not unlike the best sports sections," wrote veteran newspaper sports writer and current college professor Joe Gisondi. "The technical skills may change but the journalism approaches do not" (2011, p. 6).

That is why the authors of this book—all of whom worked in a variety of jobs encompassing nearly the entire field of sports media, and all of whom now both teach and research sports media for top universities—recognize the importance of combining our knowledge, experiences and extensive list of industry contacts to write the first true multimedia practitioner book for aspiring sports media professionals in the digital age. However, students must garner practical experience beyond the classroom if they are to gain entry into the sports media profession.

"We don't have a business where you dip your toe in, you have to jump in," Jemele Hill said. "You have to try things that make you uncomfortable to develop your skills to make it in the media world" (personal communication, 2016).

CONVERGENCE OF SPORTS MEDIA IN THE DIGITAL AGE

Mass media convergence carries two separate meanings, the first of which is the primary basis for this textbook. First, from a skills standpoint, *convergence* means the mixing of multimedia content produced and disseminated by sports media professionals and outlets. Discussing the trends in this area and teaching those skills are the primary foci of this book. As an example, television sports reporters are now generally expected to write stories and blogs for the station's website, and help promote the station and events they cover on social media. Similarly, more major U.S. newspapers are building in-house television studios and production facilities just to develop video content for their websites, while their reporters in the field are often being asked to shoot and edit mobile video (McGuire & Murray, 2013).

Second, *convergence* is also used to describe the trend toward corporate consolidation of mass media outlets and partnerships that have resulted in fewer traditional sports media jobs in magazines, newspapers, radio and television. This consolidation also often requires sports journalists to produce different types of content that overlap into other media (Pedersen, 2014). Major media corporations are now permitted to own a radio station and a newspaper in the same city, and management expects the same sports reporters to produce content for both outlets from a particular game or event. Why pay for two reporters to cover a game when you can send one and expect that one person to produce content for multiple outlets?

By 2012, more than 90 percent of the traditional three main types of media outlets (e.g., newspapers, radio, television) in the United States were collectively owned by just six corporations, which was a drop from the more than 50 media companies that owned the top 90 percent of media outlets in 1983 (Lutz, 2012). Corporate consolidation has also resulted in fewer beat reporters from traditional media outlets (especially newspapers) covering major beats. For example, the Southern California Newspaper Group (SCNG) now operates 11 daily newspapers and websites, including the *Orange County Register*, *Los Angeles Daily News*, Long Beach *Press-Telegram* and *The* Riverside *Press-Enterprise*.

When owned independently, all of those newspapers had individual beat writers covering top professional and major college sports teams in Southern California. Now, the SCNG generally shares one beat reporter with a primary responsibility of providing coverage of a major college athletics program (e.g., UCLA, USC) or professional sports team (e.g., Los Angeles Lakers and Clippers of the NBA, Anaheim Ducks and Los Angeles Kings of the NHL, etc.) for all 11 newspapers in the group and their websites.

ESPN: The King of Convergence

Multiple convergence media skills are required of many employees of the sports media international conglomerate ESPN, commonly dubbed the "Worldwide

Leader in Sports." ESPN is best known for its rights deals with almost every major sports league or association that enables its networks to televise marquee, live sporting events. ESPN's roster of live broadcasts includes regular season and play-off games from the three most popular American professional men's team sports leagues (MLB, NBA and NFL), games from every major conference in major college football and men's basketball, and nontraditional sports and events, such as the X Games, which ESPN introduced to the world.

ESPN was launched in 1979 when cable television was not yet commonplace in U.S. households and when the idea of a sports-only television network was unimaginable to most media experts. However, ESPN largely built its brand around the most popular news and highlight show ever produced, "SportsCenter." "When Bill Rasmussen, with an investment from Getty Oil, launched ESPN, it was built around a few studio shows and an awful lot of Australian Rules Football. It was the emergence of SportsCenter as a pop-cultural force in the early '90s. . . that put ESPN on the map. Although live sporting events garner ESPN's largest audiences, the culture of ESPN is still best embodied in its SportsCenter franchise" (Greenfield, 2012, ¶ 7).

However, ESPN could not rely on just "SportsCenter" and live sporting events to fill the many time slots on its expanding number of networks. ESPN television programming now includes investigative reporting shows like "Outside the Lines" and "E:60"; popular daytime sports-talk shows like "Mike & Mike," "Pardon the Interruption," and "First Take"; and sport-specific shows such as "Baseball Tonight, College GameDay" for college football and basketball, and "NFL Insiders." Programming that entails nearly all sports of interest across the globe played at all levels from Little League Baseball to pro sports are broadcast in more than 200 countries by the 26 ESPN television networks, a list that includes ESPN, ESPN2, EPSNEWS, ESPN Deportes and the SEC Network.

ESPN has fully embraced media convergence through multiple forms of electronic and digital media, including ESPN Radio, ESPN Broadband, ESPN Wireless and ESPN Video-On-Demand. ESPN Internet regularly has the most unique visitors and page views than any other sport-focused website and the ESPN app is by far the most downloaded app for sports content (Fisher, 2015). ESPN also publishes one of the two leading U.S. sport magazines, "ESPN The Magazine." "When you work at ESPN, you are expected to contribute through multiple platforms," said Mark Schlabach, a senior investigative reporter and columnist, who largely focuses on college sports (personal communication, 2015). Schlabach, who previously worked as a sports writer for *The Washington Post* and *The Atlanta Journal-Constitution*, primarily writes for ESPN Internet and "ESPN The Magazine," but also is a regular on a variety of ESPN television and radio programming, particularly television shows "Outside the Lines," "The Experts" (college football) and "SportsCenter."

ESPN's embrace of media convergence, new technologies and innovative ideas was best exemplified by the impact of Bill Simmons on ESPN, as Simmons emerged as arguably the most influential person thus far in the 21st-century sports media due to avenues provided by ESPN. Simmons's rise and impact symbolizes the need to develop multimedia skills and embrace new types of media quickly. Simmons, who departed ESPN in 2015 after repeated disputes with ESPN management and now hosts a television shown on HBO, founded the sports and pop-culture ESPN blog, Grantland. He was largely responsible for introducing and making podcasts popular in sports media. The B.S. Report podcast he hosted regularly on ESPN Internet was downloaded more than 10 million times in just the first six months of 2009 (Ourand, 2009). Simmons also was executive producer of ESPN Films' popular and award-winning series "30 for 30," which has been the primary impetus for the boom of popular sport documentaries now dominating cable television on networks like HBO and Showtime.

Many sports professors appreciate the "30 for 30" series for telling the stories of major past events in sports. Many of the students reading this book now know much more about past sport stories because they were featured in the "30 for 30" series. Such stories include the SMU college football recruiting scandals of the 1980s ("Pony Expresses"), the cultural influence of the University of Michigan men's basketball team of the 1990s ("The Fab Five"), and Tonya Harding's involvement in the Nancy Kerrigan attack ("The Price of Gold"). That attack led to a media maelstrom and was the reason why the 1994 Winter Olympics figure skating competition remain the most watched women's sporting event in U.S. television history.

Television and Multimedia Rights Deals Still Dominate Sports Media in the Digital Age

In this digital era, sports fans can go online to watch live-stream sports events, video highlights and sports news shows from across the world at any time. They can go online to listen to numerous sports-talk and all-sports radio stations from around the world, download podcasts on every sport or major athlete of interest, and read all types of content specifically on their favorite sport, sports league, team or athletes through a variety of online and print sources. Finally, sports fans can now follow and maybe even interact with their favorite athletes, teams, other sports fans and even sports media members on social media, all while living out fantasies as faux sports team general managers and coaches through fantasy sports and video games.

Because there is an endless array of multimedia content available at all times, the influence and popularity of live and cable television is dwindling in the digital age. Few people watch their favorite television shows at the time they are initially shown. People record the season series on a DVR and watch at their own leisure— often fast-forwarding through any commercials in the process, or they may watch multiple episodes of the same show through Netflix, Hulu or another streaming service. In reality, unless you are a sports fan or (to a lesser extent) a television news junkie, there is little reason to watch live television in the digital age. Increasingly more Americans are canceling (or "cord-cutting") their cable or satellite television subscriptions, opting to instead use viewing options through the Internet. In an even scarier trend for the cable and satellite television industries, younger adults are increasingly not even initially subscribing to their services (Heisler, 2015).

However, most sports fans want to watch their teams live on television, often in groups alongside friends and family with similar interests. According to ESPN sports business reporter Darren Rovell, 99 percent of ESPN television programming is consumed live. "While most other forms of television are commonly watched on demand or DVR'd, allowing viewers to fast forward through commercials, sports programming is one of the few sectors remaining in which watching live is crucial for most audiences," Rovell wrote (2014, ¶ 6). Moreover, these sports fans are also often online and on social media as they watch the game, discussing the game they are simultaneously watching on television. Research by Nielsen found that more than 50 percent of all television-related tweets in the United States involved sports in 2013 (Nielsen Research, 2014). The phenomenon of watching a live sporting event on television while also using a mobile device or computer to follow or discuss the same game is called "second screen usage," and it is becoming increasingly popular among sports fans.

As a result of these trends, advertisers wanting to reach television viewers are increasingly focusing on sports to find live-television viewers who can still be exposed to commercials. In turn, television rights deals for major sports properties have exploded in recent years. Television "networks are finding the appetite for televised live offerings to be seemingly insatiable" when it comes to sports (Billings, Butterworth & Turman, 2015, p. 53). The money involved in some of these recent deals is staggering. For example, the NCAA opened itself up to criticism in 2010 after opting out of an 11-year, $6 billion deal with CBS to televise March Madness (the three-week, Division I men's basketball tournament). However, the NCAA was able to quickly renegotiate with CBS and Time Warner on a deal worth $10.8 billion for 14 years that also included exclusive wireless rights for CBS and Turner Broadcasting System. In April 2016, shortly after a captivating tournament culminated by Villanova beating North Carolina in the national final on a last-second 3-pointer, that deal was extended for eight more years (through 2032) for another $8.8B paid by CBS and Time Warner.

"The new pact is a big bet that sports will continue to hold value at a time when changing viewing patterns and emerging platforms are straining the traditional television networks and pay-TV businesses," sports media reporter Joe Flint (2016, ¶ 4) wrote in *The Wall Street Journal*. "CBS Sports Chairman Sean McManus said regardless of how people are getting content in the years ahead, the deal will be a success. 'Whatever new platforms develop, we have all of those rights. If people are watching on a skinny bundle, a phone or Apple TV, we have the ability to exploit all of those rights going forward.' "

The NBA renegotiated television deals in 2014 with ESPN and Turner for a total of $2.66B annually, marking a 186 percent increase from the NBA's previous contracts with those same two television partners. As part of the deal, the NBA granted ESPN enhanced digital rights for its online platforms and apps (Berr, 2014).

The most recent national television deals for America's three most popular professional men's team sports are shown in Table 1.1. The NFL dominates U.S. television ratings (sport or nonsport), with Super Bowls accounting for 25 of the 26 most-watched television events in U.S. history through 2017 (Smith, 2015). These contracts are indicative of the major television sports deals now common for all popular professional and collegiate sports.

All of these national contracts are shared equally by teams in the three major professional sports leagues. However, MLB teams also individually negotiate

TABLE 1.1   U.S. Television Rights Deals for "Big 3" American Professional Men's Team Sports

League	Television Networks	Contract Specifics	Average Per Year
Major League Baseball (MLB)	ESPN	8 years (2014–21) for $5.6B	$700 Million
	Fox	8 years (201–21) for $4B	$500 Million
	Turner	8 years (2014–21) for $2.8B	
National Basketball Association (NBA)	ESPN/ABC	9 seasons (2016–17 through 2024–25) for $12.6B	$1.4 Billion
	Turner	9 seasons (2016–17 through 2024–25) for $10.8B	$1.2 Billion
National Football League (NFL	CBS	9 years (2014–22) for $9.72B	$1.08 Billion
	CBS	2 years (2016–17) for $900M for half of Thursday games, which will also be shown at same time on NFL network	$450 Million
	DirectTV	8 years (2015–22) for $12B	$1.5 Billion
	ESPN	8 years (2014–21) for $15.2B	$1.9 Billion
	Fox	9 years (2014–22) for $10.35B	$1.15 Billion
	NBC	9 years (2014–22) for $9.45B	$1.05 Billion
		2 years (2016–17) for $900M for half of Thursday games, which will also be shown at same time on NFL network	$450 Million

Compiled from various reports. All figures confirmed by at least two different media reports.

lucrative local rights deals that generally provide far greater revenue for teams in bigger markets, such as the New York Yankees and Los Angeles Dodgers. In 2013, the Yankees reached a 20-year rights deal with the YES Network valued at a total of $7.7B in a series of escalators that average out to $385 million annually that is paid to the Yankees (Settimi, 2014).

With the exception of most NFL deals, these sports rights deals usually now include Web-exclusive and television rights to other digital properties, some of which are loosely defined in the contract details to account for new social media platforms that have yet to be developed. The best example of this move came from NBC, which had paid the International Olympic Committee and the U.S. Olympic Committee $4.38B for the rights to televise four summer and winter Olympic Games from 2014 to 2020. However, in just the first year of that deal, NBC paid an additional of $7.75B to secure the multimedia television rights for six more summer and winter Olympic Games from 2020 to 2032. *The New York Times* sports media industry reporter Richard Sandomir wrote that NBC structured this deal to secure its dominance of the Olympics regardless of changes in how media is delivered and consumed over the next two decades.

"The agreement between NBC Universal and the International Olympic Committee also captures just how technologically frenetic the media landscape is. Once, such deals had to contemplate only television, but smartphones and tablets have become an increasingly large segment of the viewing audience, and no one can guess how people will watch sports in 2032. The new Olympic contract acknowledges this, stipulating that NBC will have the exclusive rights to broadcast the Games on whatever technology emerges between now and then" (Sandomir, 2014, ¶ 3).

These different types of media convergence discussed in this section, coupled with corporate consolidation and the impact of new media technologies (e.g., Internet and social media) has drastically transformed nearly every job in sports media/journalism/communication. This is a radical change when compared to the history of sports media in the United States.

HISTORY OF U.S. SPORTS MEDIA

The United States has always been a society based on capitalism. Therefore, it is not surprising that most major developments in the history of sports media were influenced by the pursuit of monetary gain in a competitive marketplace (McChesney, 1989). However, sociocultural environmental trends and norms, as well as shifts in journalism practices, have all greatly impacted the historical evolution of sports media in the United States (Bryant & Holt, 2006). The greatest influence has likely been in advancements in technology that impact media consumption. Specifically, sports media evolution has gone from newspapers to radio to television to the World Wide Web to social media and other new media platforms (Pedersen et al., 2016).

The First Newspaper Sports Sections and the Start of Symbiotic Relationships

The Boston Gazette published a story on a boxing match in 1733, which is the first known sports article to appear in an American daily newspaper (Sowell, 2008). However, it was not until the late 19th century that sports content was regularly published in American newspapers. This occurred during the Industrial Revolution, a period when more people started living in cities, literacy rates grew, enrollment in secondary schools increased, individuals had more free time and multiple daily newspapers were flourishing in most major American cities (Bryant & Holt, 2006). This era also correlated with baseball becoming the first sport with a mass following as populations in cities, increasingly composed of immigrants and other ethnic groups, began to identify with their local professional teams. These teams needed media coverage to reach potential patrons, while newspapers needed events and people of interest to cover that would sell newspapers and appeal to potential advertisers. Thus, a "symbiotic relationship" formed between profit-driven sports teams and mass media, where both sides benefited from each other. This relationship remains in place today.

Sports coverage, though, still appeared sporadically in many newspapers, with some news editors mocking sports content as trivial. But readers wanted sports coverage. Accordingly, Joseph Pulitzer created the initial U.S. newspaper sports department for his *New York World* in 1883. A dozen years later, William Randolph Hearst established the first stand-alone, regular sports section for his *New York Journal*, which quickly helped to boost its circulation in a New York City newspaper war (Pedersen et al., 2016). But it was not until the 1920s that sports departments became entrenched as a vital section in most major newspapers, in part because following teams and athletes emerged as America's favorite hobby during the "golden age of sports" (McChesney, 1989). During this era, sports writers used colorful language to describe events that most of the public could not see in person. They essentially made heroes out of athletes and their feats, elevating the likes of Babe Ruth, Jack Dempsey and Red Grange into national household names and the first superstars of American sports.

No journalist better exemplified the "Golden Age of Sportswriting" than Grantland Rice, who is most famous for penning this lead paragraph for the *New York Herald Tribune* from his story on the 1924 Army–Notre Dame football game. Ironically, Rice got the idea for the "Four Horsemen" nickname from a Notre Dame publicity director, showing the symbiotic relationship between sports teams and schools and sports media (Stoldt, Dittmore, & Branvold, 2012).

THE FOUR HORSEMEN OF NOTRE DAME BY GRANTLAND RICE PUBLISHED INITIALLY IN THE *NEW YORK HERALD TRIBUNE*, OCTOBER 18, 1924

Outlined against a blue-gray October sky, the Four Horsemen rode again. In dramatic lore they are known as Famine, Pestilence, Destruction and Death. These are only aliases. Their real names are Stuhldreher, Miller, Crowley and Layden. They formed the crest of the South Bend cyclone before which another fighting Army football team was swept over the precipice at the Polo Grounds yesterday afternoon as 55,000 spectators peered down on the bewildering panorama spread on the green plain below.

(University of Notre Dame Archives)

A sense of realism that set in during the Great Depression and World War II essentially ended the "Age of Sports Heroes" as the American public was justifiably more focused on serious issues. They began to question the veracity of newspaper reporters who too often served as cheerleaders and promoters for the teams and athletes they covered. At the same time, newspaper sports departments had earned the unflattering nickname "The Toy Department" for their cheerleading efforts and a perceived lack of serious reporting, a stigma that stayed with sports journalism for a century (Pedersen et al., 2016; Wanta, 2006).

Following World War II, a new, realistic "perspective" in sports journalism emerged in major outlets that began taking a more objective and often cynical approach to covering sports leagues, teams and athletes (Garrison & Sabljak, 1993). This was further enhanced by the 1954 launch of Sports Illustrated, a magazine that has long served as a leader in investigative sports journalism, as well as the rise of the "alternative" press, which included many sports writers at leftist and African-American newspapers who campaigned heavily for racial integration in Major League Baseball (Lamb, 2012).

Today's print journalism is a mixture of objective, good and investigative reporting that is marred too often by an abundance of "homerism," where sports reporters seem to write too favorably about the local teams they cover. The advent of the Internet and social media, coupled with the continued financial problems and decline of the newspaper industry, has often blurred the lines between traditional journalists and fans (Kian, Ketterer, Nichols, & Poling, 2014). Therefore, it is very important for aspiring sports media professionals to learn the ethics of this vocation, which are discussed in detail in Chapter 2.

Radio Provides the First "Live" Sports Media Coverage

In 1921, KDKA in Pittsburgh, Pennsylvania, broadcast a boxing match, marking the first full radio broadcast of a sporting event to a large audience, although radio sportscasts in the United States actually dated back to at least 1912 (Schultz & Wei, 2013). Shortly after the KDKA broadcast, radio stations across the country began regularly airing sports programs, with baseball, boxing and college football the most popular broadcasts through the 1920s and 1930s (Pedersen et al., 2016). Sports radio enabled fans to listen to local teams' games live.

Sports radio attained mainstream popularity in the 1930s and 1940s, and competed well with television for media consumers during the early 1950s. However, sports radio's popularity began to fade significantly afterward as most consumers concluded they would rather watch and listen to sporting events on television rather than just listen to the radio.

Today radio has re-emerged as a major player in the sports media landscape due to the rapid rise of sports-talk radio over the last two decades. While sports-talk shows had been on radio stations dating back to the 1920s, it was not until 1987 when WFAN in New York became the first all-sports radio station in the United States (Pedersen et al., 2016). As of 2012, there were at least 677 all-sports radio stations in the United States, with almost every midsize market having at least an ESPN Radio affiliate among its sports-focused radio stations (Adgate, 2013).

Television Brings Sports to the Masses and Solidifies the Symbiotic Relationship

By far, television has had the greatest influence on the growth, popularity and commoditization of sports (e.g., professional and revenue-producing college sports in the United States) since the 1950s. "Television's love affair with sports . . . was the most important factor in creating a sports-oriented American society" (Garrison & Sabljak, 1993, p. 235).

Newsreels of sports stars and games were shown regularly in movie theaters in the 1920s and 1930s (Bryant & Holt, 2006), which for the first time exposed many Americans to sports on film. However, it was not until the 1950s that sports on television became a standard in American culture. Only 0.4 percent of American homes owned a television by 1948, but that figure would increase to 83.2 percent by 1958 (Baughman, 1993).

Baseball was first telecast in the United States in 1939, but only one camera was used for the first game (a college matchup between Columbia and Princeton), while just two cameras were employed for the first MLB telecast that same year (Pedersen et al., 2016; Schultz & Wei, 2016). The production quality of each was extremely primitive by today's standards. Early telecasts of football, which also debuted in 1939, were even worse due to the difficulty of shooting a sport like football with just one or two cameras. However, by the late 1950s, sports on television had become more common and the quality of production continuously improved. It was in the 1960s, though, that televised sports truly transformed American culture and altered the sports media landscape.

Roone Arledge, former president of ABC Sports television, arguably had more influence on the evolution of American sports media than any individual. Arledge introduced Americans to global sport by debuting ABC's "Wide World of Sports" in 1961 that showed many lesser-known sports and events hosted in other countries and by making ABC's coverage of the Olympic Games a major television event that was shown in primetime regardless of the games' location.

His greatest influence, though, was going against then-standard assumptions by being the first executive to believe that prime-time sports on a regular basis could compete for ratings with network shows (Vogan, 2014). In 1970, ABC debuted "Monday Night Football" (MNF). Although MNF moved from ABC to its Disney partner ESPN for the 2006 season, it remains the second longest running primetime television show behind CBS' "60 Minutes" and is regularly ranked as the most-watched broadcast on television each week (Vogan, 2014). Among the many other innovations during Arledge's tenure at ABC Sports were (1) creating the celebrity sports announcer (starting with Howard Cossell); (2) using storylines to help frame sports games, events and athletes; (3) increasing the number of cameras used to film games to show different angles; (4) introducing slow-motion replay for televised sporting events; and (5) broadcasting the historic "Battle of the Sexes" tennis match where Billie Jean King's win over Bobby Riggs helped launch the women's sports movement (Pedersen et al., 2016).

New Media Transforms All Sports Media

Traditional media outlets (i.e., newspapers, radio and television) seemingly did not know how to respond to the rapid rise of the Internet in the 1990s, with newspapers the most negatively affected. Massive layoffs have been commonplace in the newspaper industry since the late 1990s as younger people stopped reading newspapers and migrated to free online news and sports. The advent of Craigslist, which provided advertisers the ability to reach target demographics that visit specific websites, also led to declines in newspapers' advertising revenues (Kian & Zimmerman, 2012).

The Internet of the 1990s relied on slow, dial-up technology, and was largely text-based with static screens and limited features. Media consumers were not giving up television to watch videos on the World Wide Web. In contrast, the high-speed, interconnected, interactive and easily accessible Internet and social media platforms that are prevalent today have impacted all of sports media, because consumers can find any type of media they want (e.g., videos, highlight reels, live-streaming of sports-talk shows, etc.) online and through social media, often for free (Butler et al., 2013). This text is designed largely to prepare students and aspiring sports multimedia professionals for the Web 2.0 era.

FEATURE INTERVIEW

J. J. COOPER

Managing Editor, *Baseball America*

Like many other top print sports journalists who grew up before the advent of the Internet, J. J. Cooper began his professional journalism career with a modest job — as a prep football freelance writer for his hometown weekly newspaper, the *Houston Home Journal* in Perry, Georgia. During his high school days, Cooper had stints as interim sports editor and as a full-time sports and news writer for the local weekly before attending the University of Georgia, where he worked in a variety of roles (e.g., sports editor, football and baseball beat writer, etc.) for two campus newspapers and did a pair of summer internships with *The Atlanta Journal-Constitution*. After graduating from UGA in 1994, Cooper landed a coveted first job as a full-time sports writer with *The* Macon (Georgia) *Telegraph*, where about 95 percent of his duties were focused on writing and reporting, most of which were game stories, features, game previews and roundups.

Photo 1.4 J. J. Cooper started his career before the advent of the Internet, but now uses it daily in his various roles as managing editor of Baseball America. Photo courtesy of J. J. Cooper

Now, more than 20 years later, Cooper has his dream job, serving as managing editor for *Baseball America*, one of the most respected niche outlets in U.S. sports media. Despite numerous technological changes and several down periods that resulted in widespread industry layoffs, Cooper has remain gainfully employed and continued to advance upward throughout his career, serving as a preps and later college football/pro sports beat writer for *The Telegraph* and then sports editor for the *Leaf-Chronicle* newspaper in Clarksville, Tennessee, before returning to *The Telegraph* as assistant sports editor.

He moved on to *Baseball America* in 2002 as news editor, and later was promoted to Web editor. He now serves as managing editor, helping to plan and write for the company's magazine and website. In addition, Cooper wrote for AOL FanHouse from its inception until its demise and served as a statistical/film analyst for Football Outsiders. Now only about a third of Cooper's multimedia job duties include the traditional sports writing he did for *The Telegraph* in his first full-time job. His copy-editing, page-layout and assignment responsibilities for the magazine largely mirror what he did as a newspaper editor, but that's where the similarities end.

Since coming to *Baseball America*, Cooper has learned to shoot, cut, and upload video, make highlight films, and produce video features and stories, some of which he narrates. He regularly produces and participates in podcasts. Cooper appears on radio shows across the country and has been a guest expert on MLB Network multiple times. And like nearly all sports journalists, Cooper is expected to be active and proficient on social media, building and interacting with followers. For work, he uses Twitter, Facebook, Instagram, Snapchat, LinkedIn and Periscope, but is always looking to adapt to new social media as an early innovator. Finally, he and his co-authors have reached *The New York Times'* best-sellers list with the *Baseball America Prospect Handbook*.

"In this day and age, you have to become comfortable with whatever changes happen in mass media," Cooper said. "That's what we do at *Baseball America*. It kind of baffled me when some newspaper reporters didn't want to get involved with social media when it was obvious that's where the industry was headed. You are still reporting and telling stories. But you are just using different and new tools that best allow you to do that while reaching even more audiences. That now has to include video and social media for most print-based reporters."

Many sports magazines have struggled or folded entirely in the age of the Internet. However, *Baseball America* is not only financially stable but thriving in many ways, in part because it still fulfills its motto of largely providing "baseball news you can't find anywhere else." Just as important to its sustained success is that the magazine was an early adapter to delivering Web-based content to consumers — it had a paywall beginning in 1999 — and has embraced new technologies and multimedia, evident by *Baseball America* building its own video production and television studio in its headquarters at Durham, North Carolina.

"We know that part of our success is that we fill a niche," Cooper said. "But I think a lot of our success is because we weren't always focused on protecting the magazine, but instead focused more on reaching people who are interested in what we do. Baseball America is not just a magazine; instead we consider ourselves a content-producing company and that content can come in a wide variety of forms. That's not just important to readers, but also potential advertisers. Some want an ad in the magazine, but others want to reach our digital audience through the website or our social media."

CHAPTER WRAP-UP

Convergence, which is a term used to describe the mixing and crossover of multimedia content produced and disseminated by media and outlets, has required that nearly all types of sports communication professionals become adept at new skills in the digital age.

Students entering the sports media profession must have the ability to produce content for a variety of different types of media. Those fortunate to work for

ESPN best exemplify the need to have diverse skill sets. Corporate consolidation of mass media outlets and partnerships across media have impacted the number and types of traditional sports journalism.

Sports are primarily the only type of television programming still mostly consumed live, so sports broadcasting rights deals for the most popular professional and collegiate sports have exploded in the Internet age. These deals now increasingly include multimedia exclusive rights for the networks to better protect their investments as different types of social and new media develop, altering how sports fans consume media.

The history and evolution of sports media is far less complex. However, changes have occurred far more rapidly in the 21st century following 20th-century transition of U.S. sports media slowly from newspapers to radio to television, the latter having by far the greatest impact in making sports such an important part of American culture. The impact of the Internet and social media, however, is transforming the field today.

REVIEW QUESTIONS

1. Describe and provide examples of the two types of media convergence in the digital age described in this chapter.
2. How has corporate consolidation impacted jobs in the sports media profession?
3. What are some of the recent trends in major television/network sports rights deals?
4. Describe and give at least three examples of the symbiotic relationship between sport organizations/teams/athletes and sports media.
5. What was the order of the evolution of different types of major sports media in the United States?

GROUP ACTIVITIES

1. Assign each group of students a different major sports league, and then have each group analyze the coverage their assigned league receives on the various ESPN multimedia platforms.
2. Have each student write down in descending order her or his best multimedia skills and then have them write down what skills they think are most needed in their desired vocation, in order from most needed to least. Have students in groups discuss these two rankings and have them provide feedback for each other.
3. Have students, working in groups, come up with five primary ways that they expect sports media content to be consumed in 2025. What do they think will remain largely unchanged? What do they think will be most changed?

CHAPTER 2

Ethical, Legal and Minority Issues

In June 1994, the deaths of Nicole Brown Simpson and Ronald Goldman touched off a media firestorm that lasted for the next 16 months. At the center of the storm was former NFL star O.J. Simpson, the primary suspect in the murder. Simpson's arrest, trial and exoneration dominated media headlines across the nation.

Major news magazines put Simpson's mugshot on their covers, but it was *Time* that darkened his face to make him appear more sinister, and in some eyes, guilty. The photo manipulation raised charges of racism. "It seems to me you could argue that it's racist to say that blacker is more sinister," said *Time*'s managing editor James R. Gaines, "but be that as it may: To the extent that this caused offense to anyone, I obviously regret it" (Carmody, 1994).

The ensuing trial became a circus, thanks in large part to the presence of television cameras that turned the judicial proceedings into a daily soap opera. "It spawned mottos ('If the glove doesn't fit, you must acquit!'), reality stars (Kato Kaelin, the Kardashian empire) and dinner table arguments across America," observed reporter Lilah Raptopolous (2014, ¶ 1) in England's *Guardian*. The Simpson saga seemed to be the perfect intersection of sports, law, ethics and diversity. More than 20 years later, these issues have become even murkier in the modern world of sports media.

ETHICS

In the Simpson case, news media had a legal right to have cameras in the courtroom, but was that the right ethical decision? Could excessive coverage have altered the outcome or impacted Simpson's guaranteed right to a fair trial?

Even though the case itself was unique, sports media organizations and reporters must make ethical decisions like this all the time. Such decisions are much more difficult because of long-standing deficiencies in media ethics. Specifically:

- *There are very few written ethical standards in place.* Some organizations have written standards, but most ethical rules are vague, not communicated effectively, and changeable in that they are determined by organizational dictates at the time. Most ethical decisions are made retroactively once a crisis occurs, rather than addressed proactively.
- *Such standards vary from organization to organization.* What one outlet may discourage as unethical behavior, another may applaud as "good,

hard-hitting journalism." One of the strongest ethical attitudes today, especially in light of increasing media competition, is the idea that "if we don't do it, surely someone else will." Tabloids, both in print and on television, have been criticized for this attitude, but they have broken several major stories in recent years that other media were afraid to be the first to publish.

- *Most organizations have no process for ethical training.* The process of creating, producing and disseminating the news is the main focus of any media outlet, and thus ethical considerations are often an afterthought. Most organizations simply lack the time or resources to adequately train reporters in ethics, preferring to handle issues on an as-needed basis.

The result of all this is a haphazard, inconsistent approach to ethical situations in which decisions are often based more on personal than professional ethics. Individual reporters often have to rely on their own ethical framework, especially in situations that demand an immediate response. The following is not meant to be a complete list of ethical problem areas, but certainly they are the issues that are most pressing in today's sports media world.

Conflict of Interest

One of the most common ethical situations in sports is conflict of interest, which can be defined as any relationship that threatens the integrity or objectivity of the reporting. Conflict of interest can take many forms and come from many directions, both inside and outside an organization. The Madison Square Garden network let go longtime broadcaster Marv Albert in 2004, ostensibly to avoid paying him a large salary. In truth, Albert had been very critical of the team in his broadcasts, and that did not sit well with Knicks owner James Dolan, who also owned MSG. *The New York Times'* Richard Sandomir (2004) quoted an anonymous Knicks official as saying, "Jim felt all broadcasters had to be cheerleaders and sell tickets," and the paper went on to observe that "Dolan embraced the belief that announcers should call games with a more positive, upbeat approach" (¶ 5).

It is more common for the conflict of interest to come from outside the organization. Reporters can develop friendships with athletes or coaches that make it difficult to report critical information. This is particularly problematic when the reporter or announcer works for the team rather than for an independent outlet, which is still very common in today's sports landscape. "Boosterism" or "homerism" are also potential conflicts for reporters, especially those who work in small towns with passionate fan bases. In an effort to address questionable industry practices, especially among local journalists, the Associated Press Sports Editors adopted a code of ethics, which prohibits journalists from openly supporting particular teams or players (Hardin & Zhong, 2010). Media outlets depend on local fans for advertising dollars, so often the coverage will be supportive so as not to offend potential customers. In some extreme cases, outlets go so far as to refer to the team as "we" and "us," which is a blatant ethical lapse.

"Of course, we're all sports fans; that's what drew us to this business, but you have to remain professional at all times," said Berry Tramel, longtime lead sports columnist for *The Oklahoman* newspaper. "And of course it would be nice if the home teams are big winners. That makes everyone happy and sells more papers. But you have to remain objective at all times" (personal communication, 2015). As Tramel noted, nothing brings out boosterism like a winning team. One year when the Detroit Tigers were in the midst of a pennant race, *Detroit Free Press* columnist Joe Falls wrote an article that made the team look bad. Angry callers deluged the newspaper and "the *Free Press* was accused of trying to blow the pennant, of wrecking the team's harmony. Under the direct order of the managing editor, there were to be no more negative stories. (The paper) simply could not afford to offend its readers with negative news (or, if you choose, honest reporting)" (Cantor, 1997, p. 97).

Advertising is the main revenue source for the sports media, but with those billions of dollars in revenue comes the potential for conflict of interest. Advertisers want a return on their huge investment, and have been willing to try to influence content going back to before the days of the television quiz show scandals. Advertising slogans and signage are everywhere in sports—on stadiums, in the stadium, and on player uniforms.

Sponsorships of sports reports and stories have also become increasingly common, such as the "KARE-11 Sports Report from the Mayo Clinic's Sports Medicine Sports Desk." The 2015 partnership between a Minneapolis television station and the medical group has been described as a deal that is "bolder, more direct, and is not barely sliding over the ad-edit wall but tearing down the wall itself" (Lieberman, 2015, ¶ 6). Even if such arrangements do not compromise content, at the very least they give the appearance of impropriety.

Digital Manipulation

The mugshot of O.J. Simpson used by magazines and newspapers vividly demonstrated the power of the media to alter reality, a power that has only grown with technological advances. With today's Photoshop and other editing tools it becomes very easy to change, manipulate and create a visual impression. "At almost every stage in photographic practice from image capture to circulation there is the potential for manipulation," says David Campbell of World Press Photo. "The mere fact of going to place A rather than place B to produce an image involves a choice that might represent reality in a partial manner" ("Debating the," 2015, ¶ 34)

There are two schools of thought on digital manipulation. One says that changing a photo is not a big deal; after all, newspapers have been cropping pictures for years. Media outlets routinely change the size, framing, and perspective of pictures, and often use the term "illustration" to distinguish them from untouched photographs. Others in the industry strongly disagree with this practice, believing that any manipulation alters the perception of reality. "You can't explain it away by calling it an illustration," says John Long, former ethics chair at the National Press Photographers Association. "What you're trying to do is use words to explain a visual lie. No self-respecting journalist would do that with a story" (as cited in Schultz and Arke, 2015, p. 180).

Some manipulations, like the O.J. Simpson covers, can have important consequences, while others seem more trivial. In its coverage of a Baylor football game in 2012, *Sports Illustrated* changed the color of the team's jerseys from black to green. When a controversy broke out, *SI* representatives rather lamely answered that the problem was due to a production error. "It bothers me when a magazine whose history is built on the credibility of sports photography just kisses off the photojournalism world when the profession dares to question an image that's been as clearly messed with as this picture has been," says Donald Winslow (2012, ¶ 10) of the National Press Photographers Association.

Rush to Publish

While technology has impacted the nature of sports photography, perhaps nowhere has its ethical impact been felt more than in the shortening of the news cycle. Where once newspapers had a day to mull over content, and television stations had a few hours before the next broadcast, today the news cycle is instantaneous. Content goes up on the Internet and social media in seconds, not minutes, and with precious little consideration beforehand.

Combined with increased media competition, the shortened news cycle has resulted in some embarrassing ethical lapses. In 2015, Chris Broussard of ESPN tweeted a report that Dallas Mavericks owner Mark Cuban was desperately driving around Houston looking for the home of DeAndre Jordan, who Cuban wanted to sign in free agency. Cuban denied the report and said that Broussard had never bothered to contact him to get the details. That led Broussard to tweet a red-faced apology: "I should have attempted to contact Mark Cuban before reporting what my sources were telling me. I always try to carry myself with honesty and integrity both personally and professionally. I recognize that I tweeted hastily, I'm sorry for it, and I will learn from my mistake" (Mandell, 2015, ¶ 2).

Citizen Journalism

The other effect of technology is the growth of citizen journalism. Platforms like YouTube, Facebook and other social media allow average fans to create and distribute their own sports content. Some of this content, especially blogs dedicated to a particular team, have become extremely popular and have rivaled mainstream media coverage.

However, there is a dangerous downside to citizen journalism. Typically, citizen journalists are not "journalists" in the classic sense — they have not studied, trained or learned how to be reporters. This includes a lack of ethical training, and because these contributors are often volunteers or paid very little, they are not beholden to outlets, corporations or audiences. Speaking on the growth of bloggers, one veteran newspaper writer commented:

> It's the worst kind of insidious, stupid-creep to have ever infected our profession. Blogging blurs the lines between journalism and pajama-wearing nitwits sitting in their mothers' basements firing off bile-filled opinions. Newspaper editors and managers sit around at meetings and wonder why their circulation is falling and they have themselves to blame for lowering all of us into the foul-smelling muck of the blogworld (Schultz & Sheffer, 2007, p. 71).

Rumor, gossip and innuendo are commonplace on the Internet, and in the case of citizen journalism it's becoming more difficult to separate fact from fiction. Did they properly source their information? Did they get two independent sources to verify information before publishing it? What accountability, if any, do they have and to whom? Even as many citizen journalism sports sites strive for credibility and acceptance, these difficult questions remain unanswered.

LAW

The same media laws that apply to journalists generally also apply to sports journalists. The areas that seem to directly involve sports journalists most often are libel, sources and privacy.

Libel

Libel is the publication of false information about someone that injures or damages that individual in some way. It usually refers to written defamation, but has also come to include slander, which is spoken. The laws on libel have evolved through a series of court cases, most notably NY Times v. Sullivan (376 U.S. 254, 1964), which established the distinction between a private citizen and a public figure. A private citizen only needs to demonstrate injury or damage to reputation in a libel case, while the public figure must prove actual malice on the part of the media. That is, the public figure must show: (1) the information was false, (2) the media outlet that published it knew it was false and (3) the outlet published the material in a deliberate attempt to injure the person involved. Actual malice has been designed to be difficult to prove in order to protect the media's right to report and comment on public figures.

The key to interpreting libel law is trying to decide what exactly constitutes a public figure as opposed to a private citizen. Almost everyone would agree that the head coach of a big-time college football program is a public figure. He is seen quite often on the sidelines, in the media and in the community at large. But what about a lesser-known assistant coach or the head athletic trainer? What about someone who does not willingly seek the spotlight, but finds himself thrust into it accidentally? These gray areas are often decided by judges and juries, and what they decide can make the difference in a libel case. In 2015, HBO won a libel suit filed by the sporting goods company Mitre, which claimed it had been defamed in a report on the network's "Real Sports" show. Mitre alleged that the show fabricated segments to make it appear that the company's soccer balls were made by kids in a sweatshop in India. Although the judge in the case ruled Mitre was not a public figure and thus did not have to prove malice on the part of HBO, it took a jury less than six hours of deliberation to find HBO not guilty of libeling Mitre (Gardner, 2015, ¶ 8).

Truth is always the first and best defense for libel—if a report is true, it can't be libelous. Do not think of a retraction as a defense. Apologizing is fine, but if the damage is already done there may still be legal consequences. However, retractions do often make the libeled party more agreeable to a settlement.

Sources

Journalists often want to protect confidential sources, and that is especially true for investigative work. It took three years for *San Francisco Chronicle* reporters Lance Williams and Mark Fainaru-Wada to uncover the BALCO/baseball steroids scandal, but their efforts resulted in a Pulitzer Prize and a best-selling book. During the course of the investigation they relied heavily on confidential sources. They defied a U.S. District Court judge by refusing to identify those sources, and although they were sentenced in September 2006 to 18 months in prison, they never served any time. In his statement before the court, Fainaru-Wada said, "Throughout the BALCO affair, critics have questioned the motives of our reporting, suggesting that it has been little more than a witch hunt or an effort to profit off the big names who have been drawn into the scandal. Supporters have portrayed us as champions in the global fight against performance-enhancing drugs. For us, however, BALCO has always been an earnest and sincere effort to present the truth" ("Fainaru-Wada's," 2006, A14).

The right to protect confidential sources, also known as shield law, is not federally protected but rather is left up to the states. Thus, shield laws can vary greatly depending on the locale. In 2003, *Sports Illustrated* ran an unflattering account of new University of Alabama coach Mike Price, alleging that the coach spent a wild, drunken night in the company of strippers. Price denied most of the allegations, which were based in large part on a confidential source. The 11th U.S. Circuit Court of Appeals eventually ruled that while Alabama law protected newspapers and broadcasters, it did not cover magazines. The case was settled out of court before the source was publicly identified ("Time Inc.," 2005).

The extent to which sports reporters can protect sources is completely determined by state law. All sports reporters, and especially those engaged in investigative work, should acquaint themselves with the laws of the specific locales in which they work.

Privacy

Issues regarding an individual's right to privacy mostly center on physical location. People have the right to protect their privacy within private settings, such as a home, backyard or a privately owned facility. Once the person steps on to public property, such as a street or public building, that right usually ends. Paparazzi can stalk celebrities right up to the doors of their homes, but can't take their cameras inside without the consent of the occupants.

Privacy has become more difficult to control and interpret because of the evolution of camera technology. Drone cameras now easily circumvent borders and fences. It's also very easy to snap a picture with a cell phone inside a private club catching a famous athlete who seems to be drunk, but does that make it legal to publish it? There is also something called "the expectation of privacy." If there is an understanding in the club that there are no cameras allowed, and the club may even have signs posted forbidding them, then people in the club have an expectation of privacy and legal protection from being photographed. Regardless, these lines are often crossed in the digital age. One popular site, http://www.drunkathlete.com, regularly publishes photos of inebriated athletes and coaches in private settings.

Some privacy issues go beyond physical location. In 1992, *USA Today* believed it had a major story—the newspaper had reason to believe that former tennis great Arthur Ashe had the AIDS virus. When a sports reporter from *USA Today* called Ashe for confirmation, Ashe stalled. He asked executive sports editor Gene Policinski to delay the story for 36 hours. Policinski would not give a guarantee, so Ashe held a press conference the next day to announce that he did indeed have the AIDS virus, most likely contracted during a blood transfusion. The situation provided a textbook case of media and privacy. "I am sorry that I have been forced to make this revelation at this time," said Ashe, who died in 1993. "After all, I am not running for some office of public trust, nor do I have stockholders to account to. Keeping my AIDS status private enabled me to control my life" (Rhoden, 1992, ¶ 10). But on the other side of the argument was *USA Today*. "When the press has kept secrets . . . that conspiracy of silence has not served the public," said *USA Today* editor Peter Prichard. "Journalists serve the public by reporting news, not hiding it. By sharing his story, Arthur Ashe and his family are free of a great weight. In the days ahead, they will help us better understand AIDS and how to defeat it" (as cited in Schultz and Arke, 2015, p. 182).

Modern Issues

The advances in journalism technology have created some interesting legal situations for today's sports reporter, most of which concern access. Sports organizations and teams strictly control access to particular events in terms of who gets in, what they can shoot, where they can stand and so on. For example, huge events like the Olympic Games and the NCAA basketball tournament do not allow any television video of the action other than the official game feed supplied by the network broadcaster. The idea is that networks have paid millions of dollars for the rights to televise the game and the networks want that coverage to be exclusive.

The problem is that technology is making it easier to get around the rules. Fans, for example, can shoot video of the event with their phones or hand-held cameras and post the video to a service such as YouTube. They can also tweet or blog details of the event in real time. Why should reporters be held to a different standard? Reporters have answered this question by live blogging events, which amounts to a real-time description of specific play-by-play information. Many organizations protested, saying that live blogging of an event is a violation of the exclusive broadcast rights agreement, and in 2007 a newspaper reporter for the Louisville *Courier-Journal* was ejected from an NCAA baseball game for live blogging game action. The NCAA only later backed down when the paper threatened a lawsuit. The NFL tried to limit live blogging to 90 seconds per day of audio and/or video of interviews, press conferences and team practices that may be posted on a website. However, many reporters and outlets simply ignored the rules, including *The Wall Street Journal*, which in 2009 had one of its reporters sit at home and live blog a game between the Tennessee Titans and New York Jets as a means of testing the NFL's resolve (Figure 2.1).

One of the legal issues sports reporters must face is live blogging. Some organizations severely try to limit the practice, while others have a more open attitude, like the PGA Tour. This is a short section of the live blog conducted by Golf.com during the final round of the 2015 U.S. Open. Golf.com's coverage not only included descriptions of shots and action, but comments from readers and even players.

The controversy also pointed out the NFL's double standard in trying to limit the social media activity of journalists at the stadium while ignoring fans at home or in the stands. For example, when former Denver Broncos pass rusher Elvis Dumervil was injured in an August 2010 practice, reporters could not tweet that information from the practice field, but instead had to return to the press area.

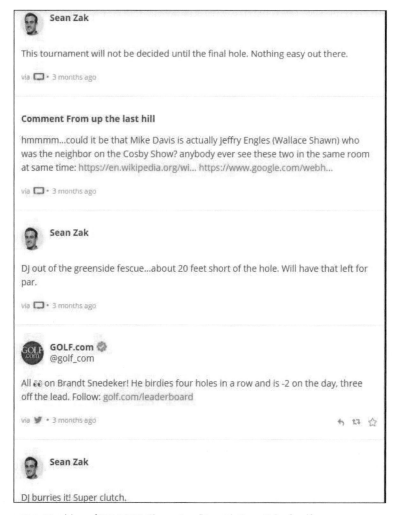

Figure 2.1 Live blog of 2016 PGA Championship with Sean Zak of golf.com.
Courtesy of Golf.com

Fans watching the practice had no such restrictions, and many of them immediately tweeted the information along with video of Dumervil leaving the field. The NFL does allow live blogging of the annual draft, and most other professional organizations have no live blogging restrictions. However, these rules can vary from sport to sport and even from team to team, so sports reporters should be aware of the guidelines for their particular situation.

MINORITIES AND DIVERSITY

There is no greater conversation today in sports, as well as in the culture as a whole, than that of diversity. It dominates almost every facet of life, including economics, law and government. In many ways it is the same conversation that has been going on for many, many years. There are two main groups in sports journalism affected by diversity issues—racial minorities and women.

Women

Women have long been underrepresented in the ranks of all types of sports media. Since the 1980s, some media outlets and even entire industries (e.g., newspaper sports departments) have made efforts to add more women to their sports staffs. Nevertheless, a recent survey of North American sports employees at newspapers and mainstream Internet sites found that men comprised 90 percent of sports editors, 88 percent of columnists, 87 percent of reporters and 81 percent of copy editors/designers (Lapchick, 2015).

The lack of women in both sports and sports reporting traces directly to men long dominating mediated sports consumption. Almost all research indicates that men are the primary consumers of sports through the media, with a few exceptions (e.g., gymnastics, figure skating, some Olympic sports, etc.). As such, men are the audience advertisers are trying to reach. Similarly, sports journalism has been traditionally considered a largely male club (Halberstam, 1989). Even though the industry is more open today, the attitude still remains.

Change has come through legal efforts such as Title IX. Since being signed into law in 1972, Title IX has led to more female participation in athletics at all levels, even though it only affects schools that receive public funding (e.g., secondary schools, like high schools, and colleges and universities). It also came through pioneers who were willing to break down the doors of the men's club of sports journalism. Women like Betty Cuniberti, Michelle Himmelberg, Melissa Ludtke and Claire Smith blazed the trail, but were usually ridiculed, ignored and marginalized. "Fenway Park (in Boston) would not allow women into the room where the male reporters ate," said Jane Gross, who began covering sports for *The New York Times*. "They would bring us food on trays on the roof of the old Fenway Park, which was outdoors." When the *Detroit Free Press* sent Mary Ann Weston to cover the Tigers in 1968, "I couldn't go in the clubhouse, of course," she said, "but they also barred me from the press box and the dugout and the field. They told me each time that 'it was no place for a woman,' and that my presence might 'inhibit' some of the players" ("Nine for," 2013).

Women have not only faced difficulty gaining acceptance from the male colleagues in sports journalism, they have also faced sexist and chauvinistic attitudes in the locker room. The most infamous incident took place in 1990 when Lisa Olson, then a reporter for the *Boston Herald*, claimed that players from the New England Patriots exposed themselves and made lewd comments. Olson complained to the team and the NFL, and filed a lawsuit after neither took action. Olson was spit upon, mocked and received death threats and physical abuse that made it impossible to work, so she ultimately left to take a job in Australia. Her lawsuit was settled out of court and she eventually returned to the United States as a freelance writer.

Sexual harassment is a common concern among female sports reporters. Networks and television stations figure men want to look at attractive women (e.g., television cameras often zoom in on attractive women in crowds at sporting events, a common practice dubbed "honey shots" in the industry). Accordingly, sexual objectification has become an ongoing debate in the industry. Female sports reporters complain that objectification makes it harder for them to get jobs, diminishes their achievements and sends the wrong message to aspiring students. "It's disappointing," said Robin Roberts, who in 1990 became the first black woman to anchor at the network sports level when she went to ESPN. "It's important that you don't use your sexuality, especially since so many women sportscasters started the fight for acceptance of women in the business" ("Jocks &," 2002, ¶ 1). Jeanne Zelasko, who also worked at ESPN, sarcastically asked, "When I talk to young women about careers in this field, do I advise them to get a solid background in sports and reporting, or do I tell them to enter a beauty contest?" ("Hottie topic," 2000, p. 3). Unfortunately, the beauty contest part of the business remains, especially in television. In 2014, Pam Oliver of Fox Sports was unceremoniously replaced as the top sideline reporter on the network's NFL coverage in favor of the younger Erin Andrews. The 53-year-old Oliver was understandably upset at the demotion. "The business is very demographic-oriented," she said. "It's not difficult to notice that the new on-air people there are all young, blond and hot" (Chase, 2014).

It is a difficult Catch-22—the industry demands attractiveness for male audiences, but that opens up the reporter to potential ridicule and sexual harassment. Today's female sports reporter must somehow balance these demands while at the same time producing quality work and maintaining professionalism. The situation does not look like it's going to change any time soon.

INES SAINZ AND JENN STERGER

A 2010 incident between the New York Jets and reporter Ines Sainz of Azteca illustrates one of the problems for today's female sports reporters. Sainz has two academic degrees, including a master's in tax law, but she has become much better known for her looks. A contestant in the Miss Universe pageant, she has been featured on the "Bad Girls" section of the Azteca website, which included a photo of her modeling a swimsuit. Sainz has also appeared wearing a bikini on websites such as *Maxim*, and often conducted her work wearing tight jeans and revealing shirts.

That's what Sainz was wearing for the 2010 interview with Jets quarterback Mark Sanchez. According to ESPN, before the interview ever took place, "Half-dressed players in the Jets locker room catcalled her, yelling, 'Chica bonita!' like teenage boys on a street corner. '[People] think you're the kind of person who takes advantage of a situation and not a professional reporter,' Sainz said. 'It was a very difficult experience for me. I do not hide my sadness to tell you what happened literally shook my life' " (McManus, 2013, ¶ 3, 6).

Others did not see Sainz as the helpless victim. "She accomplished exactly what she set out to do," said Jenn Sterger. "There's plenty of pictures of her out there at football games, at basketball games, and she's not exactly appropriately dressed. And this is coming from someone like me" ("Jenn Sterger," 2010, ¶ 3). An attractive Florida State coed, Sterger turned a brief crowd shot during an ABC football game into a modeling career that included posing nude in *Playboy*. Despite no training in journalism, she was offered a job contributing articles to *Sports Illustrated*, hosted a cable television show, and regularly contributed stories for a weekly sports show on ABC. In 2008, the New York Jets hired her to be a reporter for the team's "Gameday Host." Her main qualifications for the job? "I have to admit, I look good in green," she said (Begley, 2009, ¶ 7).

Jets quarterback Brett Favre may have thought so, too. In 2010, he was accused of texting sexual comments and images to Sterger, which became the centerpiece of an NFL investigation. Like Sainz, Sterger was fond of wearing revealing attire at work, but she says she never encouraged Favre or accepted any of his advances. The NFL fined Favre $50,000 for the incident, but Sterger remains convinced the league had no real interest in confronting the problem. "Men will never understand what women go through on a daily basis," she lamented. "The NFL and the owners don't care about individuals. The only thing they care about is money" (O'Keefe, 2014, ¶ 13).

Sexual Orientation

Negative stereotypes of what are socially construed as nonmasculine men or masculine women have long been regularly taught and reinforced through sports media content. This was most evident through a lack of coverage (i.e., "symbolic annihilation") of sports deemed gender-inappropriate for men (e.g., diving, figure skating, gymnastics, etc.) or gender-inappropriate for women (e.g., golf, hockey, wrestling, weightlifting, etc.) (Bishop, 2003; Tuchman, 1978).

However, LGBT (lesbian, gay, bisexual, transgender) individuals or issues were largely absent from sports media up through the beginning of the 21st century, in large part because very few athletes ever came out from any of the most popular team sports, and no prominent sports media members were out as gay or bisexual. Cultural acceptance of gays and lesbians is now commonplace in U.S. society. As a result, more athletes and coaches are coming out publicly. However, most who are doing so compete in individual sports or if in team sports not at the highest levels. The National Basketball Association's Jason Collins became the first openly gay athlete to ever compete in a regular-season and playoff games from any of the "Big Four" American professional team sports. In 2014, Michael Sam became the first openly gay player to be selected in the NFL draft, but never played in a regular season game.

In the 20th century, a male sports journalist coming out publicly had to fear being ostracized in the press box or by those he needed to interview in locker rooms, while an open lesbian would face even more difficulties and scorn than many women in the profession already endure. However, several prominent journalists (e.g., ESPN's Kate Fagan and Israel Gutierrez, *The Washington Post*'s Chuck Culpepper) have come out publicly in recent years, with most receiving overwhelming praise and congratulations from their colleagues and media consumers via social media.

Accordingly, young sports reporters need to be conscientious toward LGBT individuals and issues at all times, and not use any potentially offensive language or stereotypes around anyone, or they risk losing their employment.

Racial and Ethnic Minorities

Like women, minorities have long been underrepresented in the sports media profession, although not to the same degree when compared to minority representation of the overall U.S. population. However, most minorities in sports media are men, particularly African Americans. Lapchick (2015) found that people of color made up 14.7 percent of newspaper and mainstream Internet sport website staffs, compared to the 37 percent of the United States that is nonwhite, a demographic that is growing rapidly (Yen, 2013).

In one sense, minorities and women in sports media face a similar problem: lack of representation in ownership. The idea is that if women and minorities owned media companies they would have greater representation in reporting positions. The problem, mainly because of government deregulation that has encouraged corporate ownership, is they don't own much media. Recent figures suggest that while Latinos, African Americans, Asian Americans, and Native Americans combine to constitute a full third of the American population, these groups only represent less than 5 percent of the ownership of all television stations and only 7 percent in radio (Papper, 2013). Similarly, women make up more than half of the U.S. population, but own less than 6 percent of commercial radio and television stations. "I firmly believe people hire in their own likeness," says James Brown, an African American and host of the NFL pregame show on CBS. "That's what network executives always have done," said Brown. "All we're asking for is an opportunity to succeed and fail like everyone else" (as cited in Schultz and Arke, 2015, p. 197).

The percentage of the minority media workforce has actually dropped. In television in 2013 it dropped to 21.4 percent, and the decline was especially drastic in radio, which saw numbers for black workers fall from 5.2 to 2.3 percent (Allen, 2013). That decrease was somewhat offset by gains in the Hispanic workforce. In the last 23 years, the minority population in the United States has risen 10.7 percent, but the minority workforce in TV news is up only 3.6, while the minority workforce in radio is up 0.1 percent. "These reports highlight the urgent need for news organizations to go further to make newsrooms inclusive, and to clearly demonstrate that they truly value diversity in the workplace," says Gregory Lee Jr., president of the National Association of Black Journalists (Turner, 2012, ¶ 6).

What may reverse these trends is the growing economic power of minority populations, especially Spanish-speaking groups. ESPN's Deportes is now a 24-hour network, reaching 45 percent of the country's Hispanic population. ESPN also offers Sunday night baseball games and Sunday night NFL telecasts in Spanish. In affiliation with Spanish-language mega-broadcaster Univision, the NFL launched "NFL en Espanol," and other outlets have begun to seek out the burgeoning Hispanic audience. In 2014, CBS hired former NFL star Tony Gonzalez for its national pregame show, making Gonzalez one of the most visible Hispanic faces on American sports television.

Jessica Mendoza scored a double victory for both Hispanics and women by becoming a regular analyst on ESPN's "Sunday Night Baseball" in 2015. Ted Berg (2015) of *USA Today* observed, "(Her) presence in the booth made for a refreshing change from the *Sunday Night Baseball* norm, which too often seems to feature harrumphing ex-MLB players and executives prattling on about their own playing days, giggling over inside jokes, or masquerading nonsense as baseball insight" (¶ 5). As Berg noted, all analysts are former athletes and/or coaches, which represent the most common avenue for minorities to get into sports reporting.

While minority representation in sports media is certainly an important issue, it has been dwarfed in recent years by the reporting of race. In an age that puts a premium on tolerance and diversity, sports reporters must be mindful of what they say, especially on social media. Several high-profile incidents have occurred in which members of the media have been punished for untoward comments about minorities. One of the most famous occurred in 2007 when popular talk-show host Don Imus referred to the Rutgers women's basketball team as a "some nappy-headed hos there. And the girls from Tennessee, they all look cute" (Miller, 2013, p. 30). Imus was immediately condemned and lost his job, but has since come back to regain much of his former presence. In 2015, ESPN host Colin Cowherd was fired after commenting, "I've never bought into that baseball is too complex. Really? A third of the sport is from the Dominican Republic" (Manahan, 2015, ¶ 11). Like Imus, Cowherd simply moved on to another media outlet.

Both situations involved commentators rather than sports reporters, but today there is an obvious limit on how far racial commentary can go. This includes any and all material published on social media, whether it is a professional or personal account. In 2014, Fox Deportes suspended reporter Erika Reidt for her tweet at an NBA game. When it was reported that Los Angeles Lakers players were wearing "I Can't Breathe" t-shirts in warmups to support Eric Garner, Reidt tweeted, "I'm gonna start wearing a shirt that says I can breathe because I obey the law" (Dalrymple, 2014, ¶ 1). In addition to the suspension, Reidt faced a tremendous backlash on social media.

There is no doubt that the sports media have become more racially sensitive. Several individual reporters and media outlets have discontinued language and symbols considered offensive to Native Americans, such as the Cleveland Indians' logo "Chief Wahoo" and the Washington Redskins nickname. The New York *Daily News* announced in 2014 that it would no longer use Chief Wahoo or the Redskins. "While the team ownership and many fans hold such a belief in good faith," the paper editorialized, "the inescapable truth is that the term Redskin derives solely from the racial characteristic of skin tone in a society that is struggling mightily to be color blind" ("New York," 2014, ¶ 4; see also Table 2.1).

TABLE 2.1   Fail to the Redskins?

Media Outlet	Year Decided	Comment
Seattle Times	2014	"We're banning the name for one reason: It's offensive."
New York Daily News	2014	"No new franchise would consider adopting a name based on pigmentation—Whiteskins, Blackskins, Yellowskins or Redskins—today. The time has come to leave the word behind."
Detroit News	2014	"The Detroit News will no longer use the team's nickname, 'Redskins,' in routine football coverage, reflecting the growing view that the term is offensive to many Americans."
Orange County Register	2013	"It is the Register's policy to avoid using such slurs, so we will not use this one, except in stories about the controversy surrounding its use."
San Francisco Chronicle	2013	"We are not the first media outlet to make this change, and I know we will not be the last."
Richmond (Va.) Free Press	2013	"The name stems from the fact that Native Americans were scalped and butchered and a profit was made from it."
Kansas City Star	2012	"(We) see no compelling reason for any publisher to reprint an egregiously offensive term as a casual matter of course."

Source: Beujon, 2014

The controversy over the Washington Redskins nickname has intensified in recent years. Team owner Dan Snyder vows he will never change the name, so many in the media have made the decision to change it for him, at least by avoiding it in their reporting. Some individual reporters who said they will no longer use the name include Peter King of *Sports Illustrated* and William Rhoden of *The New York Times*. Ironically, while *The Washington Post* editorial board will not use the name, it is still used in the newspaper's sports section.

FINAL THOUGHTS

The issues of ethics, law and diversity presented in this chapter are complex and ever-evolving. They are constantly being influenced by the larger forces of economics, technology and culture. From an economic perspective, Daniel Snyder continues to resist changing the Redskins team name because he has not suffered financially. If various groups, including major advertisers and corporate sponsors, could ever work together to stage a powerful boycott, it might change Snyder's mind or he might be forced to change by other NFL owners concerned about revenue loss. Perhaps such a movement could be conducted through technologies like the social media. "I can't breathe," the final words of Eric Garner in a fatal confrontation with New York police officers who were choking the arrestee, ignited a social media firestorm. The Twitter hashtag #ICantBreathe was consistently in the Top Ten hashtags for that time period and on Google Trends. It is not inconceivable that a similar movement regarding the Redskins name could ignite.

Of course, all of this is driven by the culture, and for the moment the backlash against the name seems to have died down to some degree. That can change quickly, especially if Snyder were to make a racially insensitive remark or if a major celebrity got on board the name-change bandwagon. It is a culture based on the transitory, and one in which trends now move in minutes due to social media and the Internet, and not days or weeks as before. Good sports reporters are part of that culture, but more importantly, they recognize its importance in their work. Having a good understanding of culture, technology and economics can help the reporter navigate the minefield of sports ethics, law and diversity.

FEATURE INTERVIEW

HANNAH CHALKER

The obstacles facing women in sports media did not stop Hannah Chalker, or even slow her down. Right out of college, Chalker got a prestigious reporting job for XOS Digital and the SEC Digital Network working out of Orlando, Florida. From there it was on to Comcast Sports Southeast, and finally to her current spot with Crimson Tide Productions and the SEC Network. "My original focus was on news broadcasting and my dream was to be a nightly news anchor," she says. "(But) I had the opportunity to be an on-air reporter during the Southern Miss vs. Ole Miss men's basketball game, and it was there on the court, with the camera lights blinding my eyes and the fans screaming in the background of my shot, that my career took a turn for the best."

Her duties now include not only sideline reporting but also in-studio hosting and field reporting for the University of Alabama's Crimson Tide

Photo 2.1 Hannah Chalker of Crimson Tide Productions and Comcast Sports Southeast.
Photo courtesy of Robert Sutton Photography

continued

Productions and SEC Network productions. Chalker is also a host for the Alabama Crimson Tide Sports Network alongside longtime announcer Eli Gold. "I was always told that I needed thick skin if I wanted to be a female sports broadcaster, and that has rung true," she says. "In this male dominated industry it's almost a standard for women to be treated differently and I have seen and experienced prejudices first hand. My best advice is to act, dress and carry yourself as professionally as possible. That includes when you're off the clock too."

Chalker is most visible when doing her sideline reporting for SEC football games, and she has certainly noticed the double standard that affected contemporaries such as Erin Andrews, Pam Oliver and Ines Sainz. "I do feel like there's a greater pressure on women in the industry to be more attractive or to conform to the industry standards, but those standards are put on men as well," Chalker says. "If you are in the business of being on-camera, it's absolutely expected that you keep up your physical appearance. As for women having higher standards than the men though . . . of course they do. The ratio of men to women reporting on the sidelines is very lopsided, and there's a reason for that."

The future is wide open for Chalker, who could one day move into a coveted NFL sideline reporting spot or choose to become a fixture reporting on the Crimson Tide. Whatever her path, she feels like she owes something to the women sports reporters who come after her. "I absolutely see myself as a role model for other women aspiring to get into the sports media industry," she said. "I say that because I am constantly answering questions, via phone and email, about how I got to where I am and what advice I can give. The mountain is steep but the climb is worth it. Your best memories will come from the journey to the top."

Hannah can be reached on Twitter at @HannahChalker.

CHAPTER WRAP-UP

As it relates to sports media, ethics is a constantly evolving issue. There are no universal standards across the media, which often creates confusion and results in ethical decisions often being made on an ad hoc basis. Common ethical issues in sports media include conflict of interest, digital manipulation and citizen journalism.

The legal aspects of sports media are a bit clearer, but practitioners should be aware of potential problem areas such as libel, protecting sources and privacy. New technologies impact all of these areas as well.

Diversity, whether in terms of race or gender, is an increasingly important issue for today's sports media. Representation of women and minorities in the field is improving, but many are still concerned at the slow speed at which change is taking place. Women entering the field often face a double standard of having to look attractive for male audiences, yet having that attractiveness work against them in terms of sexual objectification. Another evolving issue is the decision by many sports media outlets to not use team nicknames that are considered racially offensive.

REVIEW QUESTIONS

1. What was the ethical issue involving *Time* magazine and the O.J. Simpson magazine cover? Do you think *Time* did the right thing? Why or why not?
2. What ethical issues are raised by the increasing speed and flexibility of new media technologies? What are the good and bad points of technological advances as they relate to sports media ethics?
3. Technological advances have also greatly impacted sports media legal issues. List some specific examples of how increased technology is making it easier for the sports media to skirt laws on privacy and access.
4. How is reporting in the sports media often a "Catch-22" for today's female reporters?
5. How does minority ownership of sports media directly relate to the representation of minorities as reporters and broadcasters?

GROUP ACTIVITIES

1. Discuss your personal ethical decision-making process. Where did that come from? How does it compare with others in the group? If you have starkly different values from someone else, how can you arrive at an ethical consensus?
2. As a group, work through various ethical scenarios (such as the O.J. Simpson magazine cover, the Baylor football jersey color, the Arthur Ashe privacy situation). Try to come to a group decision about handling each situation and what, if anything, you would have done differently.
3. Invite a female or minority sports reporter to meet with the group. Discuss what specific issues and difficulties this person faces on the job in contrast to other types of sports reporters.
4. Record a sporting event in which a female personality figures prominently (studio host, play-by-play, sideline reporter, color commentator). Review and discuss her demeanor, presentation and style in relation to issues discussed earlier in the chapter.

CHAPTER 3

Preparing for Careers in Multimedia Sports Journalism

Prior to the advent of the digital age, aspiring sports media professionals would generally pick a field to focus on in college, and then begin garnering experience from classroom assignments and student media and through internships and freelance work with professional outlets. They would still need to learn multiple skills; a prospective television sports reporter, for example, would need to learn how to shoot and edit video. But predigital television reporters were not expected to master Associated Press sports style or to write for a website and engage followers on social media as they are today.

Aspiring sports media professionals today must exhibit an array of multimedia skills and are generally expected to produce quality content for multiple types of media. They still are expected, however, to become an expert in one primary media (e.g., Internet, print reporting, television broadcasting, social media, video production) in which they apply for jobs. Fortunately, after decades of ignoring and/or belittling desires of their students, colleges and universities are finally recognizing the need for courses and specialized training in sports media.

GETTING EDUCATIONAL TRAINING IN SPORTS MEDIA

Course and major names in sport(s) media are often used interchangeably with sports communication and sports journalism. Regardless of course and degree titles, sports media is one of the fastest growing areas in communication/journalism schools and colleges (Wenner, 2015). Moreover, at least one general course on sports media or sports communication is included in most sports management and sports studies program curricula, which is often in addition to a course in sports public relations. Some sports management programs (e.g., Drexel University, Ferris State University, New York University, University of North Alabama, Winston-Salem State University) even offer full tracks or cognates in sports communication/sports media. But the greatest growth in sports media academia offerings this century has been in journalism/communication schools and colleges (Hardin, Pedersen, Laucella, Kian, & Geurin, 2016; "Pennsylvania State University," 2012).

The major universities now offering a stand-alone major, track, cognate, concentration, minor or certificate in sports media/sports journalism include the

Photo 3.1 Oklahoma State Sports Media students garner practical experiences in a video-production course.

University of Alabama, Arizona State University, Clemson University, University of Georgia, Indiana University-Bloomington, University of Kansas, University of North Carolina, Oklahoma State University, Penn State University, Syracuse University and the University of Texas at Austin, among others.

Several smaller colleges and universities were forerunners in developing strong sports media or related programs and thus aided their overall national student recruitment by doing so, such as Ashland University in Ohio, Butler University in Indiana, Marist University in New York, Morehouse College in Georgia and Quinnipiac University in Connecticut. But the greatest example of such success is Bradley University in Illinois, which in 2015 created the Charley Steiner School of Sports Communication, the first college or school dedicated fully to the study of sports communication.

However, many more universities and colleges are now offering coursework in sports media. Regardless of where these courses are housed, aspiring sports media professionals should take as many of these courses as possible. In other words, if you are majoring in communications/journalism, take whatever sports courses you can find offered in your college/school. Additionally, try to do sports media projects in some of your more general communications/journalism courses and take a sports-focused outside cognate or minor courses offered from the entire campus. A key, though, is to take as many writing courses as possible, because industry bosses from a variety of sports media list writing as the No. 1 skills needed in their fields (Ketterer, McGuire, & Murray, 2014).

GARNERING PRACTICAL INDUSTRY EXPERIENCE AS A STUDENT

Regardless of one's major, the No. 1 key for entry into the sports media profession is garnering practical and experiential experiences through student media, and especially through internships and freelance work with professional media outlets. Accordingly, students should take advantage of any internship credits offered through their programs.

"Grades are important, but when we are hiring student assistants, we look much more at work experience and skills, especially writing," said Gavin Lang, an assistant athletic director who usually employs 10 to 15 student assistants annually in the Oklahoma State University athletics communications office. "Other than making sure applicants actually graduated, we really don't even look at grades when hiring for full-time positions. Experience and talent are what counts."

We recommend that students garner experiences in a variety of student media to add variety to their portfolios and resumes, and help determine which areas they most want to focus on for their careers. For example, a student could write for the campus newspaper one semester, and then co-host a sports show on the campus radio station and serve as a production assistant for a television show the next term. After they have this experience, students would have a better idea of which of these fields they would most like to focus on going forward.

Students are strongly urged to take advantage of any professional or freelance opportunities available, such as covering area high school football games on Friday nights for a newspaper, television, radio or websites. They need to actively seek out such opportunities. Additionally, television and radio stations covering college football and basketball games often pay for student assistants on game day to help the production crew in a variety of roles, serve as utility runners, or even as spotters for television or radio broadcasts from the press box.

PROFESSIONAL ORGANIZATIONS

As in any other field, contacts matter in sports media. It is imperative that aspiring professionals network with those already in the field and with their classmates, who will also form contacts throughout their careers and could end up hiring other classmates down the road. Politely approaching and asking questions of industry professionals before games start is advisable. But the easiest way to meet sport media industry professionals is to join their organizations, some of which have student chapters at various universities or at least offer discount memberships for college students. Some of these organizations have regional meetings, and most have an annual national convention or conference, which provide tremendous venues for students to meet and interact with those who hire in various sectors of sports media.

The following are some of the major professional, industry-focused sports media organizations:

- Associated Press Sports Editors (APSE)
- Association for Women in Sports Media (AWSM)

Photo 3.2 Joining professional organizations provide networking opportunities. Here, Oklahoma State University AWSM (Association for Women in Sports Media) members meet with ESPN's Jemele Hill.

Photo courtesy of Courtney Bay

- College Sports Information Directors of America (COSIDA)
- National Sportscasters and Sportswriters Association (NSSA)
- Sportscasters Talent Agency of America (STAA)

In addition to these organizations, there are sports-specific professional media organizations such as Baseball Writers Association of America (BWAA), Football Writers Association of America (FWAA) and the United States Basketball Writers Association (USBWA). Students are also encouraged to consider joining professional media/communications organizations of a more general nature based on their interests, such as Public Relations Student Society of America (PRSSA), Radio Television Digital News Association (RTDNA) and Society of Professional Journalists (SPJ).

Finally, students from minority groups are strongly advised to join, place on their résumés and network in professional organizations such as the National Association of Black Journalists (NABJ), National Association of Hispanic Journalists (NAHJ) and the Asian American Journalists Association (AAJA), the latter of which recently started its own sports division.

RÉSUMÉ PREPARATION AND REFERENCES

In sports journalism, job application materials consist of more than just a résumé. Most job listings will also require a cover letter and a portfolio of the applicant's work. Résumés should be short, focused and descriptive of abilities of the sports journalist and/or sports communication professional. Résumé styles that are standard in other career pursuits (such as business) are not necessarily the best styles to use in sports journalism. In other words, going to a campus career service office will help in developing your résumé, but do not follow the formats you find there. Most job openings in sports media draw literally hundreds of applications, and it is thus important to prepare résumés in a way that gives the people looking at those applications a concise illustration of who you are and what you bring to the table.

When starting out in sports media, applicants should prepare résumés not exceeding one page in length, excluding references. Some news directors and editors will not look seriously at young professionals who cannot condense their résumés to one page. The following textbox provides an example résumé of an aspiring sports media professional.

RACHEL MARTINEZ
623 S. Main Street
Denver, CO 80123
303-421-4420
rachmart@gmail.com

EXPERIENCE

DAILY BUFFALO, Sports Editor   September 2015 – May 2016
- Managed sports staff of 13 writers.
- Assigned beats to writers and provided training and feedback on coverage.
- Managed branding of digital content, including utilization of social media platforms.
- Oversaw a 15 percent increase in sports-related web traffic.

PAC-12 NETWORK, Student Affiliate Reporter   October 2014 – May 2016
- Broadcasted 10 games for PAC-12 Network as sideline reporter or color commentator.
- Anchored coverage of games from Boulder studio.
- Interviewed high-profile coaches and athletes on live television.

LOS ANGELES TIMES, Sports Intern   May 2015 – August 2015
- Wrote and edited sports stories, with an emphasis on prep sports and small college baseball.
- Assisted sports writers with on-site gathering of player quotes and video.
- Operated sports department Twitter and Facebook accounts.

KUSA TELEVISION, Sports Intern   May 2014 – August 2014
- Produced packages and appeared in stand-ups for high school sports stories.

- Assisted videographers and reporters in filming and editing stories.
- Assisted producers in creating show rundowns.

DAILY BUFFALO, Sports Writer   **August 2012 – May 2016**
- Beat writer for four years at newspaper, covering six sports during that time.
- Covered football, men's basketball, baseball and women's soccer.
- Utilized social media to provide daily updates of team news, injuries and opponent information.

SKILLS
- **Web Analytics**: Proficient in Omniture, Chartbeat and Google Analytics.
- **Software**: Proficient in Windows and Apple software. Expert knowledge of Adobe Production Suite, Adobe Creative Suite, Microsoft Office Suite, iMovie, WordPress, TweetDeck, HootSuite, Facebook Ad Manager and Slack.
- **Social Media**: Regularly use Twitter (over 6k followers), Facebook, Instagram, Snapchat, LinkedIn and YouTube.
- Working knowledge of AP Style. Able to shoot and edit video. Comfortable on camera.

EDUCATION
UNIVERSITY OF COLORADO BOULDER   **August 2012 – May 2016**
- Bachelor of Arts in Journalism (May 2016)
- 3.31 GPA
- Minor in Broadcast Studies

Ideally the experience section of the resume will be filled with sports media jobs and internships completed while in college, including during summer and winter breaks. Student media roles, paid positions and volunteer work in sports media are all perfectly acceptable in this section. Also include any nonsports media or communication roles in your background, as well as select roles that demonstrate leadership, decision-making and creative skills. In general, though, remove entries on your résumé that deal with experiences unrelated to sports, media and communications, unless there is something exemplary on your record like university class president. The average newsroom is not interested in your three years of experience working at the campus bookstore as an extra during the first two weeks of class; instead they want to see if applicants have garnered the skills and experiences necessary to write on deadline, cover a beat, shoot and edit video and write press releases.

In most cases résumés should be in reverse chronological order, with the most recent experiences appearing at the top of the list. However, do not be afraid to put a really exciting or prestigious media position at the top of the list, even if it is not the most recent thing that you did. Your goal with the résumé is to impress potential employers with your accomplishments in sports media, so bending the norm to emphasize something unique is a good thing, particularly since those hiring will likely stop reading as soon as they lose interest. For example, a summer internship at a professional media outlet should go above student media experience even if the latter is more recent and you (likely) held more prominent positions.

Be sure to include two to four descriptive bullet points for each sports media experience on the résumé. These should be clearly written, brief and to the point. For current jobs, write them in the present tense. For former jobs, write them in the past tense. Make sure each bullet point highlights skills and responsibilities. If you have one that does not, then delete it. You will need the extra space.

For résumés in sports media, always put experiences at the top of the sheet, just below your name and contact information. Briefly list skills beneath your experiences, with education at the bottom. This is different from most résumés guides, which advise placing education at the top. Ultimately, in sports media it is far more important to demonstrate what you have done in the field than in the classroom. Education is still important and almost every full-time job in the industry now requires a college degree. However, the director or editor evaluating your application materials is going to be more interested in your abilities than where you went to school or your GPA, which should only be listed if 3.5 or above and never listed after you attained a full-time job in the field unless you graduated summa or magna cum laude. If you do not know what those terms mean, do not list your GPA.

Do not forget to include skills relevant to the specific position advertised. Employers in the digital age are looking for students with knowledge, experiences and skills in a wide variety of areas, including software, production, technical operation of equipment and social media, although writing remains the No. 1 skill desired by bosses in nearly all realms of sports media and communication as noted throughout this text. Make space in your résumé to focus on the most important skills that you possess. If you are proficient in using Twitter for marketing or publicity, or if you have regularly used Adobe Premiere or if you know how to effectively produce a podcast, then those items should find their way into the skills section of your résumé where each can be listed in one word or a short phrase.

Normally it is prudent to include references on a separate sheet, rather than trying to cram them onto a one-page résumé. Make sure listed references are people that a hiring manager or news director is going to consider worthwhile. Working professional journalists or editors who know you well enough to give a positive recommendation are always the best kinds of references to list. You should have networked well enough at your internship(s) to be able to list at least one such reference. Student media advisors are also good fits for a reference list. University professors are fine, particularly if their specialty is in journalism or media and they have practical industry experience. However, understand that professors' recommendations likely will not carry as much weight as those of practicing journalists or editors.

Remember to tailor application materials to the job that you are applying for. Send your best content regardless, but also send supplementary materials that demonstrate proficiency in something specific to that job. For example, if you are applying for a sports television job that requires a lot of editing and production, be sure to include items that demonstrate those skills in addition to your regular anchoring and reporting clips (e.g., listing your duties next to an embedded video on your online portfolio).

DEVELOPING AN ONLINE PORTFOLIO

Many journalism/communications schools and colleges now require undergraduate students to build and maintain an online portfolio to house their résumés and sample works during their studies. Generally, such individual websites must meet certain criteria and standards set by departments/schools for students to graduate. These are inaccurately often referred to as online résumés, but that is too limited. Instead, online portfolios display your best works, a variety of samples from multimedia, your résumé and sometimes references.

Some journalism schools require specific hosts for your portfolios, but several options are available if given a choice, with WordPress, Wix and Squarespace among the most popular. WordPress offers a free option, although it is recommended that you purchase your own domain name or something as close to your name as possible (e.g., adding numbers after your last name if your first and last name are already taken on a domain, such as JimSmith1999.com).

Regardless if required or not, students should start building an online portfolio early in their careers to house their best multimedia projects, which ideally could impress prospective employers. Portfolios of aspiring media/communications professionals should expand to include multiple Web pages under various headings and occasional subheadings (e.g., having a category for print articles, and then breaking down subheads by types: game stories, features, enterprise work, hard news, etc.). However, internal data at one large public university in the American Southwest revealed that more than 90 percent of visitors to student online portfolios only viewed the front/home page. Accordingly, put examples of some of your best work on the front page of your online portfolio.

TIPS FOR ONLINE PORTFOLIO

1. Purchase your own URL for this portfolio and make it as close to your name as possible (e.g., AmirRymer.com, HeatherJohnsonSportsJournalist.com, etc.).
2. Your name, educational status (e.g., name of institution, subject major, graduation date or projected graduation date) and current job should be prominent on the home page.
3. Use headers (top of page preferred) to house other pages and for easy navigation.
4. Attach a PDF version of a full résumé under a résumé tab and/or on your home page.
5. However, also place an abridged résumé of key work experiences and education (e.g., listing places worked and job titles, but not duties) on your home page.
6. Have various tabs for different types of multimedia works.
7. However, display two or three of your best works on your home page, which can, for example, be an embedded YouTube video, a clickable PDF of a brochure or media guide or a screen shot of a newspaper article with a hyperlink to the digital version of that same article.
8. Display links to your other professional pages, which could include your Vimeo page, YouTube page, a newspaper link to all of your electronic articles, a collection of podcasts housed on one page, LinkedIn, Twitter or other appropriate links.
9. Make sure your contact info (i.e., email and cell phone) is visible on several pages, including the home page. Do not require any visitor to fill out an online form to contact you; that person could be someone who wants to quickly contact you about freelance work.
10. Only include professional photos (e.g., headshot) if you include any at all. However, if your goal is to be a television broadcaster, a gallery of various portraits is acceptable, especially if you are female.
11. Whereas you want multiple items on the front page of your website, make sure that front page is not drowned out with too many items and that you have good spacing between items.
12. All of your pages should be geometrically aligned and aesthetically pleasing. Learn by looking at other (older) classmates' portfolios and those of industry professionals, which can often be linked to from their LinkedIn or social media.

WRITING COVER LETTERS AND APPLYING THROUGH EMAIL

Many of the same rules that apply to résumés also apply to cover letters. Always include a cover letter that focuses on why you are a great candidate for a particular position. Cover letters should not be long — generally one page of length is plenty — but the contents of the letter should demonstrate to the person reading it that you are both qualified for the job and excited about the prospect of working for this organization. Sending a generic cover letter is a surefire way to let a potential employer know that you are not that interested in the specific position being advertised.

Always proofread materials before submitting. Nothing can derail a job application in sports media faster than sending in a résumé or cover letter that is full of misspellings or poor grammar. Some news directors go over résumés with a fine-toothed comb, looking for any small mistakes, and then using those mistakes as justification for throwing that person's application out. Do not fall victim to something that is easily controlled, often by just proofreading and using spell check.

EXAMPLE EMAIL INQUIRY TO SEND TO A PROSPECTIVE EMPLOYER

From: John Fontaine <jayfont@gmail.com>
To: newsdirector@nbc5.com
Subject: Sports Reporter Position
Dear Mr. Carson,

My name is John Fontaine, a sports multimedia journalist who recently graduated from the University of Texas at Austin. I am writing to inquire whether there are any current or anticipated future job openings for a sports reporter at your station. I am a great admirer of your station and its reputation as a news leader in the marketplace, and would love to start my career with your organization.

It has been my lifelong goal to be a television sports reporter, and I have accrued a significant amount of experience in order to make that dream a reality. I have worked for the last four years as a student broadcaster with the Longhorn Network, serving in a variety of on-air and production roles, including sideline reporter and in-studio host. I have interned at ESPN for a summer, as well as with the local NBC affiliate in Austin. I have also gotten considerable on-air experience with our student television station, writing and reporting my own packages.

I have included a link to my YouTube channel, which contains my most recent standups and packages. You can find it here: http://www.youtube.com/jayfont/.

continued

Please let me know if you have any current or future openings. Thank you for taking the time to read this letter and hope you have a great day.

Sincerely,
John Fontaine

HOW TO LOOK FOR JOBS

So you have concluded that you want to work in sports media. But how exactly do you find that first job? Where do you look? And what do you do once you find the job you want? Sports media jobs are not likely to appear in the same places that you find most other jobs. Due to the small supply of jobs and the high demand of people looking to work in this field, you have to be entrepreneurial in approaching the job search process. Early in your career, that normally means going outside of the normal job search approach that your friends in accounting and engineering are using.

Before You Start Looking

One of the best things you can do is to start looking at job listings in areas that you are most interested in working in long before it is time for you to actually apply for full-time jobs.

Why so early? There are several reasons. First, looking for job listings long before applying provides a sense of where those job listings are located. We have already included links to some websites that list sports media jobs, but those links can change very quickly as time goes by. The more familiar you are with the actual process of searching for job listings online, the better you will be able to handle the process of looking for listings when the time comes for you to actually apply for a job.

Second, looking at job listings early allows you to get a sense for what employers are looking for in applicants. Are there particular technical skills that an employer wants? Do you need to be familiarizing yourself with new types of software? Are employers asking for expertise with certain social media networks? How much experience do you need from internships or student media? Searching job listings provides those answers, and thus can provide direction for your educational and skill development processes while you are still in school.

Third, viewing job listings early can help develop a realistic expectation of what sorts of jobs are out there before you start applying. Lots of people in sports media want to land their dream job at ESPN, FOX Sports or a major newspaper. But in reality, the majority of entry-level jobs available to most students are going to be lower-tier positions in less-than-ideal locations that pay less money than desired. There is nothing wrong with those jobs; in fact, that is where most people get their start. But it certainly helps to be familiar with the types of jobs that dominate the entry-level marketplace, and where those jobs are located.

One last important thing to do before beginning to look for jobs: Clean up your social media accounts. Go through your Twitter account and delete tweets that sound foolish or questionable in retrospect. On Facebook, change your privacy settings so that you are only showing the world the side of you that you want to be seen. If you have any sexualized pictures of yourself or any that include alcohol, take them down altogether. You should strongly consider creating a separate, professional Facebook page for yourself with links to your online materials, and changing your Facebook profile to something that does not reveal your full name.

Please note that this does not mean you should delete your social media entirely. Quite the contrary; sports media employers today want to see proof that potential employees can handle social media professionally and effectively. A job applicant without any social media accounts will not be considered for most sports media jobs today.

In addition to the major media companies' human resources Internet pages and general sites like Monster and CareerBuilder, among the best job sites to check regularly include:

JournalismJobs.com
http://JournalismJobs.com

SportsJournalists.com
http://SportsJournalists.com

STAA Message Boards
http://staatalent.com

TVJobs.com
http://tvjobs.com

COSIDA Job Center
http://forms.cosida.com/jobs.aspx

TeamWorkOnline
http://www.teamworkonline.com

The Job Search

You are finally ready to start applying for jobs. You have done your homework on job listings, prepared all application materials and are ready to land your first job in the field. What now?

First, keep in mind that timing when it comes to job applications can be tricky for college graduates. Since most students graduate in May, there is a glut of applicants looking for work during that time. However, summer months also see the most job postings because people who primarily cover high school or college sports often move during summer months, and people with children who change jobs generally try to do so between school years. Nevertheless, with so many people looking for work, the job market can be flooded and make your materials have a harder time standing out.

Regardless of when you graduate, you should avoid applying for jobs too early. It makes sense to start the process about two to three months before your graduation date, but not before. Most employers will not consider hiring you until right before graduation, and even if one does, you could end up in the uncomfortable position of getting a dream first job offer with a start date two months before you are actually able to start working.

Do not apply for jobs that you are not ready for. A lot of broadcast journalism students want to work at ESPN at some point in their careers, but are simply not ready or qualified to do so right after graduating from college. Applying to lower- and middle-tier openings is a better use of time and resources.

Do not restrict your search to only media outlets that post job listings. Contact media organizations in places where you are interested in living and speak with their human resources departments about available job opportunities. Reach out to sports directors and sports editors to see if there are any openings, or even possibilities for part-time work near your hometown, where you could likely live cheaply or free. Be professional and polite and try to make a good impression. Even if those organizations do not have anything at that moment, they might remember you for a future opening.

Make sure you apply to many jobs in many geographic regions for your first job, with the understanding most will either not contact you and that some will only send a rejection letter after their search is complete. That is normal and natural when there are literally hundreds of applicants for each position. As noted, the field is highly competitive, and just because you are not getting called about your application does not mean that you did anything wrong. Try not to get discouraged; understand that this happens to everybody and that your first full-time job will be the toughest to attain.

The Interview Process

Congratulations, one of the places you applied wants to set up an interview. This is an exciting development, but there is still plenty of work left to do before you get a job offer. Before you do any interviews, you need to do exhaustive research on the organization that is interviewing you. Read through their website and evaluate what their business or coverage approach is. Try to find online bios of leadership and employees at the company, and read those bios to get a better sense of the people. Make sure you know the names and backgrounds of everyone in the sports department. Search the Internet for stories about the company. Any information you can find will make you more knowledgeable in the interview, and will hopefully impress the person interviewing you with your level of preparation and knowledge.

The Phone or Skype Interview

In most cases, your first job interview will be by phone or Skype. If you are fortunate to have an interview with a company close by, then it might be in person.

Phone and Skype interviews are often intended to screen out applicants whose credentials look good on paper, but may not fit the profile that the employer is looking for. In sports media, this could involve a number of different factors, such as attitude towards the job, vocal quality or answers to certain questions. Approach every phone interview with a positive attitude that indicates your interest in the job, but try to pick up on cues from the interviewer about what the company is interested in. Essentially, you are generally among five to 12 semifinalists for a position when you get this type of interview. However, most companies will only bring in two to three finalists for actual in-person interviews.

Do not provide prospective employers an obvious reason to cut you from their list. Be prepared to answer a series of questions about yourself. Why are you interested in this job? Why do you feel you are qualified for this job? What do you feel are your strengths and weaknesses? Many media companies will also ask you specific questions about their media market and coverage strategies. These questions are often designed to see whether you have done any preparation for the phone interview.

Do not be afraid to ask questions of your own during a phone interview. However, only do this at the end if provided the opportunity or at an appropriate time as a follow-up. Do not interrupt those asking you questions or divert away from answering their questions to ask your own. However, it is fine to ask about the work environment, the company's core values and what they most want out of this hire. Then, try to tie their answers back into your qualifications, strengths and desires to make you stand out as an attractive candidate.

It is unlikely that you will receive a job offer during an initial phone interview. Instead, you will probably be told that they will be in touch with you in the near future if you are selected to move on to the next round of interviews. This can create a waiting game for you that is uncomfortable, but unfortunately hard to avoid. Try not to let it bother you, and just accept that the decision is largely out of your hands at this point. If you have not received any news about another interview within a week of that initial phone interview, do not hesitate to email (do this first) and then call (only if you did not hear back from your email) the company back and ask about the status of the position you applied for.

The In-Person Interview

If you make it through the phone interview, you will almost certainly be brought in for an in-person interview. This is an exciting step because it likely means that you are among the final two or three people in competition for the job. Your odds of landing this job just went way up. In-person interviews tend to last several hours or a full day, occasionally being done over two days. The in-person interview is often the company's only chance to watch you in action, interacting with several different people in the organization and seeing how well you fit in.

Make sure to dress impeccably and very professionally in business attire for your in-person interview (e.g., suit and tie for men, with dress shoes). Be charming and personable when talking with people. Ask them questions about themselves, their jobs and their accomplishments. Be prepared to answer the same questions from different people throughout the day. Above all else, keep in mind that the people you talk to during the day are going to be asked to report back to the person doing the hiring about what they thought of you.

You will normally finish your in-person interview with the person in charge of hiring. If you have any major questions left to ask, this is the time to do it. While you should not hesitate to ask about benefits, work expectations and job evaluations, it is recommended that you do not ask about salaries until you are actually offered the position. If you broach that topic, you can talk your way out of a job by expressing salary demands that are too high or end up being offered less than you would have by setting you salary goals too low. Regardless, be sure to ask them about the timetable for hiring the position. Most importantly, be sure to express your interest in the position and exhibit excitement about potentially working there.

ADAPTING TO THE FUTURE

The future of sports journalism will see many changes to the job landscape. We are already seeing the field change, as traditional entry-level positions at newspapers pay less money and more media outlets consolidate or go out of business. The lack of certainty can be frightening to an aspiring sports journalist, but there are several things you can do to prepare yourself for the future.

Audience Adaptation

The sports media audience continues to evolve, and it is part of your job as a sports journalist to understand and relate to that audience. But this is easier said than done. The digital age has created an audience with many different facets, which makes it difficult for journalists to satisfy all parts of the audience simultaneously. Younger audiences are considerably tech-savvy, and they expect rapidly delivered information, multimedia presentation, opportunities for interaction with the journalist, and data and statistics to back up arguments. On the other hand, older audiences are often deterred by complicated statistics, and tend to prefer simple presentation of content over multimedia content. Trying to reconcile these opposing preferences is difficult for even seasoned journalists.

Fortunately for the aspiring sports journalist, media outlets in this field tend to focus on younger consumers. More than that, media outlets look to young sports journalists as the key to connecting with younger audiences. Use that to your advantage. Study audience trends across media by reading media analyses online. Stay up to date on technology changes. Understand the impact of things such as streaming video, DVRs, and news aggregation on media consumption, and stay abreast of emerging technologies that further change the landscape.

Changing Job Expectations

As mentioned earlier in this chapter, the expectations of those employed in sports journalism are growing in the digital age, with social media duties added on top of traditional responsibilities without significant pay increases to offset the extra work. You can expect that process to continue, as sports journalism professionals will be expected to have experience in multiple media fields, and to use that experience in crafting a wide array of content on a regular basis.

We have entered an era where the distinctions between media types are becoming irrelevant to media employers. Writers are now expected to be able to podcast and shoot video, broadcasters are expected to write and everybody is expected to be proficient at social media. While it is still important to have an area of focus, it is also paramount that you develop multimedia skills in other areas. For example, while you may want to specialize in writing features and game stories, you need to take the time in school to learn your way around video editing software.

Emerging Technology

If the last decade has taught us anything, it is that media technologies are going to constantly reinvent themselves. This represents a huge change for journalists of all types, who grew comfortable in the 20th century with traditional technologies such as the printing press, radio broadcasts and television towers, none of which changed significantly for decades.

However, media technologies are not changing as rapidly as some people claim, and a fairly stable group of brand names such as Facebook, Instagram and Twitter have dominated the landscape since at least 2012. Some of the features have changed, but the core concepts have not. Facebook has added live video, Instagram has added features to compete with Snapchat and Twitter has tried to increase its relevance by altering its timeline algorithm.

Become a power user of social media. Maximize your presence on Twitter, Facebook, Snapchat and elsewhere. Establish your social media brand before you leave college. Communication on social networks will only become more important as the years go by, and media companies will continue to focus their attention on cultivating audiences on established networks like Facebook and Twitter. If you can make that kind of communication seem like second nature, you will have an advantage in the sports media field. As a young person in sports journalism, try to stay current on social media trends. Follow trade journals that cover the tech industry and try out new apps before they become big. If you find an app or two that helps you do your job more easily or efficiently, then you will have an advantage over many others in the field.

WHAT TO PUT ON A REEL

In broadcasting, we call the collections of work that job applicants send to potential employers a "reel" or "demo tape." Both of those terms refer back to a now-bygone era where job seekers would send in an actual physical cassette tape with their material on it. Fortunately, those days are long gone, and your demo tape is going to be a collection of clips that you organize and send online. Here are some tips and tricks to making a quality demo tape:

- Start cultivating your materials long before you need to put together a demo tape. Get a digital recording of everything you do. Then watch or listen to those digital recordings, and choose the best one- to two-minute clips out of each one. Put those items aside in a folder on your computer's hard drive, and label them well enough for you to go back and find them later.
- Get comfortable with using editing software to piece together your materials. For audio, this means programs like Adobe Audition. For video, this means programs like Adobe Premiere. Take the time to learn how to use the functions in these programs.
- For video reels, always put a graphical slate at the start of your demo reel that lists your name, area of focus (i.e., "Sports broadcaster" or "Multimedia journalist"), permanent email address and phone number. Have this slate appear for four to six seconds at the start of your reel.
- The most important part of your demo tape is the first minute. If the material in that opening 60 seconds does not captivate the person viewing it, they are not going to watch anything else that you have. Be sure to put your absolute best at the beginning. For radio, this might be your best play-by-play segment, part of a great interview or the heart of a dynamite talk radio monologue. For video, this might be your best couple of standups.
- Then, move on to providing longer segments of your materials. Put your materials into categories (e.g., "Anchoring," "Play-by-play"), and ideally line up two to five minutes of material for each category.
- Do not put anything on your demo reel that is not of high quality. You want them to see you at your best all the way through.
- Cut out the parts of the clips where you are not talking. Busy, prospective employers do not want to hear your color commentator talking; they want to hear what you sound like. They may decide to hire the other broadcaster instead, whom they may have not known about had you not included that person in your materials.
- Constantly upgrade your demo tape as you get newer clips. Your newer stuff is almost always going to sound better than what came before.
- Tailor your demo tape to the job you are applying for. Do not send a bunch of talk radio clips to a play-by-play job.

FEATURE INTERVIEW

JOHN READ

**Basketball Communications
Manager, Oklahoma City Thunder**

Growing up in Southern California, John Read dreamed of working for the Los Angeles Lakers so much that he faxed over his résumé to the Lakers more than 100 times while he was a college student at nearby Loyola Marymount. But after initially being ignored by the Lakers' front office, Read set about garnering other practical experiences. He did an internship for Penske Racing, where he formed industry contacts who were impressed by his work ethic and who knew higher-ups with the Lakers. This led to Read landing his dream college internship with the Lakers.

Photo 3.3 In his duties as basketball communications manager for the Oklahoma City Thunder, John Read (left) works closely with superstar players like Russell Westbrook (right). Photo courtesy of John Read

However, showing the competitiveness of the field, Read was unable to a land full-time position in sports after graduating. Read was set to begin working with nonsport companies when he received a call to see if he had interest in a one-year, full-time internship with the Mavericks. He immediately accepted the offer, packed up his car and moved to Dallas, where he knew no one. But once again through hard work, determination and consistent skills improvement, he succeeded and has since worked his way to his current position as basketball communications manager with the Oklahoma City Thunder. There he oversees the hiring and management of student interns and is heavily involved in all public relations hires.

What does Read and his Thunder colleagues look for in trying to sift through application materials from thousands of applicants? "We are mainly looking at your experience," Read said. "You need to have done things to set yourself apart and you need to get whatever experience you can while in school. Your references also matter."

CHAPTER WRAP-UP

Sports media education and courses have grown considerably in the past decade. Regardless whether your school offers a major in this area, you should take as many sports media, journalism skills, and sports-management/sports-studies courses as you can. But while you do need a college degree to meet the minimum requirements for most full-time jobs, practical experience is the most important key to entering the sports media profession, with industry contacts arguably the No. 2 key. Accordingly, students need to garner practical experiences through outlets like student media and through internship opportunities. They also need to keep a one-page résumé constantly updated and begin building an online portfolio to house a variety of their best multimedia works.

Even long before they begin looking for full-time jobs, students should begin preparing for this process by following job listings on the most relevant sites toward their particular interest. They should always dress and act professionally, both in the field and especially while searching for and interviewing for jobs. And although they are likely to be skilled and knowledgeable on the newest social media platforms and apps, aspiring sports media professionals must not only keep up with emerging trends and technological changes, but be early adopters who quickly master new skills to better position themselves for multimedia jobs.

REVIEW QUESTIONS

1. What is the No. 1 skill that you need to improve upon for most sports media jobs?
2. What is the No. 1 key to enter the sports media profession?
3. How many pages should there be in a sports media résumé for a college student?
4. What are some of the emerging technologies in sports media and how can you best prepare for unpredictable changes in this area?

GROUP ACTIVITIES

1. Each student in a group should list three potential work/internship opportunities, with one member focusing on on-campus media and the others researching off-campus opportunities, such as local newspapers, television and radio stations. The group should compare results to compile a list.
2. Each student in the group should research at least two professional sports media and/or media/communications organizations that are of interest. The person should then list potential benefits of joining these organizations; this will be read to the rest of the group.
3. All students in the group should bring a copy of their résumé to share with others. All should offer critiques and copy-edit each résumé in the group for feedback.

CHAPTER 4

Basics of Sports Reporting

WHY SPORTS REPORTING?

A generation ago, colleges and universities that offered specialized programs in sports journalism were extremely rare. Today, the number of sports journalism programs, along with the number of students wanting to go into the industry, has exploded. There has been an even greater rise in school programs for sports marketing and sports management, many of which offer courses in sports media.

There are a variety of explanations for this, but from a supply and demand perspective the supply of schools offering these programs continues to rise because student demand keeps increasing. Many of these students grew up as sports fans and see reporting as a way to turn their passion into a career. Others view it as a quick ticket to fame and fortune, and they envision themselves traveling first class to major sports events and broadcasting to millions of fans. Still others figure it has to be a pretty easy way to make a living. After all, it's only "sports," which for years has been ridiculed as the "toy department" of real journalism.

While these perceptions may contain a kernel of truth, they are for the most part very wrong. And certainly none of them is a reason to go into sports reporting as a career. Former television executive and news director Griff Potter says, "It's about journalism, not sports. If you are in it for the sports, you're not a journalist but a fan. Get a job in another industry and buy season tickets" (personal communication, 2000). News director Dennis Fisher at WHTM-TV, the ABC affiliate in Harrisburg, Pennsylvania, is even blunter. "Don't get in the business," he says. "There is too much competition and not enough jobs to go around. If you insist on going into it, then be resigned to hard work and little glory" (personal communication, 2000).

That's the harsh reality of the industry — sports reporting is often a difficult, unglamorous job with lots of competition, long hours and low pay. Certainly, some make it to the very top and enjoy the perks of a successful sports journalism career. However, many never get the chance to regularly cover big-time sports or, more likely, they drop out of the business to find a better paying career with more stable hours.

Although the average annual salary for a sports radio anchor is relatively low at $33,700, these positions are highly competitive because of the large number of individuals who desire careers in this area. For television sports anchors and reporters, the pay is only slightly higher compared to their radio counterparts.

The average annual salary for television sport anchors is $60,000 and for television sports reporters it is $38,300 (Papper, 2012). Keep in mind, however, that because sports reporting jobs are highly coveted, many starting salaries will be below the average. It is not unusual for those going into smaller television markets to make a starting salary between $20,000 and $25,000. The point here is not to scare off budding sports reporters, but rather to make sure you go into the field with eyes wide open. The fame, big salary and other perks may come later in a career, but for those just getting into the business, the first years are very difficult ones.

That said, if you have a love for sports, and can learn how to objectively report, tell a story, write and, increasingly, add multimedia skills throughout your career, working in sports media can be an ideal vocation. "I absolutely love my job," says Ryan Wilson, a blogger, writer and podcaster for CBSSports.com. "My friends can't believe I get to sit around and write and talk about sports, which have been a life-long passion" (personal communication, 2015).

A BRIEF HISTORY

The "toy department" criticism began almost as soon as sports became a regular part of newspaper coverage in the late 19th century. By the 1920s, sports reporters played an important role in shaping public opinion about athletes, creating a mythology that celebrated their successes and ignored their weaknesses. "When a sports writer stops making heroes out of athletes, it's time to get out of the business," sports writer Grantland Rice once said (Inabinett, 1994, p. 14).

The hero worship began to fade in the 1950s and '60s as new cultural attitudes took hold. Sportscaster Howard Cosell became known for a hard-hitting, honest style of reporting with his work for ABC Sports. "I am simply trying to bring the tenets of good journalism to television," Cosell once said. "It is difficult because sportscasting is a bottle that was put to sea many years ago and has been lost" (Twombly, 1970, p. 14). It took a ballplayer to finally strip away many of the old beliefs about sports journalism, as baseball pitcher Jim Bouton's *Ball Four* became a sensation. The diary of the 1969 season showed ballplayers as they really were — sometimes heroic, but often narcissistic, immature and sexually obsessed. Bouton (1981, p. xii) later wrote, "People were simply not used to reading the truth about professional sports. By establishing new boundaries, *Ball Four* changed sports reporting … it was no longer possible to sell the milk and cookies image again."

Since that time, reporters have become more willing to turn over rocks and expose the unpleasant, hidden side of sports. This included looking into areas that had been previously ignored, such as gender issues, economics and ownership. The sports reporting of some media outlets, notably the *San Francisco Chronicle*, *Lexington* (Ky.) *Herald-Leader* and *St. Paul* (Minn.) *Pioneer Press*, uncovered scandals that led to significant change. The popular ESPN television show "Outside the Lines" is an example of the commitment to cover sports in a serious, meaningful way.

But in this digital era highlighted by social media, websites and an endless array of choices for sports media consumers, increasingly more of the sports media are filled with gossip and innuendo, especially regarding sex and scandal.

The modern cultural emphasis on celebrity has combined with audience demand and advances in technology to create a perfect storm that threatens to overwhelm the profession. Some of the biggest sports scandals in recent years — Lance Armstrong, Manti Te'o and Deflategate — engendered an audience passion that few other news stories could match.

SPORTS REPORTING BASICS

You can see the close connection between cultural values and sports reporting style. The protective hero worship of the 1920s has now shifted dramatically as the modern sports media typically seek to tear down athletes rather than build them up. But there are rules to good sports reporting that transcend cultural time periods, and we discuss some here.

Fairness, Balance and Objectivity

All people in the media, especially sports reporters who typically grew up as fans, bring their own unique biases and perspectives to their reporting. The key is understanding your own biases and not letting them creep into your reporting. It's just common sense that a sports reporter should not take sides, show favoritism or be biased.

Fairness sounds great in theory, but it can get tricky in practice. Local reporters, especially those in small towns or in places with passionate fan bases, can drift into rooting for the home team. Known as "boosterism" or "homerism," this type of reporting can also occur when a reporter befriends a player or coach through regular coverage of the team. Such reporting may be popular with the home folks, but it makes it very difficult to report controversial or unpleasant material.

One of the most famous reporter–coach relationships involved Indiana University Hoosiers' basketball coach Bob Knight and Bob Hamel, a long-time reporter for the The (Bloomington, Ind.) Herald-Times. In his excellent book A Season on the Brink, author John Feinstein described the relationship between the two as unusually strong, almost like brothers. In this situation, one could understand how Hamel would be reluctant to report any damaging information about Knight or the basketball program. According to Feinstein, Hamel never considered it a serious ethical issue, but he did admit to having a rooting interest in Hoosier games.

Several media outlets have taken a courageous stand to report fairly and without bias, even in the face of local criticism. In 1986, the Lexington (Ky.) Herald-Leader uncovered a scandal involving the beloved hometown University of Kentucky basketball program. The newspaper won a Pulitzer Prize for its work, but received thousands of cancellations and death threats from angry readers who didn't want to see the team penalized. That same year, WFAA-TV, an ABC affiliate for the Dallas-Fort Worth Metroplex, broke news on payments from Dallas-based college football power SMU to football prospects, which ultimately resulted in SMU receiving the "death penalty" from the NCAA, canceling its football program for two years in the process.

Today, the trend is toward having more opinion in sports media, such as in sports talk radio, social media interaction and popular television shows like "Pardon the Interruption" and "Around the Horn" on ESPN. Many of those involved in these shows, such as Tony Kornheiser and Michael Wilbon of "Pardon the Interruption," have crossed over from newspaper reporting. It's important to remember that such content is clearly labeled as commentary or opinion and should not be confused with objective sports reporting.

The goal of commentary and opinion is to build and keep an audience through the force of on-air personalities. "I have to be interesting more than anything," said radio sports talk show host Mike Gastineau, known locally as "The Gasman," of KJR-AM sports talk radio in Seattle. "For example, how many preset buttons do you have on your car radio? Ten or15? It takes two seconds for you to be driving along and say this is boring and go to another station" ("Sports talk," 1999). The goal of sports reporting is to tell fair, balanced and objective stories in an interesting way.

Beginning students often gravitate to opinion and commentary because it seems fun and easy, but very few people in the industry start out as commentators. Media outlets are looking for solid reporters who can tell compelling stories, and only the most experienced reporters eventually work their way into commentary.

Have a Story to Tell

Having a story to tell may seems like the easiest and most basic part of reporting, but it often gets lost or ignored. Reporters are in the storytelling business and all stories must have a point or theme. Sometimes the theme is blatantly obvious: "Henrik Lundqvist stopped all 31 shots last night, and Ryan McDonough scored twice to lead the New York Rangers to a 4-0 shutout win over Tampa Bay."

However, sometimes the theme is harder to identify, especially for feature stories. Good reporters can build themes around common emotions that everyone understands, such as overcoming hardship, perseverance, courage or tragedy. All people, not just sports fans, can connect with the kid who comes off the bench and becomes a hero with a game-winning kick.

IS THAT MY SON? YES, AND A HERO TO BOOT

The following excerpt is from a 2006 story on University of Texas football player Ryan Bailey, who kicked a last-second field goal to beat the University of Nebraska. Even in this short selection you can get an idea of the theme that writer Geoff Ketchum had in mind—a kid who never got off the bench gets his chance and becomes a sudden hero.

> Cindy Bailey stared at the television.
> Ryan?
> Steve Bailey stared at the television.
> Ryan?

Millions of Americans stared at their televisions.

Who's Ryan?

Nearly no one watching Texas and Nebraska play football Saturday recognized Ryan Bailey, jogging into swift and surprising fame through a swirl of Midwestern snow.

But his parents knew their son, and when they witnessed Longhorns head coach Mack Brown pat Ryan's helmet on the sidelines, they began to accept the sudden and thrilling and agonizing truth.

Soon, everyone would remember Ryan.

Ryan Bailey — 19 years old, walk-on sophomore placekicker, Anderson High School graduate, No. 39 on the Texas travel roster — had never played in a college football game.

"Never even smelled the field," said his father, Steve.

But there he was Saturday. Kicking a 22-yard field goal. With 23 seconds left and the fate of the game resting on his shoe.

Source/Courtesy: Ketchum (2006). *Austin American-Statesman*

Themes that are overly complex or try to go in too many directions only confuse audiences. The simpler and more narrowly focused the theme, the better. Once you establish the theme, support it with the materials you have to tell the story. For print stories, this would primarily be the writing and images, while for broadcast stories, it is a combination of video, sound and writing. Online stories are a hybrid of print and broadcast, offering both the depth of print reporting with supplementary video and sound. No matter what platform, the materials should support the theme. In the Ryan Bailey story, for example, the best photo to accompany the story would be Bailey celebrating the winning kick with his teammates, not one of him sitting dejectedly on the bench.

All stories and themes should lead the audience to the same place. That is, they should tell a story that is engaging and easily understood. Audiences don't necessarily have to "agree" with the story, only to find it compelling and understandable. University of Nebraska fans probably didn't like the approach taken in the Ryan Bailey story, but they certainly understood the point the author was trying to make.

Research and Background

Sports reporters cover lots of different types of stories. One day the story might involve a track meet, the next day the resignation of a local coach, and then the following day tougher penalties are announced for players caught using performance-enhancing drugs. Even the biggest of sports fans can't be an expert in all these areas, which means there will often be the need for additional research. In the pre-Internet days, this meant making phone calls, looking up newspaper stories and records, and getting out to talk with people. That's still very much the case, but the Internet has changed much of the process. Computer-assisted reporting makes it easy to find statistics, background, and contact information.

As great as they are in aiding research, computers and the Internet come with a warning. There's a ton of information on the Internet, much of it unverified and unreliable. Simply cutting and pasting a Web story, or using the information in a broadcast report, violates one of the basic tenets of journalism: All information should be confirmed by two independent sources. Even something as routine as a game score or spelling of a name can be problematic, and it's best to double check any and all information.

In 2010, *Washington Post* sports writer Mike Wise got into trouble for deliberately tweeting a phony report on Steelers' quarterback Ben Roethlisberger just to see how many other reporters would retweet it without verification. A number of Web sites, from *The Miami Herald* to NBC's "ProFootball-Talk," passed on the tweet to their audiences. After he received a month-long suspension from *The Post*, Wise acknowledged his mistake: "My own stupid, irresponsible experiment has cost me a chunk of my own credibility. I'm paying the price I should for careless, dumb behavior" (Kurtz, 2010, ¶ 9). But Wise apparently didn't take his own advice. In 2017, now working for ESPN, Wise was disciplined for attributing phony Twitter comments to University of Alabama football coach Nick Saban.

Identify the Stakeholders

Once the theme of a story has been established, the reporter needs to identify the stakeholders that will be necessary to help tell that story. One reason a narrow, focused theme is so important is that it leads the reporter right to the one or two main stakeholders for the story.

Let's take a look at a hypothetical story with a theme that is too broad: "Steroids have become a problem in high school athletics." That may be true, but it is such a complex story that there are dozens of stakeholders involved, including athletes, coaches, parents, schools, doctors and lawyers, among others. It would be impossible to track down and interview all the various stakeholders, and even if you could your story would likely turn into a jumbled mess. Instead, narrow the theme so as to make the story more focused, and thus more manageable. Consider the theme "An increase in steroid use among high school athletes is resulting in serious medical problems." Now, we can target specific stakeholders — such as athletes, parents and doctors — and not worry about others (such as lawyers or school administrators).

The same process is used when covering a particular game, although it's a bit easier because the important stakeholders are more obvious and all in one place. Go back to our hockey story — "Henrik Lundqvist stopped all 31 shots last night, and Ryan McDonough scored twice to lead the New York Rangers to a 4-0 shutout win over Tampa Bay." The stakeholders stand out — Lundqvist and McDonough — and these are the ones the reporter is likely to zero in on after the game for interviews and further information.

Learn to Keep Stats

Sports are competitive, with winners and losers in every game, match and event. Some type of scoring mechanism generally decides sporting events, either through points scored or a judging system, the latter of which is also usually based on points. The basics of sports reporting entail detailing the 5 Ws (who, what, where, when and why). When covering games, the most important of those are who played and who won (e.g., always make the final score the first numbers to appear in any type of sports story). Individual and team statistics help convey what happened for any type of sports game story regardless of the type of media outlet where it is delivered (e.g., television, newspaper, radio, website, social media). Therefore, reporters should keep their own statistics for any type of sporting event or game they cover. The basic rules and scoring system for just about any sport can be found through Google searches. Do not rely on scorekeepers, especially at high school or youth contests. Keep your own stats. Get rosters before games at high school and youth contests, and check with coaches to assure accuracies of names and jersey numbers. You can practice keeping statistics at home while watching games on television, or better yet, by attending amateur sporting events.

At least early in your career, do not try to do too much when keeping stats, particularly with sports you do not understand or that move fast, such as basketball. Make sure you keep a running score chart and stats for who scored and how. For some sports that are more slow-moving by nature (e.g., baseball) or without much scoring, stats are easier to keep. Other sports require more in-game work. Individual stats are also very helpful in building a sports story for print, broadcast or online. However, do not bog down your sports story with too many statistics, particularly for games where anyone can access a box score via the Internet. See the accompanying website for this book (http://www.oup.com/us/kian) for more overall tips on keeping stats, sports terminology and rules for specific sports.

Personalize the Story

Stressing the personal can't be overstated enough. To some degree, sports are about scores and statistics, but the main story is the people behind the numbers. That's what is so compelling about sports — the people behind the records and the numbers. Good reporters recognize that good stories are always about people. In the 1960s, ABC's "Wide World of Sports" called it "the human drama of athletic competition," and Roone Arledge pioneered the idea of showing athletes "up close and personal" (Wasko, 2010, p. 341). That style still works today, whether you're covering the Olympics or the high school volleyball match. Get people to care about the games and athletes on a personal level.

At the 2014 Winter Olympics, U.S. skier Bode Miller, who had come under previous criticism for not performing well, won an unexpected bronze medal in the super-giant slalom. Winning a medal and proving his critics wrong, along with the recent death of his brother, all made it a very emotional moment for Miller. That's what NBC reporter Christin Cooper focused on in her interview with Miller right after the race.

GOING TOO FAR?

NBC's Christin Cooper came under intense criticism of her post-race interview with Bode Miller at the 2014 Winter Olympics for pushing him too hard. The transcript below suggests that Cooper knew to focus on the emotion of the moment, rather than the facts and figures of the race.

> BODE MILLER: This was a little different. With my brother passing away, I really wanted to come back here and race the way he sends it. So this was a little different.
>
> CHRISTIN COOPER: Bode, you're showing so much emotion down here. What's going through your mind?
>
> BM: (Long pause) A lot, obviously. A long struggle coming in here. And, uh, just a tough year.
>
> CC: I know you wanted to be here with Chilly experiencing these games, how much does it mean to you to come up with a great performance for him? And was it for him?
>
> BM: I mean, I don't know it's really for him. But I wanted to come here and uh—I don't know, I guess make myself proud. (Pauses, then wipes away tears.)
>
> CC: When you're looking up in the sky at the start, we see you there and it just looks like you're talking to somebody. What's going on there?
>
> BM: (Falls to his knees and rests himself on a fence separating him from Cooper.)
>
> CC: (Whispers "sorry" and puts her hand on Miller's shoulder before he walked away a few seconds later.)

Courtesy of NBC/Universal

Cooper came under intense criticism for her handling of the interview, especially through social media outlets. Richard Sandomir (2014, ¶ 11) of *The New York Times* cuttingly remarked, "If you've made a medal winner cry, it is time to simply say 'thank you' and move on." NBC supported Cooper, saying "Our intent was to convey the emotion that Bode Miller was feeling after winning his bronze medal. We understand how some viewers thought the line of questioning went too far, but it was our judgment that his answers were a necessary part of the story" (Chase, 2014, ¶ 13). Interestingly, Miller also later supported Cooper, which helped quell some of the backlash against her.

Whether or not Cooper actually caused Miller to cry, it would have been a completely different, and obviously less compelling, interview if Cooper had only focused on such questions as, "What do you think of your time?" or "What seemed to be the most difficult part of the run for you?" She also seemed to clearly understand that the theme of the interview/story was not so much Miller winning a medal, but rather the flood of emotions that came from the victory.

Tell Your Story on Multiple Platforms

Technology, and specifically the Internet and social media, has vastly complicated the sports reporting process. Where in the pre-Internet days a newspaper reporter wrote specifically for the paper, that same reporter today must create stories for the newspaper, website, social media, and sometimes even for television. It's called multimedia reporting, and it has become the standard in the sports media industry. Today's outlets are looking for someone who can report on these multiple platforms, which means students need skills and experience in print, broadcast and social media. To better understand the process, let's consider a specific example (Figure 4.1).

Reporting on multiple platforms is essential for today's sports reporter. A single game played at night will require more than a dozen hours of reporting coverage in print, broadcast, online and social media. Say there's a big basketball game coming up tonight at 7:30. How might the multimedia sports reporter handle it? The day will start early in the morning with the reporter beginning to formulate a plan on covering the game. This would include checking newspapers, television, Internet, social media, and personal sources for updates and the latest information. If something does need to be updated it would go immediately on social media and the Internet.

Sifting and sorting through thousands of potential pieces of information related to the game has become a big part of reporting. Social media are not only ways to distribute stories, they can often be stories themselves, as athletes and coaches now use these platforms to post newsworthy information and opinions. For example, if a player in our basketball game tweeted that morning that he was not going to play because a family member died, the reporter would obviously want to pass along that big news.

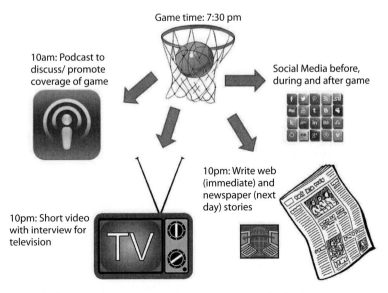

Figure 4.1 Modern sports reporting requires reporting on multiple platforms.

Photo 4.1 An example of organizing Twitter feeds in a Tweetdeck.
Photo courtesy of Twitter

One way reporters can keep up with this is a program that manages and organizes media feeds. Twitter, for example, lets the user organize, manage and prioritize particular Twitter feeds through Tweetdeck. For our basketball game, the reporter might want to create a Tweetdeck that has the feeds of the two teams involved, their star players and perhaps another media outlet such as ESPN.

A program like Tweetdeck can be helpful to a reporter in terms of sorting through potential stories and newsworthy items. It has become routine for players to make comments or pass along information on social media that has turned into a big story. The reporter will likely have to write some sort of game preview story, or multiple stories, to appear online. This may or may not be the same information that gets posted to the reporter's blog. The reporter may have recorded (or may need to record) an online podcast that talks about the upcoming game.

Throughout the day and as game time gets closer the reporter is maintaining a constant presence on social media. Some of this is cross-promotion, such as getting fans to listen to the podcast, read the blog, or remind them of upcoming coverage in the newspaper. A lot of it is simply engaging fans with discussion. Twitter has become a valuable platform in this regard because it allows for an ongoing conversation between the reporter and the audience.

The reporter will head to the arena in the afternoon to get some pregame material. This could be as simple as watching a shoot-around and passing along any relevant observations, but could also include some interviews. This material will go immediately on the Web and social media, and may be used in a television report at 5 or 6 p.m.

During the game the reporter will continue to engage fans through social media. This could include answering questions submitted to an online forum, live blogging or tweeting specific observations from the scene. When not engaged with social media, the reporter is still observing, taking notes, and starting to work the framework for the stories that will appear online as soon as the game ends. This has

A DAY IN THE MULTIMEDIA LIFE OF DERRICK GOOLD

Derrick Goold covers the St. Louis Cardinals for the *St. Louis Post-Dispatch*. His work includes print stories for the newspaper edition, an Internet blog that appears several times a week, and a podcast connected to the newspaper. And don't forget his social media accounts, including Instagram and Twitter, where he has been cited for innovative coverage. Before one particular game, Goold tweeted that the team was watching a major league baseball-related steroid video. "That's the kind of nugget that would never make it into a game story or even into a blog post," says sports blogger Patrick Thornton (2009, ¶ 20). "Goold also interacts with users via Twitter and has a Facebook page for himself and his blog."

Photo 4.2 Some of the multiple platforms reported by Derrick Goold of the *St. Louis Post-Dispatch*.

Photo courtesy of Derrick Goold

caused problems for games that run long or change dramatically toward the end. Former sports writer Rick Cleveland remembers the long night in 2001 he spent covering an Arkansas–Ole Miss football game that went into seven overtimes. As the game approached and then passed his deadline, Cleveland had two stories prepared and ready to send back to the paper — one in which Ole Miss won and the other in which Arkansas won.

After the game, the reporter finishes the online game story and heads to the locker room for interviews. This material will then be incorporated into a more developed online story and for the next day's newspaper. It will also go out on social media, which the reporter will also use to promote stories on television and the Web. There might also be the need for a quick video element in which the reporter interviews the main star of the game. This video can appear on the newspaper's website and possibly on one of the local television stations.

From start to finish, the reporter is looking at 15-plus hours of almost non-stop coverage on multiple platforms. It is a far cry from the days when newspaper reporters slept in late, spent a leisurely afternoon at the ballpark, and then wrote one story to appear in the paper the next day. Former ESPN reporter Graham Watson observed, "You wake up at 7 a.m. and put your face into the computer. It's a grueling, demanding job and burnout is a real danger" ("Ahead of," 2010).

Work on Your Writing

Even in the age of constant social media and Internet updates, the industry still requires people who can write effectively. In fact, a national survey of newspaper sports editors and television sports directors found that quality writing was the No. 1 skill desired by bosses from both types of media (Ketterer, McGuire, & Murray, 2014).

Social media are great tools for interacting, breaking news and promoting work on other media platforms, but almost any media outlet will tell you that it uses social media to drive traffic back to newspapers and television. The traditional media get a lot of criticism today as outdated and incapable of meeting the demands of today's news, but that's still where you'll find the biggest audiences, and thus the money. In other words, social media are the means, not the ends, of good reporting. Don't confuse what transpires on social media as a substitute for good writing. Sports media outlets will always need reporters who can craft interesting and compelling stories. This skill has lost none of its importance in the digital age, and in fact may be more important than ever.

INTERVIEWING

Conducting an interview has become an essential part of sports reporting. Audiences want to know what happened, how it happened and why it happened, and that means hearing from the people who made it happen. Most sports interviewing is done to give context and perspective to a story, but in some cases the interview becomes the story, such as Lance Armstrong's nationally televised interview with Oprah Winfrey in 2013, in which the disgraced cyclist finally admitted he had been doping for races.

Asking the right questions is certainly a big part of the process, but a good interview begins long before the questions are asked. If the story and time permit, the sports reporter must thoroughly *research* the interview subject. This is less important for postgame interviews, but crucial for more in-depth or feature reporting. Knowing a subject's background, history, attitudes and the like will help the reporter conduct a more meaningful interview. The reporter must then determine the *purpose* and *audience* of the interview, and usually the two are related. For example, if a late-night talk show host conducts an interview with quarterback Tom Brady, the purpose of the interview is fun and entertainment because that's what the audience is expecting. Brady would expect a much different interview following a tough loss in which he played poorly; the audience and purpose of the interview would be much more serious.

Misinterpreting the audience or purpose of the interview can lead to problems, as it did for sports reporter Jim Gray when he interviewed Pete Rose in 1999. At the time, Rose was still banned from baseball for his part in betting on games, something he consistently denied. Gray conducted an on-field interview with Rose before a World Series game and used the opportunity to grill Rose over the gambling issue. Rose thought the interview should focus more on his selection to the baseball's All-Century Team, which had been announced that night. Most of America seemed to agree, and Gray got a lot of negative reaction for the contentious interview. However, Gray was vindicated five years later when Rose admitted in an autobiography that he had bet on baseball while managing the Cincinnati Reds.

Once purpose and audience have been established, the reporter needs to determine whether the interview will be *cooperative* or *uncooperative/adversarial*. Almost all sports reporters would prefer a cooperative interview in which both sides can work together and speak openly. An exception might be sports talk host Jim Rome, who has made a career out of being the provocateur, going back to his days at ESPN when his demeaning approach led then-NFL quarterback Jim Everett to attack him during a televised interview.

Cooperation is usually determined more by the interview subject rather than the reporter. Most athletes recognize the demands of the media and will cooperate for interviews out of a sense of professional obligation, although some do it quite grudgingly. A smaller group refuses to cooperate for any interviews, whether it's because they have been burned before, face an embarrassing situation they want to avoid or simply because they don't care. In 2014, Seattle Seahawks running back Marshawn Lynch dominated Super Bowl media day, not for what he said but for what he didn't say. Required to attend the event by the NFL or face a massive fine, Lynch showed up, but his answers were so short as to be almost unusable. For several questions, he simply stared into space and did not respond at all. "Here's the embarrassing part," said Gary Myers of the New York *Daily News*, one of the reporters covering the event. "The media were lined up five deep in front of Lynch waiting him out" (Myers, 2014, ¶ 16).

While the Lynch situation is relatively harmless, other athletes have been more openly hostile, and some have threatened or even attacked reporters they believed had pushed too far. Veteran sports columnist Bill Plaschke stood his ground on several occasions when threatened by ballplayers. "Never back down," he says. "Once a player thinks he can run you out of the clubhouse, you'll never feel safe there again" (Plaschke, 2000, p. 43). There is nothing that forces a player or coach to talk, and sports reporters are not in the business of making them try to do so. But that does not mean they should not ask the questions.

Cooperative interviews are obviously much easier for the reporter, but even then the athlete or coach is likely to be suspicious and on guard. This is especially true for news conference situations where the coach or athlete answers questions from dozens of reporters. It can be a high-stress environment, especially after a loss, and some coaches and players have had spectacular meltdowns in front of the cameras. These situations are the exception rather than the rule, and for the most part nothing revealing or interesting comes out of the news conference situation.

With dozens of reporters trying to shout questions, it's already a high stress environment. Add the sting of defeat, and it's no wonder that some athletes and coaches lose their cool.

If possible, try to avoid the news conference or gang interview and get the subject in a one-on-one situation. This will allow you to increase their level of *trust and comfort* before the interview. Conduct the interview in a place where the subject feels comfortable, such as a home, office or locker room. If time allows, engage in some preinterview conversation to help the person warm up and get used to talking. Talking about the other person's interests, hobbies or families can help put him or her at ease. People are much more likely to open up and give honest answers to people they trust.

Photo 4.3 News conference interviews can be noisy, stressful and uninformative.

TABLE 4.1   Famous Sports News Conference Meltdowns

Who says nothing interesting comes out of a news conference? Many of these coaches are more well-known for what they said after the game than for any particular game they won.

Coach	Setting	Comment
Dennis Green	After his Arizona Cardinals gave up a big lead and lost a heartbreaker to the Chicago Bears in 2006	"They were who we thought they were! That's why we took the damn field (slaps microphone). If you want to crown them, then crown their ass. But they are who we thought they were, and we let them off the hook!" (Storms off podium).
Herman Edwards	A Monday news conference following a Sunday loss for his New York Jets in 2002	"This is the great thing about sports. You play to win the game. (Stares hard at reporter). Hello! You play to win the game! When you start telling me it doesn't matter, then retire. This whole conversation bothers me."
Mike Gundy	The Oklahoma State football coach used part of a postgame news conference in 2007 to rant on a reporter who had written a critical article about one of Gundy's players.	(Shouting) "Attacking an amateur athlete for doing everything right! Come after me! I'm a man! I'm 40!"
Jim Mora	A reporter asked Indianapolis Colts coach Jim Mora about his team's chances of still making the playoffs after a 2001 loss to the Saints.	"Playoffs? Don't talk about that … playoffs? You kidding me? Playoffs? I just hope we can win a game."

Sources: Edwards, H. (2002, October 30). https://en.wikiquote.org/wiki/Herm_Edwards; Green, D. (2006, October 16). https://www.youtube.com/watch?v=lh0EYgmtz4w; Gundy, M. (2007, September 22). http://www.tulsaworld.com/sportsextra/osusportsextra/the-rant-revisited-from-an-image-standpoint-mike-gundy-recovered/article_2af51ce4-7ff6-51cd-b450-21193fac41a4.html; Mora, J. (2001, November 25). http://jimmoraplayoffs.com/

Once the interview begins, try to conduct it more like a *conversation* than an interrogation. That is, have a dialogue with the person; don't just shoot questions. Dialogue means listening to the responses, and not being afraid to deviate from a predetermined list of questions. Too many reporters are so focused on the next question that they never listen to the responses. The best interviews are a give-and-take dialogue between reporter and subject.

In terms of specific questions, sports reporters certainly have to ask the "who and what," but you're much more likely to get better responses and stories asking the "how and why." *How and why questions* get to the feelings behind the statistics, which is what really interests audiences. People want to know what it feels like to miss the putt that costs the tournament, or why the coach went for it on fourth down instead of punting. "How does it feel," "talk a little about ...," or "what were you thinking when ..." are the kinds of questions most likely to result in good answers.

It's also important for reporters to remember that in any interview, the subject has an *agenda*. Sometimes, it's to protect image or reputation, which is why Pete Rose and Lance Armstrong stonewalled and lied to reporters for years. Any athlete in the middle of controversy will engage in image repair strategies to try and regain the public trust. Other times, the agenda may be no more complicated than the athlete wanting to get the interview over quickly. Reporters must realize that all people they interview have an agenda, and thus may not answer honestly. It is important to recognize such agendas and try to work through them.

FEATURE INTERVIEW

HOWARD SCHLOSSBERG

Howard Schlossberg has seen a lot and covered a lot during nearly 40 years in the newspaper sports writing business, most of it spent with the Arlington Heights *Daily Herald* in suburban Chicago, but he's certainly no dinosaur. Unlike many of his contemporaries who remain stuck in the "good old days," Schlossberg has embraced the changes and challenges of modern sports reporting.

"Newspapers aren't dying, they're evolving," he says. "There is no more print media — there are just media. As a reporter, it means you have to be adept on all platforms. At a game you have to post updates to social media, along with photos/graphics/videos. You have to be accurate, and you have to able to do it at the speed of the game, and sometimes faster than the game."

Photo 4.4   Photo courtesy of Howard Schlossberg

When Schlossberg started reporting there was no Internet and certainly no social media. But he quickly realized the importance of those tools in sports coverage, especially in terms of interacting with fans. "Social media means everything in sports today," he says. "Nothing happens in sports that doesn't go on social media first. When Tiger Woods does come back, we'll learn about it first on Instagram. When he makes his first birdie on the comeback, we'll hear about it first on Twitter. When he slams a club in frustration on that comeback round, we'll see the first images of it on Snapchat."

Technology has not only changed the way reporters gather and distribute information, it has also affected what they do with it. In today's modern sports media, simply passing along information is not enough. "Fans no longer need us to describe the action," says Schlossberg. "They need us to interpret it, analyze it, investigate it in some cases and maintain our objectivity. PEDs, WARs, Sabermetrics and the latest saber-toothed tigers in any sport means that fans need our steady expertise and insight ability so they understand not just what all that means, but why it's significant."

So while Twitter, Facebook and Instagram are great additions to the house that is sports reporting, the foundation is still based on great writing.

"If you can't write, why are you in the industry?" asks Schlossberg. "The best writing is what gets on the air. The best writing is what gets published, in print and online. The best writing is what gets talked about on social media and discussed on talk radio. If you can't write — if you can't ask the right questions at an interview, if you can't piece together the elements of a great story — if you can't make something understandable in a paraphrase out of a jumbled rant from a riled-up athlete in a postgame locker room, then everything you know about sports might be more useful for you in a fantasy league."

Schlossberg uses those same concepts at Columbia College in Chicago, where he has taught for more than 20 years. He believes it's never too early to start building a portfolio, which should include work at student media and as many internships as possible. His best advice is also the most basic. "Start writing," he says. "Start now. Start a blog. Today. Write. Every day, write. How do you expect to become a good writer if you don't practice writing?"

CHAPTER WRAP-UP

Sports reporting today is a highly competitive field that balances the traditional aspects of the job — objectivity, fairness and balance — with the demands of new technology. Today's sports reporter must be able to produce content on a variety of platforms, including video, print and online. And all of it must be done under the constant strain of a deadline.

While spread across various platforms, today's sports content must still be well written and compelling. That usually means the reporter must be able to personalize stories, and incorporate effective interviewing as part of the storytelling process. Keeping statistics is an undervalued, but essential, part of the job for today's sports reporter.

REVIEW QUESTIONS

1. How has the nature of sports reporting changed over the decades? If Babe Ruth were playing today, how would he be covered differently by sports reporters? How would LeBron James have been covered in a different period, such as the 1920s?
2. How would you define boosterism in the sports media? Can you think of any examples of this in terms of the media in your area?
3. What are the dangers and advantages of the trend toward more opinion in sports reporting? Does this trend seem likely to continue in the near future?
4. Do you think NBC reporter Christin Cooper went too far in her interview with skier Bode Miller? What, if anything, would you have done differently than she did?

GROUP ACTIVITIES

1. Assume your station is covering an important high school playoff game this evening. Brainstorm in your group about how can you plan out a multimedia strategy for coverage that includes online, social media, and possibly even print.
2. Invite a local sports figure (player, coach, etc.) in to address the group in a news conference situation. (The scenario can either be real or hypothetical.) Have the group ask questions and video the news conference for later review.
3. Visit a local television or radio sports department to get a first-hand view of what sports reporters go through on a daily basis. This type of job shadowing can be quite revealing in terms of seeing how much work goes into producing a sports program of only a few minutes in length.
4. Tape several sports programs on different outlets such as ESPN, your local television/radio station, Fox Sports, etc. Critique and analyze the programs in terms of their similarity/difference, multimedia presentations, and content offerings.

CHAPTER 5

Sports Writing for Newspapers, Websites and Magazines

DO SPORTSWRITERS STILL EXIST IN THE DIGITAL AGE?

Just the mere use of the word "sportswriters" instead of sports writers or sports reporters hearkens back to an era before the advent of the Internet and social media. Newspaper reporters were the dominant figures in sports media through the first half of the 20th century. Few Americans of this era ever saw any professional or major college sporting events (in person or through movie reels), because there was no television. Instead, society learned of the exploits of athletes like baseball superstar Babe Ruth through embellished prose and blatant hero-worshipping in the "Golden Age" of sports storytelling from scribes like Grantland Rice and Damon Runyon (McChesney, 1989; Pedersen, Laucella, Kian, & Geurin, 2016).

Through the 20th century, the full-time responsibility of covering a marquee beat (e.g., popular professional sports franchise or major college athletics program, among others) for a major metropolitan newspaper was among the most coveted jobs in U.S. sports media, and most major pro-sports teams and universities had multiple sports writers from different papers covering them year-round. Furthermore, newspaper sports writers overwhelmingly dominated the numeric ranks of all sports media professionals, since nearly every town had a newspaper and each of those papers had a sports section that provided coverage of the local high school sport teams (Laucella, 2014; Wanta, 2006).

Working in a sports section for a daily newspaper and its website still remains a prominent job in sports media. In fact, it is probably the realm of sports media where students have the highest odds of finding full-time employment. However, almost no one holding such a position can still be dubbed just a "sportswriter." Sports reporters now must be mobile journalists who can shoot video, appear on camera and post on social media, all while handling "all the traditional responsibilities of print journalists" (Stofer, Schaffer, & Rosenthal 2010, p. 8).

Increasingly more sports writers work for stand-alone websites, with ESPN Internet and Yahoo! Sports the two most prominent in the United States. Unfortunately, the financial decline and waning influence of the newspaper industry described in Chapter 1 have created more work for a fewer number of print-focused sports writers in the newspaper industry.

The sports magazine industry has struggled even more financially than the newspaper industry in the digital age, as potential subscribers often opt for free content online. *Sports Illustrated* and *ESPN The Magazine* are the only two remaining broad-based sports publications with high circulations for their print versions ("Top 25 U.S. consumer magazines," 2014). Once-popular comprehensive publications like *The Sporting News* and *Sport* have either switched to an online-only format or folded entirely. However, jobs covering high school sports for daily newspapers or stand-alone websites remain plentiful, especially in communities where following local high school sports is akin to religion.

Finally, whereas the number of prominent beat-reporting jobs covering big-time pro sports team or major colleges have dwindled in the era of media consolidation and convergence (see Chapter 1 for descriptions of those terms), the national prominence and reach of top sports writers are now greater than ever before due to easy access to their content via the Internet and social media. "I keep hearing that I am going to lose my job because of the Internet," said Mark Purdy, a longtime sports columnist for *The Mercury News* in San Jose, California. "But yet more people are reading my columns than ever before and my readership is coming from more different places because of the Internet. I'm getting people reading my columns from all over the world, and that's something that was unimaginable before the Internet" (personal communication, 2013).

Being a sports writer is not easy, though. In fact, the life of a digital-age sports writer is far more challenging and detailed than ever before. In the digital age, television and radio reporters are increasingly being asked to write print articles for their station's websites, while media relations professionals regularly use basic Associated Press (AP) sports writing style guidelines in their game summaries, notes and feature writing. Television and radio station directors, and sports public relations professionals, all rank and cite writing as the No. 1 skill needed for success in their respective fields (Ketterer, McGuire, & Murray, 2014; Stoldt, Dittmore, & Branvold, 2012). As Schultz, Caskey and Esherick (2014) noted, "Anyone in the business of sport communication must learn the fundamentals of good writing and practice them diligently to develop proficiency in the craft. A professional cannot succeed without a thorough understanding of the parts of speech, sentence structure, grammar, spelling, punctuation, and theme development" (p. 119).

Many college and high school students dream of appearing on ESPN, even though a top-tier job as television talent is the hardest to attain in the sports media industry. However, the vast majority of the experts who initially report national news on the major professional team sports for outlets such as ESPN and Fox Sports began their careers as newspaper sports writers. ESPN's Adam Schefter breaks much of the national news on the National Football League, a professional sport that overwhelmingly dominates U.S. sports media coverage of all types. Schefter began his career as a student at the University of Michigan, serving as an editor at *The Michigan Daily* student newspaper. He interned or worked full-time for four different daily newspapers before landing with the NFL Network in 2004 and then

RAY'S RULES/MURRAY MANDATES FOR SPORTS WRITING

Ray Murray has taught introductory and advanced courses in sports writing, multimedia reporting and copy editing at Oklahoma State University for 12 years, where he serves as an associate professor of Sports Media and Multimedia Journalism. Before entering academia, Murray spent 21 years working for newspapers as a sports writer, editor and copy editor, including more than 14 years with the *Sun-Sentinel* in Fort Lauderdale, Florida. Murray has taught, worked with or helped train some of the top sports reporters in America. For aspiring sports writers, Murray provides some basic rules/guidelines that all should follow.

By Ray Murray

Photo 5.1 A veteran sportswriter and newspaper sports copy editor, Ray Murray says the type of media may change, but tenets of good sports writing remain constant.
Photo courtesy of Ray Murray

1. The final score, with few exceptions, should be the first number in the story. It often fits well in the second to fifth paragraphs.

2. Don't put partial scores before the final score (i.e., the first score you use should *not* be the halftime score).

3. Be more creative than starting stories like this: "The Southwestern Area High School football team. . ." That is seven words without saying anything relevant.

4. In writing lead-ins for game stories that often work, use a turning point or how the game was won or lost. Stay away from quote/question mark leads, and don't put the score in the lead.

5. A team is an it. "Chicago won its game" or "Los Angeles traded its top pick." City names are singular. Nicknames, with a few exceptions depending on editors' preferences, are plural.

6. Avoid putting the score in the same paragraph as a team record. Also, avoid putting both teams' records in the same paragraph. Too many numbers slow readers.

continued

7. If it is a conference game, say so, and say which conference. If it is nonconference, say so.

8. Do not write chronologically. Get to how the game was won/lost early and fill in later.

9. No need to account for *every* score. Some football games will be 56-49, and some baseball games will end 14-11, but you do not need to write about each touchdown or run.

10. Use numbers and statistics sparingly; make them count. Numbers are hard to digest, so spread them out.

11. Get rosters for both teams before the game. Do not write, "Steve Smith scored when the Midwest City shortstop committed an error." Name the shortstop.

12. If a player is injured, get specifics. "He left with a leg injury" says nothing. Which leg? Which part? What is the injury? Prognosis?

13. Do not end game stories with "advances." "Next week, East High travels to West High on Friday at 7 p.m. in West High Stadium." Save that for advances.

ESPN in 2009 (Maese, 2014). Similarly, past or present ESPN NBA insiders Chris Broussard, Rachel Nichols, Marc Stein and Brian Windhorst all worked their way up through the media ranks, initially learning their reporting techniques as sports writers for daily newspapers.

Excluding those who were ex-players or coaches, even many of the most known sports television personalities began their careers as newspaper sports writers, including the likes of Skip Bayless, Dan Le Betard, Jemele Hill and Stephen A. Smith. Hill, who co-hosts the television talk show "Numbers Never Lie" on ESPN2, dreamed of being a newspaper sports writer since middle school (personal communication, 2015). She worked for several major newspapers (i.e., Raleigh (N.C.) *News & Observer, Detroit Free Press, Orlando Sentinel*) before joining ESPN in 2006, initially as a print columnist for ESPN Internet. "I will always credit newspapers for making me into the journalist that I am, because I learned basically everything in an old-school way that serves me very well in the new medium," Hill said. "I don't feel like I abandoned newspapers. Instead I feel like they were my foundation and I used that foundation in another medium to still perform many of the same job duties" (Kian & Zimmerman, 2012, p. 298).

In other words, while writing copy for television and radio differs in many ways from writing for newspapers, all aspiring sports media professionals need to learn the basics of print sports writing in the digital age. Most will have to write sports articles at some point in their careers, regardless of their area of specialization within the broad and perpetually evolving field of sports communication.

This chapter now briefly introduces the basics of sports writing for newspapers, websites and magazines. Topics broached include AP style guidelines, how to write various types of sports articles (e.g., game stories, features, advances, columns, enterprise reporting), as well as basics such as rules/tenets of sports writing, the inverted pyramid, developing creative leads and writing on deadline. But first, let's set some rules that cover some of the basics.

SPORTS WRITING BASICS

Know Sports and Read Regularly from a Variety of Subjects (Both Sports and Non-sports)

Attaining a job in sports media is more difficult than any other type of media due to the sheer number of people who dream of covering or being around their hobby for a living. Thus, it is assumed that anyone taking a course in sports reporting has an interest in sports. But do you follow the sports industry as a whole, including trends and the business of sport? Do you follow, watch and — most important — read about a variety of sports, so that you can correctly write and speak about the rules and terminology for each sport? If not, start now. This is especially concerning for those raised in the digital age, because media consumers now regularly pick and choose what specific sports and teams to watch and read about through their

Photo 5.2 Jenni Carlson, past president of the Association for Women in Sports Media (AWSM), began her career as a high school sportswriter before becoming a top-tier columnist.
Photo courtesy of Jenni Carlson/*The Oklahoman*

favorite media instead of skimming through at least the first few paragraphs of all sports content in a daily newspaper.

A knowledge of sports and sports terminology is even more important for women due to historic sexism rooted in sports organizations and structures, gender differences in the sports media industry and its content, and within sports culture as a whole, including its largely male fan base (e.g., Billings, Butterworth, & Turman, 2015; Cooky, Messner, & Hextrum, 2013; Hardin & Whiteside, 2006).

"Young women, you better know your sports," said Jenni Carlson, ex-president of the Association for Women in Sports Media (AWSM), an organization that aspiring female sports media professionals are advised to join for networking and mentoring. "All journalists get criticized if they make mistakes and rightfully so. But it's a lot worse if you are women. Sadly, a lot of men are going to assume that you know nothing about sports and don't appreciate reading from a woman in their sports pages."

Regardless of what type of media you work in, you will have to cover all types of sports from all levels. The glossary in this text provides some basic terminology for most organized U.S. sports and more information is available on the corresponding website for this book. However, if you are unfamiliar with a sport that you are assigned to cover, Google to learn about the basics before leaving to cover the event and do not be afraid to ask questions of others with more knowledge of that sport. There should be no embarrassment in doing so, but there will be if your boss relays criticism you received for mistakes in your articles because you had too much hubris to ask questions on a sport you knew little about.

Beat reporters must be experts on the teams, leagues and sports they follow. In general, sports media professionals should try to follow all types of sports at various levels, especially focusing on *reading* other sports writers' articles. However, this does not provide an excuse for general ignorance of the world around you. Read from a variety of sources on multiple subjects and make sure to stay abreast of news of the world and your community. Most sports media outlets will not hire a reporter who does not have experience covering hard news, which is increasingly more paramount to sports journalists' jobs, especially at higher levels. Accordingly, all students interested in a career in any realm of media must learn how to file a FOIA (Freedom of Information Act) to attain government documents and should familiarize themselves with the various sunshine laws in their states. Learn how to read and write about police reports and judicial proceedings.

However, it would be prudent, as a rule, to keep opinions to yourself on political and social issues unrelated to sports, especially on social media. "Sports figures who publicize their political viewpoints only serve to divide the audience," said ESPN NFL reporter Adam Schefter. "People are drawn to sports as an escape from politics. . . . Politics should be kept out of reporting. People don't want political opinions from sports reporters" (Deitsch, 2016, ¶ 27, 72). Just remember that sports editors deal with enough problems; they do not want to receive complaints on their reporters stirring controversy unrelated to their jobs.

Learn and Master the *Associated Press Stylebook* and AP Sports Style

Aspiring sports writers often become frustrated by professors who routinely deduct points for AP-style errors and by editors at their student newspapers who point out similar flaws in their copy. However, it would be wise for such writers to express gratitude to anyone who takes the time to point out AP-style errors. Making these mistakes while freelancing or interning for a professional media outlet could cost you future opportunities. It could even cost you your job if you regularly make AP-style errors after entering the field full time. Even rookie reporters at the smallest outlets (e.g., weekly newspapers) are expected to be proficient in AP style. Therefore, buying the latest version of the *Associated Press Stylebook* is a wise investment. Read it through and open it frequently when you have questions on style guidelines. The *Stylebook* can also be downloaded as a smartphone app or purchased as a computer subscription via www.apstylebook.com. A simple Google search can also usually provide such answers.

However, like most things in life, the only way to become a master of AP style is to write a lot of articles and continually look up topics in the Stylebook, like what and how to abbreviate. For many years, young sports writers had to rely on a limited sports section toward the back of the *Associated Press Stylebook* that consisted of just a few pages. Fortunately, long-time Associated Press sports reporter Steve Wilstein authored the *Associated Press Sports Writing Handbook* (2001), which provides a handy reference guide. Many sport-specific AP-style questions can also be answered through a basic Google search.

Here are few basic AP-style guidelines that are particularly relevant for sports writing:

1. Spell out most numbers under 10 unless they appear in a score that includes a hyphen or indicates a team's overall record, which is also separated by a hyphen. Thus, "The Tigers beat the Dolphins, 7-6" is correct. However, you would also write, "Detroit scored all seven of its runs in a fourth-inning rally highlighted by 11 hits, including three doubles and two home runs." Another major exception is listing someone's age, which is a numeral (e.g., "A 7-year-old gymnast" or "Smith, 9, placed third in the girls 15-and-under division.")

2. Most credible media outlets largely adhere to AP style, but some have their own house style that supersedes AP style. Therefore, "Johnson rushed 22 times for 149 yards and two touchdowns" is correct, per AP style. However, some papers and websites use "Johnson rushed 22 times for 149 yards and 2 touchdowns" or "Johnson rushed 22 times for 149 yards and 2 TDs," which is even more common on stand-alone websites.

3. Capitalize proper nouns, which include team names, nicknames (e.g., Tigers, Bears, Bulldogs, etc.), and specific names of conferences, leagues, athletics associations and districts (e.g., Big Ten Conference, District 6-AAAA, etc.).

4. The name of a pro sports franchise, university or high school is usually singular, but team nicknames are usually plural. Therefore, you would write

"Auburn's rushing attack was dominant in the first half," but also "The Tigers' rushing attack was dominant in the first half."

5. Use "men" and "women" when covering sports competed in by athletes who are mostly 18 and older and "boys" and "girls" when covering minors in high school or younger. A common mistake is incorrectly using apostrophes to describe gender-specific sports. For example, when covering tennis it is correct to write "Jimmy Johnson won the boys' singles title," while "Sheila Harrison placed second in the girl's tournament" is wrong.

6. With the exception of specific years (e.g., 2012), AP style requires spelling out any number that begins a sentence, including those more than 10 (e.g., "Twelve minutes is all that separated the Cavaliers from a third consecutive Eastern Conference title"). In general, though, just try to avoid using numbers to start a sentence.

7. Use "No." in front of a team's ranking (e.g., "Alabama is No. 1 and Ohio State No. 2 in the first official College Football Playoff rankings of the season").

Learn Inverted Pyramid Style

This is the most common format for writing news and sports articles, where the most important details are toward the top of a story. After all, copy could be shortened later during the editing process when editors on deadline often just trim straight from the bottom up. Readers could also just stop reading after the first few paragraphs. Therefore, make sure the 5 Ws (who, what, where, when and why) and H (how) are answered in the first five paragraphs. Place the most important info at the top, followed by content of lesser prominence and the bottom third the least important. A common mistake young writers make is saving a great quote or anecdote for the end the story—and then finding out after publication that it was deleted for space.

Inverted pyramid-style works best for news events and games that many readers did not see in person (e.g., a local high school volleyball team's road match, but not an NBA Finals game that much of America watched live on television). A classic AP style game story using the inverted pyramid would answer the 5 Ws in the first paragraph. For example, "The Washington High girls' basketball team clinched its first district title in nearly two decades with a 61-43 win at archrival Johnson County on Tuesday." However, you can have a feature-type lead and still largely adhere to the inverted pyramid style. Just make sure the 5 Ws and how are answered in the first five paragraphs.

Thoroughly Research Whatever You Are Covering or Whom You Are Interviewing Beforehand

The amount of sports media content of all types (e.g., articles, analytics breakdowns, videos, blogs, podcasts, etc.) now freely available online provides information that can help print reporters in doing research for their reporting, but also makes their life much busier. "Sports writers can often be overwhelmed with the amount of sports information produced from content distribution digital outlets. Sports writers are increasingly expected to keep abreast of news and rumors related to stakeholders affiliated with their assigned beats, other sport media personnel, fan postings on blogs and message boards, and a plethora of social media accounts" (Pedersen, 2014, p. 103).

Accordingly, it is inexcusable to not research teams, athletes, coaches or officials prior to covering games or, especially, before leaving to interview anyone. See what others wrote about athletes, so that you do not waste time asking the same questions or repeating the same narrative in your content. Do not waste everyone's time by asking biographical and statistical information that can be easily attained through a simple Google search or by asking someone else who has that info (e.g., a college media relations staffer, a high school coach or team statistician, etc.).

When covering a game, attending a press conference, or just going to interview someone for a feature story, it is good practice to:

1. Arrive early and attain rosters, checking for accuracy and making sure that jersey numbers match what appears on paper.
2. Carry pens/pencils, notebooks, stat sheets.
3. Bring two types of recorders (a smartphone and digital recorder).
4. Do not forget your computer, and power adapters for your computer and phone.
5. Know where you are going. It is always prudent to print out a copy of directions to and from a stadium or school where you have not been before. It is wise to know at least two routes to arrive at a venue if roads are closed or congested.

Covering Games and Writing Game Stories

Sports writers produce all types of stories, but the vast majority will spend more time in the field covering and writing about games than writing all other types of articles combined. That is probably why you want to enter this field.

Photo 5.3 Dr. Kathleen McElroy, associate director of journalism at the University of Texas, worked for *The New York Times* for 29 years, mostly in sports.
Photo courtesy of Dr. Kathleen McElroy

Covering games is arguably the best part of the job and your friends will be envious. Nonetheless, it is work that is competitive and pressure-filled, especially when covering games and events on deadline (i.e., your articles must be submitted by a set time). Provide analysis and insight that is not just a repeat (e.g., running play-by-play, a scoring summary that also appears in a box score on the agate page) evident to anyone who saw the game. "In simplest terms, your job as a sports reporter is to look for angles, leads and storylines so that even fans who saw the game themselves have reason to revisit through your eyes" (Gisondi, 2011, p. 11).

While you want to provide insight, try not to get too technical in a game analysis or while citing statistics. Most people reading an article on a high school basketball game will understand the meaning of a team "switched to a zone defense," but most have no clue on advanced analytics terms like PER (i.e., player efficiency rating).

"Unlike most news stories, even a basic sports game story involves a bit of analysis," said Dr. Kathleen McElroy, associate director of journalism at the University of Texas at Austin who spent 20 years in managerial roles at *The New York Times*. "But the analysis is based on the confluence of observation, facts and background information, especially from covering a beat. If you don't have significant experience with a team, player or beat, keep your analysis at a minimum and base it only on what you see and what is confirmed, usually through statistics and quotations" (personal communication, 2016).

A common practice for smaller, local outlets is to name-drop, where a few extra names get into a story (e.g., putting in the names of all players from local schools who scored in a baseball game). Just make sure not to go overboard and insert names for little or no reason, or come up with a ridiculous rationale for doing so (e.g., "Although they did not see game action, Jerome Davis, Jimmy Jenkins, Devin Morris, John Smith and Maurice Taylor provided strong encouragement from the bench and were instrumental in the Bears' landmark victory").

On a related note, even sports writers at small newspapers cannot be homers. As noted in various parts throughout this text, sports reporters must remain objective at all times, and there is no cheering allowed in the press box or on press row.

The best sports writers in the country covering the biggest games that fans watch on television generally get creative in their game stories. *The Washington Post* online published this game story from Chuck Culpepper (2016) — the first three paragraphs are below — less than 15 minutes after the end of a thrilling 2016 NCAA Division I men's basketball national championship game. "Chuck Culpepper is such a master of his craft," tweeted *The Oregonian* college sports reporter Gina Mizell in a theme that was echoed throughout social media by other top sports journalists who marveled at how Culpepper could write a story of this quality without quotes so fast.

THE WASHINGTON POST ONLINE
KRIS JENKINS HITS BUZZER-BEATING THREE-POINTER TO LIFT VILLANOVA PAST NORTH CAROLINA FOR NCAA TITLE

By Chuck Culpepper
April 4, 2016

HOUSTON — As a roaring basketball game in a roaring football stadium distilled to one final, soaring shot making its descent, 74,340 seemed almost to hush. The hush would not last. Kris Jenkins's cocksure three-pointer from the right of the top of the key swished down through the net and into deathless fame, and all manner of noise broke out and threatened to stream through the years.

Villanova's players surged into a pile. Villanova's coaches hugged and hopped. Jaws dropped. Fans boomed. Streamers fell. North Carolina's players walked off toward hard comprehension. The scoreboard suddenly read 77-74, and Villanova, a sturdy men's basketball program with an eternal Monday night glittering from its distant past, had found another Monday night all witnesses will find impossible to forget.

It had claimed its second national championship 31 Aprils after its first. It had added another pinnacle to the storied occasion of 1985 in Lexington, Ky., when a No. 8-seeded Villanova faced a towering Georgetown and rode near-perfection to the kind of 66-64 upset that lives on in memory banks and highlight reels. On this freshest Monday night, a No. 2-seeded Villanova reached a 35-5 peak in Coach Jay Wright's 15th season and looked very much like it had become, by the end — especially the very end — the nation's hardiest, most united, most resourceful team.

Courtesy of *The Washington Post*

Most sports writers will never write anywhere near the level of Chuck Culpepper. But before learning how to write a game story, you need to be able to keep and tally stats from any game you cover.

Keeping Stats During Games
Statistics are covered in-depth in Chapter 4. However, sports writers for print sources must keep sports statistics during games more so than some other types of journalists. Many print reporters are expected to file a story right after a game ends and before they can attain quotes. Those stories will largely be based on what happens in the game (e.g., key plays that resulted in or led to scores).

KEEPING STATS AT A BASKETBALL GAME

Basketball rivals volleyball as the toughest sport to keep full stats for, especially in fast-paced games. Here are some pointers to keeping stats at basketball games:

1. Start off with the basics. Try to keep a running score chart per quarter or half, noting who scored for each team, as well as points for each player on each team.

2. As you become more experienced, keep a detailed running score sheet, which includes not only who scored, but also how they scored (e.g., a 15-foot jumper) and the time on the clock. This will be important when you go back to examine the most important scoring runs that impacted the game (e.g., "a 15-3 run midway through the third quarter ignited by 3-pointer from Josh Benson propelled the Lions to a commanding 19-point lead").

3. Gradually expand your individual player stat summaries for both teams to include 2-point field-goal attempts/makes, 3-point field attempts/makes, free-throw attempts/makes, defensive and offensive rebounds, assists, steals, blocks and turnovers.

College students who learn sports writing by covering teams at their universities are generally given official statistics during and after games by those schools' sports information departments. These young reporters then take their first jobs, where they are expected to cover mostly high school and community sports, but are too often woefully unprepared to keep full stats during a game, all the while having to churn out a story near deadline. Therefore, young students interested in a career in sports reporting should be covering high school sports as a freelance reporter for a local newspaper or website to garner experience. They can also practice keeping stats for all sports while watching televised events on mute.

As noted, those covering professional and major college sports are handed official stats and anyone watching these games can attain the same through free sites like ESPN Internet's Gamecast, which offers full statistical breakdowns (team and individual) and running play-by-play summaries during most professional and major college football and men's basketball games. Nevertheless, most top reporters covering these games still keep some stats, looking for unique angles and storylines.

Interviewing and Developing Sources

Good sports articles feature great quotes and insider insights, which usually come from effective interviewing. "For sports journalists, interviews serve three main purposes: to acquire new information, to elicit an expert's opinion and to tap into a person's thoughts and feelings" (Gisondi, 2011, p. 24).

Before interviewing any athletes for a feature, write down at least 10 open-ended questions and print out a copy of this interview guide (i.e., a list of open-ended questions in an order to be potential asked) to take to your interview. Try to do the same with at least five questions before news conferences and after-game interviews of coaches and athletes. Otherwise, you may forget something important, especially during quick interviews with coaches after games. However, do not hesitate to veer away from these questions as the interview unfolds based on the respondent's answers. Make sure you do not ask questions further down the list that the subject already answered in her or his earlier responses.

Arrange interviews before going to a team's practice or media availability. Let a coach or media relations representative know (who, in turn, should let the athlete know) at least a day in advance that you want to interview specific athletes after practice for a feature story and that this will take roughly 30 minutes per subject. Give yourself extra time

If you are doing an individual feature on a specific athlete or coach, talk to others (e.g., teammates, coaches, media relations reps) about that individual first, which should be after your initial online research. If possible, do the interview for a feature one-on-one (just you and the subject), and not with other reporters asking unrelated questions and possibly using the best quotes for stories published before your feature.

Ask specific questions, but leave them somewhat open-ended in nature. Let the subjects talk—not the reporter. Therefore, the goal should be to keep questions brief, which allows interviewees to speak freely. Do not ask pointed, lead-in questions that can result in yes or no answers or where an athlete can simply rephrase your question in slightly altered language.

Another common mistake is to ask an athlete or coach to "talk about. . .". That is not a question. Do not ask run-on or compound questions. The goal is to attain a great deal of information through interviews. If responses are unclear or lead to further questions, do not be afraid to ask for clarification or offer follow-up questions.

In general, we do not recommend off-the-record or anonymous interviews. Most media outlets have their own policies on citing anonymous sources, with some prohibiting this all together and others not allowing it when using quotes. However, reporting by *The Washington Post*'s Bob Woodward and Carl Bernstein on the Watergate break-in that resulted in the eventual resignation of President Richard Nixon is arguably the most impactful investigative journalism in U.S. history. However, many of their articles relied on and cited anonymous sources. Some of the biggest sports journalism investigative series have done the same.

But for those covering major beats, some comments and even full interviews can be attained off-the-record, and in some cases quotes may need to appear anonymously. Jeff Goodman has developed a reputation as arguably the top men's college basketball reporter in the country based on his stints working for the Associated Press, *USA Today*, *The Washington Post*, CBS Sports and now ESPN. While Goodman communicates with numerous sources daily, he said some of his best information comes from off-the-record conversations with assistant coaches late in the evening and long after games end (personal communication, 2012).

"You have to learn how to work a beat, develop sources and ask the right questions from people in the know," said ESPN senior investigative reporter Mark Schlabach, who is featured in an interview at the end of this chapter. "That's still the bottom line in this business if you want to be a top reporter. That is what all the ESPN Insiders do."

Nevertheless, for most print articles and especially features, there must be a compelling or interesting lead (i.e., sometimes referred to as a "lede") for readers to want to continue. This is especially true in the age of social media, where people are used to getting their news in short snippets through platforms like Twitter.

Writing Leads

Anderson (1994) wrote that structuring a quality, effective and interesting lead is the most difficult part of writing a sports article. However, the flow of the entire story "will fall into place naturally if the article beings with a suitable lead" (p. 32). As previously noted, a basic AP sports style lead includes the five Ws. However, professional sports writers more often employ a feature lead that focuses on a star or key player in the outcome, a key turning point in the contest, the importance of an event or something unusual. Good leads can be a single paragraph or flow into four or five, although articles still need a nut graf (i.e., the paragraph that explains the focus of the story) in the first five paragraphs.

Incorporating Quotes into Stories

Mediocre writers can still write good stories through the use of interesting, colorful and unique quotes that enrich their copy. Many sports articles are built around quotes. They add perspective to game stories and are a must for good features. Quotes can provide new information, as well as insight and heartfelt perspective from athletes and coaches, especially when they are quoted shortly after games when emotions are high. Unfortunately, way too many bad or unneeded quotes appear in sports pages each day. Avoid clichés quotes like "We gave 110 percent" or any war analogies, such as "I'll go to war with these guys any day of the week."

Do not repeat stats or factual information in quotes. For example, why quote a coach as saying "We scored 41 points in the first half"? But the most annoying quotes often found in sports copy appear after redundant lead-in transitions. Why write, "Johnson said his team's clutch shooting was the key to victory" before using this quote? "Our clutch shooting is why we won the game," Johnson said. Instead, use lead-ins that complement quotes. Thus, the quote from Johnson above would be more effective by including a preceding paragraph from the writer like, "After falling behind, 49-44, early in the third quarter, Utah shot 11-of-16 from the field and 12-of-12 on free throws over the final 20 minutes."

In general, you should not modify quotes. The *Associated Press Stylebook* prohibits altering quotes in any scenario. However, be cognizant of cleaning up incorrect grammar or rambling run-ons, especially of local, younger and amateur athletes. You do not want to embarrass youngsters, or irk their families and coaches. If a high school player says "um" between each sentence, do you quote him on that? Of course not. Just take those out of the quotes.

Writing Features

Every sports reporter is assigned features. Sometimes they are told whom to interview. In other cases, they are just told that a feature from some game or team is needed, or that simply just a feature is needed. As noted when discussing interviews, talk to friends, family, coaches, teammates and others who know the people you are writing about beforehand to learn what you can before you begin the interview. Look for interesting anecdotes and human-interest stories that will compel potential readers that reading this feature is worth their time.

Jon Wilner (2015) of *The* San Jose *Mercury News* took first place in the Associated Press Sports Editors (APSE) 2015 features writing competition for circulations over 175,000 with this feature on Golden State Warriors coach Steve Kerr. Although Kerr has been a household name among sports fan since he was a teammate of Michel Jordan with the Chicago Bulls in the 1990s, Wilner adeptly drew readers in and kept them captivated with the first seven paragraphs of his feature.

THE MERCURY NEWS ONLINE
A DAD'S LEGACY: WARRIORS' KERR GUIDED BY FATHER'S EXAMPLE

By Jon Wilner
April 16, 2015

OAKLAND — Steve Kerr played with some of the NBA's greatest players and for several of its greatest coaches. But the man most responsible for Kerr's success as the Warriors' first-year coach was an understated Middle East scholar who enjoyed curing olives and had little interest in professional basketball.

"I'm grateful I had him for 18 years," Kerr said recently in a rare interview about his father. "I feel his full impact on my whole life. It's there every day."

Malcolm Kerr was assassinated in the winter of 1984, gunned down by Islamic terrorists at the American University of Beirut.

His athletic endeavors extended no further than shooting hoops with his kids in the driveway, but the upbringing Malcolm and his wife, Ann, provided would infuse Kerr with a worldly perspective and ability to adapt to anyone and any situation.

Before he learned the game from Hall of Fame coaches like Phil Jackson, Kerr learned German in a French elementary school.

Before he caught a pass from Michael Jordan and hit the shot to win the NBA title, Kerr attended a backyard barbecue with Egyptian royalty.

Before he set foot in a Warriors locker room that was reeling from the departure of his popular predecessor, Kerr spent years navigating his way around Cairo.

Courtesy of *The* San Jose *Mercury News*

Writing Game Advances

Big games call for advance stories and prominent teams in the most popular sports have their contests previewed in the sports pages beforehand. Reinardy and Wanta (2015) noted, "The advance has two functions. First, it is to inform the readers of the essentials: time, place, date, and teams involved. Second, the advance attempts to capture the game's potential meaning without predicting the outcome" (p. 148). In addition, game advances should include teams' records, injury updates, results of previous matchups between these squads, outcomes from each team's last games and keys to this contest, such as player or positional matchups.

However, a common problem in newspaper game previews is a text box often appearing alongside that repeats the same information found in the article. Thus, make sure you find out if the sports editor or design editor plans to add something alongside your article. Add quotes to the game preview to set it apart from an infographic.

Writing Sidebars

Major print outlets occasionally send two writers to big games. One may be assigned to write a sidebar, with the subject of that article usually determined during the game by what unfolds. Sidebars usually provide in-depth examination on one thing, but generally are not as long.

The focus, for example, could be on the star of the game or an unexpected contribution from a role player, a matchup between units or stars, a turning point or flurry that made a difference in the outcome, a trend for a team, a milestone or record, an injury that occurred during the game or a player's return from injury.

Photo 5.4 Veteran columnist Berry Tramel focuses on making people feel or think about the subjects he writes about.
Photo courtesy of Berry Tramel

A key is to make sure the person writing the sidebar communicates with the other reporters covering the game, so there is little overlap in content. In other words, you do not want the game story to lead with the same topic or athlete that is the focus of the entire sidebar.

Writing Columns

Lead columnists at major newspapers and national websites often write on whatever subject they choose and attend what sporting events they want to see that fall within the budget of their outlet. Accordingly, these have long been the most coveted positions in print-focused sports departments. However, columnists are less prominent and important in the digital age, where an endless array of opinions from fans and less-prominent reporters are transmitted on blogs, independent websites, sports-talk radio and especially via social media. As a result, too many lousy columns appear in too many websites and newspapers, especially in today's college newspapers. Today's college students grew up exposed to sports-talk television programming and wrongly believe that such programming is real journalism. In general, young reporters should focus more on covering news objectively than trying to share their opinions.

Writing effective columns and doing so regularly is very difficult, which is why columnists are usually among the best and most experienced reporters at a media outlet. However, the great ones can still stand out, even in the digital age. "The goal of writing a column is to make readers feel something, whether that's happiness, anger, sadness, excitement, whatever," said Berry Tramel, lead sports columnist for the *Daily Oklahoman* newspaper in Oklahoma City and NewsOkSports.com. "But if people read it and don't care and immediately forget that they read it, then you've failed in your job as a columnist."

Good columnists do not just share their opinions; they substantiate them through great reporting, research and statistics. Finally, even when writing columns, the word "I" should not appear in your copy. "I think" or "I believe" is not needed when your picture appears by a column. Readers assume it is your opinion.

Enterprise Reporting

Enterprise reporting is hard to define, but aspiring journalists will hear editors and professors constantly harping on the need for more of it from young journalists. These are generally in-depth and deeper examinations on complex, historical or culturally relevant topics that often result in a series of articles and usually involve multiple reporters. Enterprise reporting takes time and ingenuity. *Sports Illustrated* has long served as industry leader for quality enterprise reporting.

"The enterprise pieces are what impresses me most when looking through clip files and portfolios," said Mike Sherman, 2015 president of the Associated Press Sports Editors (APSE) and sports editor at the *Tampa Bay Times*. "Almost all qualified applicants have good gamers and features. But the deeper stuff is what can separate you from competition."

One advantage of the digital age is that more quality enterprise reporting is being written than ever before due to the sheer number of websites and available resources for finding information. However, far less is appearing in daily

EXAMPLE GAME DAY OF A TOP SPORTS WRITER IN THE DIGITAL ERA

* *12 a.m.–11:59 p.m.* Work or ready to work at all hours. Print and online sport reporters fortunate to serve as professional sports team or league beat writers are like dedicated family doctors in that they are devoted to their jobs and thus always on call. Most check their phones and laptops (e.g., key Internet sites, RSS feed on the players, teams and sports they cover, social media, text messages, emails, phone calls, etc.) habitually for news from the time they awake until bed. The higher-profile and more competitive the beat they cover, the more often they check their phones, tablets and computers throughout each day.

* *11 a.m.* Begin doing initial research and formulating of story ideas, possibly contacting sources for information and for news updates on teams, athletes and coaches they cover. Be active on social media all day, while also constantly checking social media feeds for updates from those you cover and other media members.

* *2:30 p.m.* If you have not already been in touch, contact the sports desk to determine what specific content is needed (e.g., multiple versions of game stories with word and deadline requirements for each, sidebars, blogs, social media during the game, video from postgame press conferences live-streamed on Periscope, video package for the media outlet's website, etc.).

* *4:00 p.m.* Beat traffic to arrive early at the stadium and head straight to the press box. Greet other media members and talk to the team's public relations representatives for any updates or news. Generally, media relations staff members try to assist reporters covering the team. In fact, team and university media relations pros are often given preferential treatment (e.g., scoops, more access to coaches, better seats in press box) to beat reporters who cover the team regularly.

* *4:30–5:30 p.m.* (at the professional level of sports) Conduct pregame interviews with coaches and athletes made available to the press, usually in a media room and/or in the locker room. College and high school athletes are rarely made available to media before games. Video-record these interviews with your phone or camera, so you can potentially upload to your media outlet's website.

* *5:30–6:30 p.m.* Write pregame blogs for the website and post updates on social media, largely based off information and quotes attained from pregame interviews. Possibly upload those videos to your media outlet's website.

* *6:30 p.m.* Eat pregame meal provided by the team's media relations staff, while reading game notes, depth charts, updated stat summaries, media guides and other materials, all while constantly checking social media.

7–10 p.m. Game time. Unlike when they covered high school games earlier in their careers, media relations staffers bring professional team sports beat writers in-game stats, in-game notes, play-by-play sheets, participation summaries, injury updates, etc., regularly throughout the game and key announcements are made to the working press. Nevertheless, most reporters covering a professional sports team still keep their own game notes and some stats. Sports writers are also now expected to share court/field/press-box insider observations and sport expertise to followers via social media during games. They may also be required to write a blog at half time, or possibly even at the end of each quarter for their website.

8–10 p.m. Write a basic, AP-style game story that focuses on the 5 Ws (i.e., who, what, where, when and why) for your media outlet's website and file it as the game ends without any quotes. Finish as much of this article as possible by the end of half time for football or basketball, or do it between baseball innings or during the course of action for soccer.

10:15–10:45 p.m. Go to the media room and/or locker room for postgame press conferences and interviews.

10:45–11 p.m. Insert quotes and rewrite article. Send it in.

11:15 p.m. Call sports desk for any questions.

11:30 p.m. Upload videos from postgame interviews to your media outlet's website. Also make sure you post updates and select quotes on social media.

11:30 p.m.–12 a.m. Write and then send in a postgame/look-ahead blog, based largely off the quotes you just attained.

12:15 a.m. Check social media and competitors' stories to make sure you did not miss anything of major importance. Update accordingly if you did, which could require new reporting.

12:15 a.m. Leave press box. You may need security or the cleanup crew to let you exit the facility, because nearly everyone has left.

8 a.m.–4 p.m. (the next day) Wake up and begin working on postgame analyses, feature stories, and advances for the next game after checking email, Twitter, and RSS feed for news on the teams, athletes, coaches and sports you cover.

newspapers due to cutbacks in staff, available resources and the number of pages dedicated to sports for print editions.

Some young reporters such as ESPN NBA writer Zach Lowe — who began his sports writing as an unpaid blogger for a Boston Celtics fan website — have circumvented traditional paths and the time it usually takes to reach the top of the profession due to outstanding and in-depth enterprise reporting.

Writing on Deadline

Some readers may assume that the dominance of the Internet in 21st-century media has made deadlines less important for print-focused sports journalists. However, we live in an impatient society where sports fans want to read or hear about a team, game, injury or whatever right after a game ends, and this is especially true for younger readers. Therefore, as noted earlier, some writers for major newspapers and websites are asked to send stories right after or shortly following the end of games. They can usually send in more enhanced versions later. Further, newspaper deadlines for the next day's print edition are earlier than ever before, because many major newspapers are now being printed far away from their main office. Young reporters thus need to learn to write on deadline. That is where keeping your own stats and a play-by-play summary can really help. Take advantage of halftime and timeouts to get paragraphs typed up. You can delete some of these scoring summaries for later editions.

FEATURE INTERVIEW

MARK SCHLABACH

Senior Investigative Reporter, ESPN

Photo 5.5   Mark Schlabach previously worked for several major metro newspapers before becoming ESPN's top investigative reporter on college football. Photo courtesy of Mark Schlabach

If you watch ESPN television networks and follow college football, you likely know of Mark Schlabach, who regularly appears on a variety of ESPN programming.

Among the many major stories on college sports Schlabach wrote since joining ESPN in 2006, his coverage of Baylor University's mishandling of sexual assault cases involving football players may have had the greatest impact. As lead investigator, Schlabach's series of reports in 2015–16 ultimately led to the firing of highly successful football coach Art Briles.

Schlabach is among America's top investigative sports reporters in large part due to his relentless work ethic, evident by his finding time to churn out

13 books on the side, including co-authoring the definitive autobiography of legendary Florida State football coach Bobby Bowden.

Although he uses various types of multimedia to deliver content, including social media, Schlabach still relies on the sports writing and reporting skills he first developed at the *Red and Black* student newspaper at the University of Georgia, and later in stints as a top college football beat writer for *The Atlanta Journal-Constitution* and *The Washington Post*.

"Everything in sports media now seems to be focusing on content being instant, quick, light and fun," Schlabach said (personal communication, 2015). "But I still say the reporting, your ability to acquire information and report the news, regardless of how good you appear on TV, is the most important thing for anyone who wants to become a national reporter."

Schlabach's advice for young reporters is poignant and sound: "Write as much as you can and read often," he said. "Cover as many games as you can. Meet veterans, watch what they do and learn from them. Most will help you and provide good advice, but they have to see you out in the field to know you."

CHAPTER WRAP-UP

Traditional print reporting (i.e., newspapers, magazines, newsletters) dominated U.S. sports media through the first half of the 20th century, but nearly all of these outlets have lost circulation and influence in the digital age. However, writing for newspapers and/or websites as a multimedia sports reporter remains a likely destination for many young sports media professionals.

Regardless of the type of sports media where you wish to work, you should learn the basics of sports writing for print sources in the digital age, where nearly all outlets host and create content for websites. However, the digital age has made researching and preparing to write sports media articles much easier due to the vast the amount of information readily available via the Internet and social media.

Aspiring sports media professionals must learn and master the *Associated Press Stylebook*, AP sports style and the inverted pyramid style of writing. They also must learn how to keep statistics and write game summaries from all types of sports events, as well as proper and effective interviewing techniques to garner the best quotes and information.

Those interested in writing for newspapers, websites and magazines for a living must also be able to produce a variety of different types of sports articles (e.g., game stories, features, advances, sidebars, notebooks, enterprise pieces, columns, etc.) depending on their position, all the while using creative leads that draw readers into stories and keep them interested.

REVIEW QUESTIONS

1. List and describe three rules for print sports writing.
2. What are some of the reasons why sports writers should read from a variety of sources and keep up with the news of the world and their communities?
3. What are the *AP Stylebook* rules for numbers under 10 and more than 10?
4. Describe the inverted pyramid style.
5. List at least three different types of sports articles that were described in this chapter.

GROUP ACTIVITIES

1. Watch a game or sporting event in class. Have students keep their own stats and then have each write different types of preassigned articles from the game.
2. Have students edit each other's work from assignments they previously prepared, looking for AP sports style errors.

CHAPTER 6

Social Media and Sports Journalism

The use of social media in sports has, in a very short time, grown from a niche activity to a required aspect of the job for most journalists and professional communicators. As recently as 2009, Twitter and Facebook were viewed primarily as personal communication networks, rather than important venues for dissemination of information. Steady growth in mobile device usage led to the development of huge potential audiences online, and social media's emphasis on immediacy and speed merged nicely with the live-event nature of major sporting events. Social media users have shown a desire to follow their favorite athletes and teams on social media, and sports journalists have had to follow their audience into that space.

Social media can be described as Internet-based applications where users can create publicly shareable content and interact with other users. In the sports journalism setting, the term "social media" generally refers to a specific set of media networks and services. The primary networks used are Twitter and Facebook, but several other applications have become popular in sports media, including Instagram, Snapchat and Periscope.

The purpose of this chapter is to introduce you to the uses of social media in sports journalism and to discuss the impact of their uses on those working in sports media. The chapter includes a breakdown of the most important social media networks used today, as well as tips and examples for effective usage of each network.

USING SOCIAL MEDIA IN SPORTS JOURNALISM

Social media have had a significant impact on sports journalism. While some have claimed that social media have hurt the sports journalism industry, others feel it has given parts of the industry a much-needed boost. "It's possible that social media has saved the newspaper industry for the time being," says Gregg Doyel, sports columnist for *The Indianapolis Star*. "On the one hand, newspapers are dying and we all know that. But on the other hand, social media, particularly Twitter and Facebook, have allowed us to almost treat our news product like a drug, where we mainline it into a reader's veins. It's easier than ever for newspapers and writers to get information right into the user's laptop or phone."

There are a myriad of social media channels at your disposal as a sports journalist, and it is important to remember that they each possess different characteristics. One of the biggest mistakes that professional social media users make is treating all social media the same. The type of content you produce, the audience

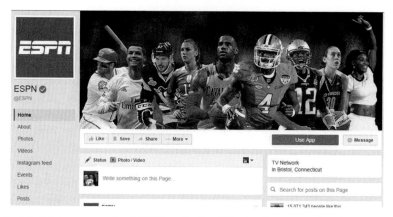

Photo 6.1 This is an example of ESPN's professional Facebook page masthead, containing clickable links to a variety of user options.

you produce it for and even the frequency with which you create it can vary widely from network to network. This section takes you through some of the major social media networks available to sports journalists today, explains their technological and audience characteristics and what makes them unique, and provides guidance on best practices for using each network.

FACEBOOK

Facebook is a data-rich social network that uses two different types of network architecture to promote the flow of information among fans, sports teams and journalists. Founded in 2004 by Mark Zuckerberg, Facebook has undergone several changes to its structure over the course of its existence. It currently stands as the most-used social media network, with a worldwide base of 1.49 billion active users as of 2015 (Facebook, 2015). Facebook enjoys a global reach while still maintaining a major presence in North America. As of 2015, there were 164 million daily active users in the United States and Canada, which only represented 17 percent of the daily active users across Facebook's worldwide network (D'Onfro, 2015).

Facebook is accessed by users through two primary means: Web browsing and mobile access. Web browsing is the original method of accessing Facebook, and the site's original look and architecture was built for traditional Web browsers. However, mobile access has grown to become the dominant form of accessing Facebook, with 78 percent of users utilizing mobile phones or tablets to access the network (Constine, 2013). This shift has important implications in how people consume media on Facebook.

When it launched in 2004, Facebook's architecture was similar to Twitter's in that all accounts were treated equally within the network. Businesses and professional services that wished to be on Facebook were required to have a personal account, the same as a normal user. This setup eventually was replaced by the current architecture, which allows businesses, organizations and popular individuals to create "Pages" on Facebook.

The advantage of the Facebook "Pages" architecture is that it allows individual users to "like" the page and create a one-way connection to the page. This allows the owner of the page to publish material that can be consumed by the user, without the owner of the page having access to private information on the user's account. Within the world of sports journalism, a television station or newspaper website can create its own Facebook page, invite their readers to like that page, and then publish stories and other content on the page that will be seen by those users and potentially shared with other users.

News Feed

The news feed is the core information feed for all Facebook users. Stories are placed into a user's news feed by a secret algorithm used by Facebook and designed to provide people with information that they will view as interesting or entertaining. The contents of the news feed are influenced by what profiles and pages that a user has chosen to like, the articles that a user has liked or commented on and the links that a user has clicked on in the past. Every user's news feed contents appears to change over time, as their own actions provide the algorithm with information about their wants and needs.

Likes, Comments and Shares

There are three primary ways that users interact with information in their news feed. The simplest interaction is the "like." Users press a button underneath a post or story that they enjoy, and that post or story keeps track of the total number of likes it receives from all users. Liking a story or post will sometimes cause it to appear in the news feeds of people who are closely tied to the user who clicked the like button, thereby spreading the visibility of the story or post to other people in that user's network.

The next type of interaction is the "comment." Users are able to write a comment underneath a post, either directly to the posting entity or in response to a comment left by another user. Commenting on a post also can cause it to appear in the commenter's news feed.

The final type of interaction is the "share." Users are able to press a button and place the post directly into their timeline, and also add a comment of their own above the post if they so desire. This is often used by people who are particularly moved by a story or who want to start a conversation on their own news feed as opposed to the original story's comment section.

Photo 6.2 Facebook users are given the option to like, comment and share posts that appear on their timeline.

Using Facebook in Sports Journalism

Facebook has often been undersold as a delivery system for sports journalism. Former *Sports Illustrated* writer Andy Glockner notes that while Twitter is useful for quick interactions and personal branding, "Facebook is vastly superior in terms of actually getting your work into the hands of readers." These advantages are largely due to Facebook's huge user base, combined with the way that the Facebook algorithm identifies items that may be of interest to particular users based on their likes and activities.

Engagement is key to increasing likes, comments and shares, and these types of interactions can help to extend the reach of your content. "I have a Facebook account and I accept almost all friend requests," says Gregg Doyel. "It's a way for people to see my work. If they like it, they might share it and that's more people who could potentially see it."

From an organizational perspective, sports journalism outlets should establish and leverage Facebook pages, and actively build their audience through that portal. Promoting your content through Facebook is a key aspect of driving eyes and ears to your website, and often allows your content to find audiences that it might not have otherwise found.

An effective social media manager should selectively promote content, utilizing a regular posting schedule that the audience can rely upon. How much content to promote via Facebook is a question that must be evaluated based upon how much overall content your organization is producing. A media outlet that publishes six to eight items a day would likely be able to promote each piece of content without its users feeling flooded by too much information, provided that posts for those items are spread out over a certain amount of time. Ideally, an outlet would leave at least an hour between postings. For organizations with more content production, it is important for the social media manager to make editorial decisions on which content is most likely to attract an audience.

Due to its versatility, Facebook is able to continually innovate, adding new features and functions that journalists can take advantage of. As an example, Facebook launched a live video feature in 2016 (Wagner, 2016), largely in response to the recent successes of sites like Periscope. Keeping track of these innovations, and making logical decisions about which ones to integrate into reporting and coverage, is an important part of Facebook usage by journalists and news organizations.

Facebook allows page owners the ability to schedule posts ahead of time, which allows journalists and social media managers to publish links to content without having to be online at that precise moment. While scheduling posts ahead of time can save time and allow for specific targeting of times of day, it is important to keep in mind that breaking news or changing storylines can sometimes make scheduled posts appear at inopportune times. If you schedule a Facebook post, be sure to stay conscious of changing news conditions that could put your post in jeopardy.

For the individual journalist, particularly one trying to build an audience, it is advisable to create your own Facebook page and post all your work to that as it is published. You can also post your work to your personal Facebook page, but you may wish to avoid interacting with audience members in that personal space. A professional Facebook page allows you to keep the audience at arm's length, while still allowing them to like, comment on, and share your work. It also allows you to keep your social media presence independent from your job status, which is important due to the likelihood that you will change jobs multiple times in your career.

BEST PRACTICES FOR FACEBOOK IN SPORTS JOURNALISM

Facebook is the most important tool for journalists in communicating with a large number of people, particularly for those working a local or regional beat. Here are some tips for utilizing Facebook effectively in that environment.

- Promote your website content on Facebook. Post stories during times of the day when people are using the service most often, and be sure to write a short one- to two-sentence blurb in the preview window of the links that you post.
- Use Facebook to conduct live video chats with your audience. Journalists can answer fan questions directly via Facebook's comment section. Using Facebook for video chats is an effective way of reaching a large group of people on social media.
- Set community policies for your audience's comments. You should clearly state on your Facebook page that civil discussion is allowed, but vulgar and/or hateful speech will be removed. However, do not delete or censor audience comments simply because they are unpopular. You want to promote free speech on Facebook while also promoting civility.
- Do not use Facebook and Twitter the same way. Avoid using your Facebook feed to provide live play-by-play of games or post links to large numbers of stories in a short time period. Use pictures and video whenever possible — remember that your audience looks to Facebook for visual material, not just text.
- For individual journalists, remember that you can and should create a Facebook page that is separate from your personal profile. Be sure to use as many of the features on your Facebook page as you can. Post photos from your reporting. Write notes that the audience can comment on. Look at link traffic reports to see who is viewing your stories the most, and when they are viewing them. And above all else, stay abreast of new features that Facebook offers.

Photo 6.3 This is a typical Twitter post, which includes an embedded picture.

TWITTER

Twitter is a social network that is streamlined and focused on fast distribution of messages. Unlike Facebook, all accounts on Twitter are considered equal. While celebrities and companies often will receive a "verified" check mark from Twitter indicating that they are who they claim to be, the actual functionality of those Twitter accounts is the same as the account of a normal person.

Founded in 2006, Twitter quickly grew into a prominent social media network, particularly in the areas of sports and entertainment. This was largely due to ease of access, early adoption by media members and celebrities and prominent use of Twitter during major world events such as disasters and political revolutions. Twitter quickly grabbed about 20 percent of the social media marketplace by 2010, and appeared poised to someday overtake Facebook as the most popular social media.

However, Twitter's star has faded a bit lately, as its user base has failed to grow in step with those of other social media networks. In fact, Twitter's total user base is now less than social media sites Instagram, LinkedIn and SnapChat. As Twitter continues to stagnate, questions have been raised about whether the service needs to change its model in order to compete. Twitter itself has moved to change the way it approaches content, including winning a bid to stream live NFL games during the 2016 season (Belson & Isaac, 2016).

Despite these concerns, Twitter maintains both importance and popularity among sports media and sports fans. Of all the social media sites, Twitter remains the best for spreading information quickly, engaging in a broad conversation around a live event and discovering topics and stories outside a user's normal area of knowledge.

Home Timeline

All Twitter users utilize a home timeline, which is a series of messages presented in reverse chronological order that have been published by the accounts that a user follows. From the timeline, Twitter users can do a variety of things, including posting their own tweets and interacting with tweets they have received. Every tweet in the timeline contains the tweet itself, the Twitter handle (or name) of the originating account and the picture (or avatar) of the originating account.

Twitter has historically limited its tweets to 140 characters, although the network started allowing 280 character posts in late 2017.

Posting

There are several different methods that can be used to post on Twitter. The most basic of these methods uses the Twitter.com website. However, most Twitter use occurs via mobile apps, either through Twitter's official app or through third-party apps such as Echofon, Tweetcaster and Twicca. There are also web-based software programs such as HootSuite and Tweetdeck that allow a variety of posting options.

Retweets and Favorites

Retweeting causes all or part of a tweet to appear in someone else's timeline. There are currently three types of retweets available to users. The first and oldest type of retweet involves a user copying all or part of an original tweet directly into a new post, placing the characters "RT" in front of it, and then either posting it directly or making a comment before the post. This method was the original form of

Photo 6.4 Changes to the Twitter retweet architecture now allow accounts to include their own messages alongside the retweeted message.

retweeting on Twitter, but often it did not allow much room for users to comment on the original tweet.

The second form of retweet causes the entire post, including the original author's name and avatar, to appear in the timelines of people who follow the retweeting user. This allowed the full text of the original tweet to be seen by a large number of users, but didn't allow the retweeting user any opportunity to comment on the tweet.

The third and newest form of retweet allows users to quote the original tweet, but still allows the user the full 140 characters to comment on the tweet. The original tweet appears as an inset box within the Twitter timeline of the retweeting user, with their additional commentary included above it.

Retweets are considered an important part of Twitter communication culture. Content that receives multiple retweets stands a better chance of being seen by a broader variety of people, due to increased exposure to other users' networks. A tweet that receives dozens or hundreds of retweets is often said to have "gone viral," and for many media companies this is an ideal outcome for tweets promoting content on their sites.

Users are also allowed to "favorite" tweets. The act of favoriting a tweet generally falls into three categories. The first category is a show of appreciation from the user to the person who tweeted the favorited content. In this way, the favorite can be similar to the "like" on Facebook.

The second usage of favoriting is for users to bookmark certain tweets for later examination. Due to the speed with which Twitter messages often scroll, it can sometimes be impractical to read linked articles or content as they appear. By using the favorite button, users can save access to the tweet and then return to it later to examine the contents.

The third usage of favoriting is as a polling mechanism. Many media companies will post a poll with two choices, and then tell their followers to retweet if they like the first option, or favorite if they like the second option. This allows for primitive public opinion polling on Twitter, and also allows the question being asked to reach a wider audience through the usage of retweets.

Hashtags

Hashtags are an important part of communication on Twitter and are perhaps the most unique part of the tweeting environment. A hashtag is any word or series of characters preceded by the "#" symbol. Hashtags are given a special status in Twitter programming; users are allowed to click on any hashtag and doing so opens a search box within Twitter where all instances of that hashtag are displayed.

This functionality means that hashtags are regularly used as grouping mechanisms for tweets that share the same topic. Journalists who cover sports teams will often use an abbreviated hashtag (such as "#MIA" or "#JETS") when posting content that relates directly to a team. This allows fans to find tweets relating to their favorite team much more easily, and allows for reporters and other media entities to occupy a shared online space while commenting on a team. Hashtags can also be used for humor or sarcasm. Hashtags used in this manner are generally used in one-off situations where the tweeting user is trying to make light of a situation.

Direct Messages

Twitter offers users the ability to communicate directly with each other through private channels. Direct messages are often used between individuals who do not wish to communicate their thoughts to a larger public. Direct messages can be quite useful for journalists, as they allow private conversation that can be used to cultivate sources, ask follow-up questions and offer contact information for potential interviews.

Dynamic Content

Although Twitter does not host any dynamic content, it does allow for certain types of content to appear directly in the Twitter news feed. Pictures, videos, GIFs (short, repeating videos, often used for comedic effect) and select other content will load directly into a user's timeline. This can be useful for sports journalists who have access to those types of content. Generally, an individual tweet should only contain one piece of dynamic content. If additional dynamic content is available, it can always be included in a separate tweet.

Twitter Usage in Sports Journalism

Twitter currently has the most applications in sports journalism of any social media network, largely because sports journalists were early adopters of Twitter. It is important for you to establish a Twitter presence early on in your sports journalism career. Ideally, you already have a Twitter account, but if you do not, then create one and start using it immediately.

Sports journalists should avoid using the name of the media organization they work for in their Twitter account. The realities of career mobility in the sports media field mean that you will likely change employers multiple times, and including part of your employer's name in your handle just means you will have to change your handle when you move on. For instance, a reporter named Sarah Diaz who works for TV station KRNO is much better off choosing a Twitter handle of @SarahDiazTV than @SarahDiaz_KRNO, because the moment she leaves that station to go to a new station, her old handle would be obsolete.

The most prominent usage of Twitter in sports journalism is as a way to report on live events, including games, press conferences, interviews and practices. Many journalists use Twitter to provide a play-by-play account of sporting events as they happen. This can help the audience to better understand what is occurring in a game, and can be used to provide coverage to certain events that are not otherwise being covered on a play-by-play basis, particularly at the high school and college level. However, it is recommended that you do not live-tweet play-by-play of games and sporting events that are readily available to watch on regular television, or you will flood users' inboxes with unneeded information and likely lose followers. In all cases, it is recommended that you refrain from mass-tweeting every detail of every game (even those not shown on television) for fear of irking users who have little or no interest in such details. Another, more appropriate route for events shown on television could be providing insight from the game that likely would not be available to those following from afar and/or providing statistical insights or trends beyond the basic in-game analyses tweets.

Sports journalists will also "live tweet" press conferences and interview sessions, providing snippets of quotes from coaches and players. Journalists will often use these tweets as the basis for longer stories that they write later, and the live tweets serve as a public notebook of sorts, allowing the journalist to keep track of what seems important and pertinent to the story as the event transpires.

Some sports journalists will provide running commentary on events as they occur, rather than providing a facts-only account. This method of using Twitter allows journalists to provide immediate context for actions or quotes, which theoretically leads to a more informed audience. Often this is an important method to use, since Twitter's text-centric approach strips away context from actions and words, and can contribute to events being misinterpreted by the public.

Sports journalists often use Twitter for primary reporting, following the accounts of players, coaches and team officials in an attempt to glean information on the sports they cover. Twitter reactions from both official sources and from fans often find their way into official stories published by sports media outlets. Even nationally prominent outlets such as *The New York Times*, *USA Today* and ESPN will often collect and publish Twitter reactions to games and events from prominent athletes as well as from ordinary fans.

Twitter is used by sports journalists as a way to publicize their content, through posting links to their work and inviting people to click through. Journalists and news organizations will often tweet links to articles two or three times a day, spread out to reach people who may have missed earlier tweets about the content. Journalists should also discuss their perspectives on issues that are important to them, and which tie in with their work. "Be yourself," says Patrick Hruby, former Contributing Editor for VICE Sports. "Talk about what you're interested in. Talk about the stories you're working on."

Sports journalists also use Twitter to communicate with other sports journalists. This process allows sports journalists to share content and links, promote other journalists' work, and discuss issues and current events with peers at other journalism outlets.

Finally, many sports journalists use Twitter to express personal aspects of their lives and careers. It is not unusual to see journalists talking on Twitter about their affinity for music, television and sports teams. This aspect of Twitter usage is helpful to journalists looking to build a personal brand, because it allows the audience to view the journalist as human and relatable to their own lives. But it is recommended that you avoid tweeting about controversial topics unrelated to sports and/or journalism.

BEST PRACTICES FOR TWITTER IN SPORTS JOURNALISM

Twitter is a different type of network than Facebook. On Twitter you have a much broader geographical reach, you'll be in contact with a lot more of your fellow sports journalists, and your audience tends to be more highly educated and tech-savvy. The following tips can help you get the most out of your work approach on Twitter.

- Did you know it is possible to buy fake followers on Twitter? And did you know that buying fake followers is a terrible idea? If you are concerned that your follower numbers on Twitter are low, you need to go about raising that number organically. The best way to do so is by regularly interacting with the audience, using retweets and including comments that can be publicly viewed.
- Interact regularly with other sports journalists on Twitter. Retweet their work as long as it does not conflict with your own. Engage them in conversation about published stories. Building a professional network with other journalists on Twitter can help your stories reach a wider audience and can provide you with networking opportunities you might not get otherwise.
- Do not overtweet. Learn how to condense your thoughts into 140 characters, rather than stretching them out over several individual tweets. If what you have to say requires several tweets, then it probably isn't something you should put on Twitter.
- Remember that starting a tweet with an @ symbol (as in when you are replying directly to someone) means that the tweet will only appear in the timeline of the other person and the timeline of any users who follow both of you. If you want a reply to be public, place a period (.) in front of the @ symbol.
- People are often mean on Twitter. Despite the temptation to respond to every attack someone tweets, it is generally best to ignore insults and anger directed at you. In most cases, the tweets are coming from people with small numbers of followers and little influence. Responding to those users will only draw attention to them, which was probably their plan from the start. If you do respond to a critical tweet of you or your work, limit yourself to just a one-tweet response.
- Be sure to follow media members whose primary role is to observe and report on the sport media industry. Popular reporters in this area as of 2015 include *Sports Illustrated*'s Richard Deitsch (@richard-deitsch), *The New York Times*' Richard Sandomir (@RichSandomir), independent writer James Andrew Miller (@JimMiller), *Sports Business Journal*'s John Ourand (@Ourand_SBJ) and the independent website Awful Announcing (@awfulannouncing).

INSTAGRAM

Instagram is a photo and video sharing app that is almost exclusively used on mobile devices. Started in 2010 and purchased by Facebook in 2012, Instagram has surged in popularity since then and is now used in the United States more widely than Twitter. It is particularly popular among users aged 18 to 25.

Compared to the relative complexity of Twitter and Facebook, Instagram is simple to use, which may explain some of its popularity. Users create an account on the service, and can choose whether other users can view their posts or not. This allows for individual users to selectively provide access to others, which is important for those concerned with privacy.

Users may post one of two types of media. The majority of posts on Instagram are pictures, but users can also choose to post videos. Once the user decides on the media they wish to post, they are given some basic editing options (e.g., cropping, rotation, zoom) and the ability to add a filter to the media, which can give it a significantly different and sometimes more professional look. Users are able to tag their media with particular terms or names, and include geolocation information indicating where the media was taken. Finally, users can post a caption under the media and tag other users in the media. Many users include hashtags in their Instagram captions, but it is important to remember that these are platform-specific; Instagram hashtags do not carry over to Twitter and vice versa.

Media organizations can use Instagram to reach younger user demographics, with 90% of Instagram users under the age of 35. Cool-looking photos,

---

BEST PRACTICES FOR INSTAGRAM IN SPORTS JOURNALISM

Instagram has a lot of unique uses for sports journalism, particularly if you have a background or interest in sports photography. Here's how to get the most out of the service.

- Do not over-post on Instagram. Users will quickly unfollow your account if you post multiple pictures or videos in a short time span. A good rule to follow is to post a maximum of one picture or video every 20 minutes during an event, a maximum of one picture or video an hour during a normal day and no more than five pictures or videos during a single day.
- You can use computer apps such as InstaPic to post to Instagram. This allows you to utilize professionally taken and/or graphically enhanced pictures in your feed.
- You can link your Facebook, Twitter and other social media accounts to your Instagram feed, and can select the option to cross-post your pictures and videos on those services. Cross-posting on Twitter is always a good idea for journalists because it provides your audience with additional dynamic content as well as servicing two platforms at once.

unique "insider" images and short video recaps are attractive to sports consumers, and journalists are often in a position to provide those types of media. Since most Instagram media is created using nothing more than a smartphone, it takes little additional effort for journalists or media organizations to use their accounts to provide supplementary information not included in their tweets or Facebook posts.

SNAPCHAT

Snapchat is a private messaging application that has gained popularity among sports teams and media companies due to its popularity among younger audiences. Snapchat allows users to send messages to individuals or groups of people, with the messages only being viewable once and then expiring.

Snapchat messages are generally either images or video. Users can draw or type on pictures and send those messages to friends, and control the amount of time that the image is viewed by the audience. Video works in a similar manner. Users are also able to stitch together multiple instances of video and/or images into "stories," which can last for several minutes in some cases.

Companies such as ESPN have used Snapchat to put together promotional videos for their media programs. For instance, ESPN's "College GameDay," a popular college football show, puts out a three- to four-minute recap of the experiences and behind-the-scenes activities of the show, its on-air personalities and the game they are covering that day.

ESPN also uses Snapchat displays a still picture with sound in the background, which is intended to advertise the story in question. The user is then invited to swipe up on the screen to display the written story or video, or swipe sideways to move to a different story.

BEST PRACTICES FOR SNAPCHAT IN SPORTS JOURNALISM

Even though Facebook has its Stories feature, Snapchat is still the preferred network for young people. Don't neglect your Snapchat audience. Here are some tips.

- Remember your audience. Most Snapchat users are interested in fun, humor and excitement. If you are not able to capture one of these items in a snap, then your audience probably will not enjoy it.
- As with Instagram, do not flood your users with snaps. It is better to string together a two-minute Snapchat story then to send four 30-second snaps.
- Snapchat is best used as a supplementary social media outlet. Use it to promote your main content or to provide context to that content, rather than using it as a stand-alone outlet.

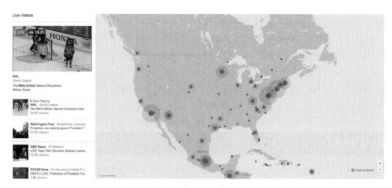

Photo 6.5 Streaming video has emerged as a powerful communications tool on social media. Here, Facebook shows where Facebook Live streams are taking place in real-time.

STREAMING VIDEO

The year 2015 saw the rise of personal video streaming on smartphones. While online video streaming had been available for several years already via Google and YouTube, the emergence of the Periscope and Facebook Live applications made it easy to stream video via hand-held devices.

These services allow users to create a video stream from their phone, to name it and then to publicize it on other social media. Viewers can join the stream live and interact with the streamer. Periscope allows for users to watch an archived version of the stream for up to 24 hours after it airs, while Facebook allows for users to comment natively within the network's architecture, by leaving comments and reactions just as one would on a normal Facebook post.

Streaming video services have a number of applications in sports journalism. Professionals have used the services to provide live commentary during or after sporting events they cover, provide analysis and information at a scheduled time every week, live-stream press conferences and give their audience an insider view of facilities they might not otherwise see.

BEST PRACTICES FOR STREAMING VIDEO IN SPORTS JOURNALISM

Streaming video continues to grow in importance, and both Facebook and Instagram have made it a key feature.

- Use it to extend your coverage. Provide the audience with insights they might not get otherwise.
- Do not be afraid to solicit questions from the audience. Streaming video is a great way to conduct Q&A sessions, and can allow the audience to feel more connected to you.
- Keep in mind some rudimentary rules about streaming good quality video. Make sure you aren't streaming from incredibly noisy places.

Be sure that your face is properly lit when you're on camera. And whenever possible, stream video with the phone held horizontally, rather than vertically.

- Facebook streaming video will stay in your feed, and can often serve as your own small "live TV show" complete with comments and likes from the audience. If you use it strategically, you'll find it an effective way to build audience interest.

TABLE 6.1   Strengths and Weaknesses of Various Social Media Platforms

Network	Strengths	Weaknesses	Best Used For. . .
Facebook	• Largest potential audience • Allows text, pictures and video • Easy-to-understand commenting system for audience	• Can be hard to reach people outside your network • Not a good network for posting multiple small updates	• Communicating directly with a wide audience • Promoting important stories • Getting your audience to share your stories with their networks
Twitter	• Best platform for breaking news • Best platform for giving live written accounts of events • Excellent for networking with other media members	• Small audience relative to other social media platforms • 280- character limit can create contextual issues with messages • Not as visually engaging as other social media	• Providing real-time news updates • Promoting stories • Being part of the online conversation surrounding a team or an event
Instagram	• Young audience • Easy to post photos and short videos • Can use caption function to include written material	• Not intended for multiple posts in short period of time • Video limited to 60 seconds max	• A supplement to other coverage • Capturing "insider" perspectives
Snapchat	• Young audience • Can tell stories using a combination of pictures and video	• Messages are only available for a short time • Will not reach most of your audience over the age of 25	• Supplementary coverage of events • Behind-the-scenes material • Humor and wit
Streaming Handheld Video	• Allows for direct communication with audience in video form • Audience can interact directly with you via written questions • Low technology requirements	• Messages are only available for a short time • Has smallest current audience of any application class	• Talking directly to audience • Streaming press conferences and other media events

IMPACT OF SOCIAL MEDIA ON MODERN-ERA SPORTS JOURNALISM

Social media have had a considerable impact on sports journalism over the past decade. Journalists are now expected to use social media to promote work, interact with audiences and supplement their content production. While there are rare instances where sports journalists refuse to use social media, the vast majority are expected to take part in multiple social media networks. "I will not hire a sports reporter who is not on Twitter," said Mike Sherman, sports editor of *The Oklahoman* newspaper and NewsOkSports.com, who also served as national president of the Associated Press Sports Editors (APSE) in 2014–2015. "How can you do your job as a reporter in this era if you are not on social media? Plus, we want you to build up a following to promote our content and interact some with your readers."

Changing Job Requirements

Almost all sports journalists are required by their employers to use social media. In fact, many media outlets will use social media evaluation as a primary component of hiring decisions for new journalists. Bill Simmons, former editor of the popular sports site Grantland, once said that his hiring process was in part based on an evaluation of their social media output. "We'll look at someone's Twitter feed and see what's on there," said Simmons, "and if it's somebody who's starting fights, I don't want to hire that person."

Many major sports media outlets have in-house rules and guidelines for social media usage among employees. As an example, ESPN has a set of policies that emphasize responsible and conservative use of Twitter and other sites (Soltys, 2011). Other sites have similar rules, and it is important for any sports journalist to clearly understand what their employer expects of them when it comes to professional and personal social media usage.

When Should You Promote Your Content on Social Media?

Content promotion on all social media should take place during the time periods when people are actively using social media. The range of time that stories should be promoted is approximately 9 a.m. until 9 p.m. local time. For national media organizations, you will want to adapt those times to your likely audience for a particular story. For instance, a story involving a West Coast team or athlete may need to be promoted later in the day due to the social media cycle starting later for that audience.

The most active times on social media for sports tends to be in the first few hours of the work day (9 a.m.–12 p.m.), as well as the post-dinner evening period (7 p.m.–9 p.m.) on days when sports programming is prominent on television. On Twitter, you will often want to promote your outlet's most interesting or popular work in both windows on a given day, in order to capture audience members who may have missed it earlier.

You may want to consider using a social media management system to help you with the process of creating and cultivating multiple audiences. These management systems allow you to post messages across multiple social media networks, schedule posts and tweets and monitor multiple streams of information. These management systems are often available in both free and subscription forms, and through both browser and app-based interfaces. The marketplace for these systems include products such as Hootsuite, Spredfast, Sprout Social and TweetDeck.

Journalists should be able to use social media to complement their work. A large amount of social media usage in sports journalism is focused on promoting content produced for other platforms. Newspaper writers will be asked to promote their stories and columns by tweeting and posting links to their content, often more than once per piece of content. They are expected to utilize hashtags on Twitter to place their work in front of a larger audience, and they are expected to interact with the audience to try and increase interest in their work.

As Doyel points out, "Aside from sending out direct links to stories, I am on social media to build up my brand, as they say. I don't mean that selfishly. The more followers I have, the more people are going to click on my work, or on my colleagues' works. We're all playing a game—whoever has the most social media followers wins. Can I get someone to see my tweet and think that I'm so clever that the person will retweet the story and get me more followers the next time I tweet out a story?"

There is also an expectation that journalists use social media to supplement their stories and reporting with additional information. In many cases, journalists are only given vague direction in this area, and may not receive support from their organization in terms of training on social media. Journalists must be entrepreneurial when it comes to social media usage, both in terms of learning how to use social media more effectively and in learning about new social media opportunities. As Hruby points out, the benefits of learning about and using emerging social media can be significant. "Anytime a new social media network takes off, if you're one of the first movers there, you reap the rewards," says Hruby.

An Information Source

Sports journalists must remember that social media is a valid and important source for news, information and potential leads for stories that they are working on. You should not view social media as simply a vehicle for interacting with fans and promoting content, but also as an information source that you need to constantly monitor. Part of your job as a reporter is to follow people who are important or potentially newsworthy on as many social media accounts as they are on. It is not enough to simply follow the Twitter accounts of players and coaches for the team you cover. You should also be sure to follow public pages of athletes and teams on Facebook, feeds on Instagram and other social media outlets. You should also learn who the opinion leaders among fans of that team are on social media, and make an effort to follow their accounts as well.

In some cases, particularly when reporting on high school recruiting and college athletics, "friending" an athlete on Facebook or mutually following accounts on Twitter is not just advisable but necessary for the type of reporting and communication necessary for that job. "Lots of teenagers don't like talking on the phone anymore," says Zach Osterman, *Indianapolis Star* beat writer and recruiting reporter. "When I covered recruiting full-time, I probably conducted as many recruiting update interviews via Facebook messaging or Twitter direct messages as I did on the phone."

Ethics

The increase in social media usage among journalists has led to questions about the ethical implications of its usage. The nature of social media often puts journalists in difficult ethical situations, and it is important to consider these potential concerns.

One of the major ethical considerations for sports journalists using social media concerns the announcement of breaking news. Due to the speed with which information travels on social media, many journalists choose to break news there first and then follow up with more information on that or other platforms. Twitter is the primary social media service for carrying breaking news, due to its unique architecture and its popularity among journalists. However, the pressure of wanting to break news first can lead journalists to be tempted to tweet out information prematurely. If this information turns out to be inaccurate and the journalist is forced to retract the report, the damage to the perceived credibility of the journalist can be tremendous.

Good sports journalists should not compromise their principles just to gain credit for posting a breaking story that they are uncertain about. While breaking important news stories is still seen as a sign of a well-connected journalist, trying to force a story that is not yet confirmed is not worth the risk. If you cannot break a story due to uncertainty, or if someone else breaks a story that is close to your beat, focus your attention on reporting the context of the story, and use social media to share those items with your audience.

Another major ethical consideration for sports journalism on social media is attribution. When information comes to light on social media that you use in reporting, the ethical thing to do is credit the source of that information publicly. Do not act like you found the information on your own. You can and should confirm stories on your beat that are broken by other sources, but acknowledge the journalist who published the news first. This is an ethical consideration for both individual journalists and media organizations. ESPN has been criticized multiple times over the past decade for not properly crediting reporters outside their organizational umbrella for breaking news, or for claiming that their own reporters broke the news story in question.

Interacting with Audiences

As has been mentioned throughout this chapter, interacting with audiences is among the most important aspects of social media usage for sports journalists. Proper and effective audience interaction can lead to larger and more interested audiences, and can create audience members who will spread your content to their own feeds.

Andy Glockner, formerlyof *Sports Illustrated,* said that connecting and interacting with audiences is even more important in today's age of sports journalism. "I think in any business where you rely on customers to drive your worth, it's important to make a connection with them," says Glockner. "Journalists are selling themselves, their ideas and their writing in a very competitive, crowded industry, and the biggest value you can have, if you're solely or mostly in print journalism, is to develop a loyal audience that's portable. Social media enables you to build that."

The uniqueness of the sports journalist's role is also an important aspect of social media usage. "I think we lose track sometimes that our readers think what we do is really cool, and it's very exciting and valuable to them to feel like a writer values their opinions," says Glocker. "If they feel they have a direct link to someone with a national or local platform, they're very eager to connect and interact."

However, sports journalists should also be cautious about dealing with audiences. While the majority of social media audience members are primarily interested in gathering information and speaking with an expert who covers their team, there will also be times when audience members react negatively to things that you say and do. Sometimes this negativity will rise to the level of vitriol and hatred. It is important for sports journalists to realize this ahead of time, and develop strategies to deal with it.

Sports fans are often very passionate people, and sometimes that passion leads them to react negatively to perceived threats to their favorite teams, coaches and athletes. Social media provides many of those fans with an impersonal outlet for their negative reactions, and often the sports journalist is the one they target. "Would I use social media in my spare time for fun?" asks Gregg Doyel. "No. I take a lot of abuse from fans on Twitter. Do I like that? No. But I don't resent social media. I understand it and why we need to use it [as journalists]." In most cases, responding to negative comments about yourself or your work is not advisable. Such responses make you appear overly sensitive or unable to deal with criticism, and can actually encourage others to make negative comments towards you in order to try and elicit a reaction.

Social media users will sometimes act far more negatively online than they would in personal conversation. This is partially due to a phenomenon known as the "online disinhibition effect," which describes a phenomenon where people abandon normal social roles and practices during online conversation due to perceived anonymity, lack of perceived danger and feelings of invisibility (Zhou, 2010). It is important to remember that online users would probably act far differently if they interacted with you in person.

Female journalists, in general, often face a frightening onslaught of negative, threatening and sexually oriented social media messages. While these messages generally only come from a small segment of the audience, they are both disturbing and unwelcome. Freelance journalist Jessica Luther was asked about why women in sports journalism are so often attacked on social media in an article published in *Sports Illustrated*. "I think attacking women who talk about sports often stems from the idea that women simply don't belong in sports, especially not in men's sports," Luther says. "Women shouldn't have an opinion, and certainly not one that challenges the systemic issues endemic in the sport or team or league someone else is invested in. But also, you just shouldn't have an opinion about who plays better at the quarterback position, or what team will make the postseason. If you dare to have one, well then, you are just asking for someone (often a man) to correct it" (DiCaro, 2015).

For any journalist facing aggressively negative audience members, normally the best option is to block that user so they cannot tweet at you directly anymore. However, if you feel personally threatened to the point of perceived danger to yourself, you should notify both Twitter and law enforcement.

FEATURE INTERVIEW

JOSH BAIRD

Director of Social Media and Audience Development, FOX Sports

Photo 6.6   Photo courtesy of Josh Baird

Josh Baird serves as Director of Social Media and Audience Development for FOX Sports. A graduate of Northeastern University, Josh took a non-traditional route to his current position. He started out working as a booking agent within the music industry, which then turned into a position in event marketing. He was able to get in on the ground floor of the marketing world's utilization of social media for audience engagement, and eventually took a job directing social media at Fuel TV. Josh assumed his current position when that station was merged into the channels known as FS1 and FS2.

Baird's duties extend across both the television and digital properties of FOX Sports, and include leveraging third-party platforms (e.g., Facebook, Instagram, Twitter) to promote content and drive traffic to the company's digital properties. Josh is also responsible for audience development within the social media sphere, working with digital partners to try and drive traffic to FOX Sports, while evaluating and using emerging technologies such as live streaming video, VR and social news products like instant articles.

Baird's perspective on social media is one that's developed over a long career of watching how user behavior intersects with product development and the process that plays out across platforms. "We prioritize content production and marketing distribution, equally. The trick is positioning our promotional content," says Baird. "And we work closely with our social media partners to effectively engage audiences and drive revenue on those platforms."

One of the biggest challenges that social media managers within sports media face is how to engage users with their content. Baird's approach focuses on trying to perceive the user's experience and interests. "We're laser focused on user experience because we want people to keep coming back.

Our philosophy is to create content for 'sports fans' that they would want to share with their friends."

"Obviously there's a lot of competition. The way we differentiate is by trying to think like a fan would. If you're going to your Twitter timeline and looking for a piece of content, we want to be the ones that are there in the moment, the ones that can deliver the type of news that you would want to read. We try to cut out a lot of the nonsense and focus on the interesting parts of a story. That memorable moment that really sticks with someone."

What does Baird consider to be the types of stories that resonate in the social media age?

"It's about being timely with a focus on what people are talking about. Instead of a game recap, we'll give you a story about the Steph Curry half-court buzzer shot that didn't count, but was still super cool. We are working to surface the stories that people will talk about the next morning."

At a media entity like FOX Sports, someone in Baird's position not only has the company's social media channels to consider, but also the individual talent that the network employs. Baird sees these accounts as a benefit to the overall social media engagement process.

"The way I see it, talent accounts are our pool of influencers. We want all of our talent to have their own voices. That's what sets them apart. We don't want to manage their accounts or tell them what to say, because that takes away from their unique qualities. Authenticity is really important in social media. It's what makes a profile worth following."

The constant struggle facing Baird and his team is how to deal with the ever-changing face of technology, and making decisions about what to ignore, what to use, and how to use it. But he says that the best approach in the current technology climate is to be at the forefront of new development.

"In order to stay competitive, you have to be willing to lean into new technology and take chances. Being an early adopter allows you to be out in front of products as they evolve. That can lead to new and innovative opportunities for driving engagement. It can also lead to big wastes of time, but that's all part of growth."

CHAPTER WRAP-UP

Social media represent the new age of reporting and journalism, and contain both promise and pitfalls for the aspiring sports journalist. Social media change constantly, with new features added and old features disappearing on a regular basis. Dealing with these changes seems easy when you are younger, because your personal communication tendencies are often changing right along with the social networks. But as your career continues, you will often find yourself dealing with new technology and methods that are difficult to learn on the fly. The successful sports journalist must learn to keep on top of these trends, understand what the audience is using, and find a way to adapt.

Social media represent a way to reach the audience directly, and to use words, pictures, audio, and video to tell stories in unique and captivating ways. The multimedia nature of social networks require young sports journalists to be comfortable with a wide variety of communication methods. Gone are the days where simply being a writer or a broadcaster is enough. You should focus on becoming adept at creating content in a variety of ways, and learning how that content is received by audiences.

REVIEW QUESTIONS

1. What are the key advantages that Facebook enjoys over other social media in terms of audience engagement?
2. Describe the two different types of hashtags on Twitter, and how they are used.
3. Which social media networks should sports media outlets use when trying to reach younger audiences?
4. How has social media increased the workload of sports journalists?
5. What are some things to be careful about when interacting with audiences on social media?

GROUP ACTIVITIES

1. Assign each group member a different sports media entity, and have them analyze how that entity is using its various social media outlets. What kinds of content are being posted on each network? How does the content differ? How much interaction is taking place with audiences on each network?
2. Choose a major sporting event taking place during the course. Assign students to groups, and have each group develop a coverage plan for that event for different social media networks (i.e., have one group create a plan for Facebook coverage, another for Twitter, etc.).
3. Have your students audit their own social media output, and compare it to the social media output of professional sports journalists. What are the major differences between the two, both in terms of content and in terms of writing tone?

CHAPTER 7

Sports Public Relations and Sports Information

We have already described how technology has influenced the sports media in a variety of areas, including broadcasting, production and economics. This is no less true in sports public relations and sports information, which has been drastically affected by advances in technology, particularly the Internet and social media. While the aims of sports public relations remain the same, its practice is undergoing significant change.

SPORTS PR: AIMS, GOALS AND THE ROLE OF AGENDA

The goal of any public relations communication is to influence opinion. Sometimes this relates simply to influencing a person's perception or attitude, while other messages may be designed to compel action. Strategies can be implemented proactively, that is before something happens, or retroactively, after a situation has occurred.

Everyone involved in the sports communication business has an *agenda*. This is the unique set of perspectives, goals and attitudes each stakeholder brings to the communication process. In order to understand sports public relations, it is important to know the different agendas involved. For any athlete, coach or sports organization the agenda is the creation of a favorable image. As with most things in sports, it directly relates to economics. Organizations that have good reputations can sell more tickets and merchandise, while athletes with positive images can make millions in endorsement dollars.

The media play a vital role in shaping sports public opinion, but their economic interest is different. Media competition means a scramble for audience attention, whether that is in the form of newspaper sales, television ratings or website clicks. Thus, the media are concerned about the reputation of the athlete or organization only so far as it helps them sell content. In today's ultra-competitive media environment full of endless consumer choices, outlets can often sell more content through criticism, sensationalism, gossip and innuendo.

"I like to write in detail on serious topics," said Ryan Wilson, an NFL writer, blogger and podcaster for CBSSports.com. "But if I write two lines on some other report on (ex-Cleveland Browns quarterback) Johnny Manziel doing something dumb, our page views and social media blow up, which is what the bosses are often pushing for because it's good for business" (personal communication, 2015).

Audiences play a dual role in this process. Traditionally, they have consumed the content provided by media outlets. In a sense, they were the umpires of the agenda tug-of-war between media outlets and athletes, coaches and organizations. Public opinion—whether audiences would be more sympathetic to critical coverage coming from the media or more positive information coming from the organizations — often dictated a story's shelf life and how it evolved.

However, now audiences are empowered beyond the ability to merely consume content. The Internet, blogs and social media allow them to become their own content creators and more directly push their own agendas. Rather than umpiring between the media and organizations, audiences have now become equal stakeholders in the process (Figure 7.1).

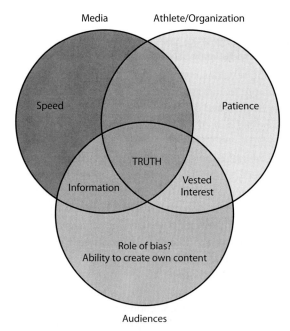

Figure 7.1 The intersection of competing agendas for audiences, sports figures and the media. In any sports communication scenario, the stakeholders will have different agendas. Sometimes these agendas intersect, such as the desire for all stakeholders to discover the truth, but how much truth gets out and on what timetable can be a source of conflict. Competition drives the media to get information out faster, while organizations want to control and slow down the information flow. Some audiences may want information out more quickly, while others that have a rooting or vested interest may side with the athlete or organization. That audiences can now create their own content signals a dramatic shift in the process.

We can better understand the role of agenda by looking at a specific example. Consider the 2014 story of Baltimore Ravens running back Ray Rice and the altercation with his girlfriend. On February 15, the two were accused of getting into a fight in a New Jersey casino; both were arrested and charged with simple assault. Four days later, the television outlet TMZ broadcast surveillance video, which showed Rice dragging his unconscious then-girlfriend, Janay Palmer, out of the casino elevator. While charges against Palmer were dropped, Rice was indicted by a grand jury on third-degree aggravated assault charges (Table 7.1).

What unfolded over the next nine months was an example of the role of agenda in sports public relations. Rice's agenda was to clear his name, protect his livelihood and rebuild his reputation in the eyes of the public. To that end, his news conference on July 31 was an admission of guilt in which he took responsibility for his actions. His entrance into a program for domestic violence also signaled a desire to repair his public image. Interestingly, Palmer also engaged in these repair strategies, defending Rice on several occasions and complaining about media coverage that had made her life a "nightmare" (Alonso, 2014, ¶ 10).

Given its vested interest in Rice, the Ravens also engaged in image-repair strategies. The team sponsored a news conference with both Rice and Palmer on May 23, although their efforts at live-tweeting the event were roundly criticized by national media figures (Bien, 2014; Van Bibber, 2015). In early interactions with the media, Ravens officials consistently supported Rice, including head

TABLE 7.1   Timeline of Ray Rice Incident

February 15	Incident takes place in Atlantic City, N.J.
February 19	TMZ releases video of Rice dragging Palmer from elevator.
February 21	Ravens coach John Harbaugh offers team's first public comments on Rice since the video, expressing support for Rice, touting his character, and saying he expects Rice to remain with the Ravens.
March 24	Offering his first public comments since the video release, Ravens owner Steve Biscotti touts Rice's community involvement, states that Rice "will definitely be back" with the Ravens that fall and also said, "When you drink too much in public, those kind of things happen."
March 27	Rice is charged by an Atlantic City grand jury.
March 28	Rice and Palmer marry.
May 1	Rice pleads not guilty.
May 20	Rice is accepted into a diversionary program for domestic violence.
May 23	The Baltimore Ravens hold a news conference with both Rice and Palmer. Rice apologizes for his actions (although never to Palmer) and Palmer defends him. The Ravens' public relations department is widely criticized for live-tweeting the press conference and quoting insensitive comments made by Rice such as "I won't call myself a failure. Failure is not getting knocked down. It's not getting up."
July 24	NFL Commissioner Roger Goodell announces a two-game suspension for Rice starting August 30.

continued

TABLE 7.1 Timeline of Ray Rice Incident *continued*

July 31	Rice conducts a news conference where he calls his actions "inexcusable."
August 28	With criticism mounting over what is considered a light punishment, Goodell announces a new harsher (six game) punishment for future domestic violence. He also admits that in the Rice decision, "I didn't get it right. Simply put, we have to do better. And we will."
September 8	TMZ releases another video, this time showing Rice punching and knocking out Palmer in the elevator. That same day the Baltimore Ravens release Rice and the NFL suspends him for the rest of the season. The NFL claims it had not previously seen the new video.
September 9	TMZ reports that the NFL never contacted the casino to request the new video. The NFL responds that "the video was never made available to us."
September 10	The Associated Press reports that the NFL received the tape back in April and that the NFL confirmed it had the video. The NFL announces an independent investigation.
September 11	*The Wall Street Journal* reports that Goodell and the NFL didn't pursue an investigation earlier because of concerns over how it would be perceived.
September 16	Rice appeals his indefinite suspension.
November 28	An independent arbiter overturns Rice's suspension. Despite his eligibility, Rice sits out the entire season because no team will pick him up.

Sources: "Key events," 2014; "A complete timeline," 2014.

coach John Harbaugh, who repeatedly praised his character, and owner Steve Bisciotti, who publicly said, "He's just been lauded as the nicest, hardest working, greatest guy on the team and in the community. So we have to support him" (Mink, 2014, ¶ 11).

But when the new video of Rice came out in September, the agendas of the team and Rice diverged. Quick to realize the negative public relations potential of not taking domestic violence seriously — protests, media scrutiny, and lower ticket and merchandising sales — the team released Rice and said that like the NFL it had not seen the new video until TMZ released it. Instead of lauding Rice, Bisciotti now said, "The decision to let Ray Rice go was unanimous. Seeing that video changed everything. We should have seen it earlier. We should have pursued our own investigation more vigorously. We didn't and we were wrong" (Sessler, 2014, ¶ 18).

The NFL changed its position on the incident several times to fit its public relations needs. The main agenda of the NFL, or any other organization, is to promote a positive image in the mind of the public. Goodell has called this "protecting the shield" in reference to the NFL logo. The NFL believed that its initial response would handle the situation, but when the new video surfaced the league and Goodell looked incompetent. Only when the public relations backlash got so hot that there were some calls for Goodell to resign did the league counter with the six-game suspension. When reports came out that the NFL had the videotape for months and did not act on it, the league rather weakly maintained the position that such reports were wrong. All in all, it was a serious public relations black eye for the NFL in terms of maintaining its image.

The agenda of the media was to get information out quickly, and TMZ played a major role in that. Tabloid outlets such as TMZ and the *National Enquirer* come under constant criticism for their sensational, celebrity-oriented approach, but such outlets are increasingly breaking stories that mainstream media sites are afraid to touch. Mainstream media will also pay for video taken by bystanders and then uploaded to websites like TMZSports.com. In this case, TMZ drove coverage of the event, both at the beginning and the end. Once the events were established, other media outlets joined in the efforts to publicize the story.

The media had no vested interest in protecting Ray Rice or Roger Goodell, and in this situation the ability to find not one, but two villains made for extremely compelling coverage. The story dominated the sports media for almost its entire duration, driving audiences to newspapers, television broadcasts and websites. The media found other ways to create interest beyond the salacious details, such as using the incident to spark discussion on domestic violence.

There were multiple audience agendas in the Ray Rice incident, just as there are in any sports story. Many fans simply wanted the truth to come out and to understand what happened. To them, the main agenda was to determine guilt or innocence. Other audiences, especially fans of the Ravens, may have been more sympathetic to Rice. They wanted to avoid the initial "rush to judgment" and let the process play out. No doubt some of them simply wished that the story would just go away and they stopped consuming content on the matter. Another audience segment perhaps used the incident to bring the issue of domestic violence into the national conversation. Each of these audiences promoted their agendas on personal blogs, websites and social media accounts.

Media analyst Marie Alonso (2014) noted, "The matrix of social media tightened around the Rice drama, as a cumulative and assembled voice raised loudly with everything from criticisms of the NFL to insults cast at Rice's expense, and even posts by Rice's wife conveying anger, humiliation, and disgust at the public ridicule and professional damage done to her husband. Would Rice have continued to play on as a gridiron hero, inspiring youths and receiving cheers, if social media did not exist? Quite possibly. *Correction: Make that probably*" (emphasis original) (¶ 5).

Audiences are in a unique situation in this process, at least for those who choose to produce content. Some of their work, especially on social media, blogs and start-up websites, is nothing more than blatant homerism and a desire to support a particular team. They are, in essence, just meeting market demands, since many fans only want to read slanted news on their favorite teams, which the Internet and social media now afford them the opportunity to do. Others have taken a more objective approach and created an agenda of trying to compete with the established media. Many of them have cultivated large and loyal audiences.

PUBLIC RELATIONS STRATEGIES

The Ray Rice incident also highlights the specific strategies used in sports public relations. These strategies can vary depending on whether they are proactive or reactive.

Proactive strategies are developed before a specific event or situation takes place. Almost everyone who engages in public relations acknowledges the value of "getting ahead" of a situation and not letting events dictate strategy. There are a variety of proactive strategies, including cultivating and establishing relationships in the media industry, integrating new technologies such as social media into the public relations message and developing specific events to create positive public opinion. For example, the NFL has several programs designed to positively influence its female audience. Many teams implement a "Football 101: NFL Workshop for Women" program that is designed to introduce women to the rules, strategy and nuances of the game. The league also works with the Susan G. Komen Foundation to promote awareness of breast cancer. During the month of October the program reaches maximum visibility as players wear pink game attire.

One of the most important proactive strategies is to create a crisis communications plan. Crises are increasingly common in sports media, whether it's an athlete arrested, a personal scandal or an ill-advised social media post. Sometimes the organization will have lead time on how to handle the situation, but more often than not it will get blind-sided.

IN TIME OF CRISIS

What should go into a sports crisis communications plan? There are no definitive rules, but the following guidelines are fairly standard in sports public relations:

- *Have a list of media contacts already developed.* Know who and what outlets to target when news needs to get out. Cultivating relationships with those in the media prior to a crisis can help mitigate some of the fallout. Of course, the media member ranks have greatly expanded in the digital age and not all sport public relations professionals are recognizing the influence of bloggers and those in social media.
- *Develop and maintain a consistent media message.* It is essential that organizations communicate a single message during the crisis. Mixed messages coming from within the organization raise suspicions for the media and the public, and cast doubt on the organization's ability to handle the situation.
- *Determine who will be the singular point of contact for the organization.* To maintain a single message usually means having just one public spokesperson. Allowing multiple parties to speak to the media increases the chances of giving out information that is incorrect, premature or damaging. Those not designated to speak to the public should stay silent, so that the organization stays on message. European soccer clubs do this well by designating an official spokesperson who regularly speaks to media.

- *Have social media guidelines already in place.* Many crises have become even more inflamed because of careless social media usage. Organizational policies about social media—including who can use them and what message goes out—should be well established before a crisis occurs. There should also be someone responsible for checking on the organization's social media output.
- *Determine the flow of information, including regular media contact.* How much information goes out? When will it go out? What platforms will be used for dissemination? Those issues will be largely determined by the nature of the crisis. Some crises require daily, if not more frequent, updates, while other situations are slower paced. In any situation, the organization should plan for consistent contact with media outlets. Those organizations that do not only raise suspicions of "stonewalling" or hiding information, and become even bigger targets of media investigation.

In terms of specific crisis strategies, several common responses have emerged. *Denial* is fairly self-explanatory in that the person or organization simply denies that any problem has occurred. For 15 years, former baseball star Pete Rose denied that he had bet on baseball games while manager of the Cincinnati Reds, only to come clean with the publication of an autobiography in 2004. "I feel he has embarrassed me," said veteran sports writer Roger Kahn. "I must have asked Pete 20 times, 'Did you bet on baseball?' He would look at me, blink his eyes and say, 'I didn't bet baseball. I have too much respect for the game'" (Blum, 2004, ¶ 25).

Blame shifting or *scapegoating* occurs when blame is shifted to someone else. During the Deflategate scandal in 2015 in which the New England Patriots were accused of deflating footballs before an NFL playoff game, Patriots coach Bill Belichick denied any responsibility, but hinted superstar quarterback Tom Brady might know something more. "Tom's personal preferences on his footballs are something that he can talk about in much better detail and information than I could possibly provide," said the coach. The Boston *Globe* responded, "(Belichick's) message to the media, fans and the NFL at large? Hey, don't look at me. Blame the other guy" (Volin, 2015, ¶ 2, 8).

Other evasive strategies include *evasion of responsibility* ("It's not my fault"), *reducing offensiveness* ("It's not that big of a deal"), *defensibility* ("I didn't know the rules involved"), *accident* and *good intention* ("We tried to do the right thing. . .") (Benoit, 1995). Perhaps the strongest and most ill-advised evasive response is *stonewalling*. This is where the organization or athlete cuts off all communication on the issue in hopes that it will eventually blow over. When golfer Tiger Woods went through his personal scandal in 2009, he tried this tactic, essentially refusing to cooperate with the media, other than a brief "press conference" in which he read a statement and took no questions. David Hinckley (2010, ¶ 12) in the

New York Daily News wrote on Woods, "He clearly hoped that by bypassing the media . . . he can tamp down the volume of the questions and make the press look petty for asking, thus shifting some of the attention away from himself." But while Woods would not talk, the women involved did, and despite reports that Woods offered millions in hush money, they painted an unflattering picture of Woods as a sexually voracious predator.

As Woods found out, stonewalling rarely works, in part because it encourages the media to seek its information elsewhere (Smithson & Venette, 2013). In 2014, the University of North Carolina became engulfed in a scandal when reports surfaced of widespread academic fraud committed over decades. It was alleged that players were taking bogus classes and had tutors write their term papers for them. Basketball coach Roy Williams immediately denied the reports, as did the university administration. "UNC's initial response to all these charges has been stonewall and deny, stonewall and deny, right out of the Richard Nixon playbook," said author Gregg Easterbrook (Tiberii, 2014, ¶ 18). Only when events spiraled out of control, and the evidence became incontrovertible, did the university administration finally come clean and start to repair the mess. Despite all its efforts, UNC lost its ability to control the story. Sometimes that happens because the media pushes so hard that the organizational stonewall finally gives way.

Not all responses to crises are negative or evasive. In some cases, the organization will use *bolstering* or emphasizing positive traits, such as was previously mentioned in the Ravens' initial response to the Ray Rice situation. An organization also might try to *reduce credibility* or attack the accuser. In 2015, it was reporters in Indianapolis who brought the Deflategate scandal to light, and in doing so called for coach Bill Belichick to resign. That prompted a response from a CBS television affiliate in Boston: "If prominent voices in the Indianapolis media like Bob Kravitz and Gregg Doyel can outright call for the firing of Belichick," wrote Michael Hurley, "despite having no basis for such a ludicrous opinion, then I can say this: It's time to kick (Colts' owner) Jim Irsay out of the league. Heck, ban (head coach) Chuck Pagano for a year, too. It's the only fair response to this situation, right?" (Hurley, 2015, ¶ 12).

Sometimes, athletes and organizations find it easier to simply admit guilt and move on. *Accepting responsibility* often builds goodwill with the public because those involved are perceived as "stand up" and accountable for their actions. *Corrective action* can also be used as a follow-up strategy after guilt is admitted. The violator undertakes some sort of action that suggests a willingness to fix the problem and make sure it doesn't happen again. An athlete checking into rehab, as Johnny Manziel did in 2015, is an example of corrective action.

All these strategies are multilayered and can intersect or change as the situation warrants. For years, bicycling champion Lance Armstrong used denial, blame shifting and scapegoating to refute the many doping charges against him. Only after media reports conclusively proved that he had used performance-enhancing drugs did Armstrong shift his tactics, accepting responsibility and taking corrective action in a televised interview with Oprah Winfrey.

Armstrong, Tiger Woods, and Ray Rice have all gone through highly pub-licized scandals in recent years, but no single situation demonstrated the role of crisis communications more than the Penn State football scandal of 2011.

Maybe it is better to say that no situation better demonstrates how *not* to engage in crisis communications. Allegations surfaced that former assistant foot-ball coach Jerry Sandusky — the architect of Penn State's famed "Linebacker U" defense as its longtime coordinator — had sexually molested young boys for decades, including while he coached at Penn State and at university athletics facili-ties after he had retired to emeritus status. Further, reports stated that Penn State officials, including revered head coach Joe Paterno, knew about the abuse but did nothing to stop the crimes, making this a major national news story that Penn State mishandled from the start.

As it apparently had done for years with details of the incident, Penn State tried to delay, hide and stonewall the media as the story broke. During the height of the story, Lynn Zinser (2011, ¶ 1) at *The* New York *Times* observed:

> Anyone with an ounce of sense happening by the Penn State campus these days might want to deliver a message to the people ostensibly running the place: Your scandal isn't going away. With hundreds of reporters roaming their campus look-ing for answers to the obvious questions that come with a sexual abuse case uni-versity officials — including Coach Joe Paterno — allegedly sat on for years, and a public cry for some defense for what appears to be an institution-wide moral collapse, the university brain trust has found a very large sand pit for those brains and decided not to deal with it. So, on top of a crisis, the university has heaped a public relations catastrophe.

But no amount of delay could deter the media, whose ranks quickly expanded, and they relentlessly dug into the story. Their work contributed to the firing of Paterno, university president Graham Spanier and several other Penn State ad-ministrative figures. Sandusky was convicted and sent to prison. The university suffered extensive damage to its brand and public image that will take years to overcome. Part of it was a failed institutional culture that allowed such activities to take place and then covered them up, but another part was a failed public relations effort by isolated university and athletics communications departments that obvi-ously had no idea how quickly a story like this could become the No. 1 national news items in the age of digital and social media.

SPORTS INFORMATION

One of the most visible areas of sports public relations is the person at an orga-nization in charge of handling sports information. This position can have a vari-ety of designations and is now often an assistant or associate athletics director in charge of athletics communications at the college level and or director of media relations at the pro level. But historically this position was dubbed the sports infor-mation director (SID), a term still regularly used by colleges and even more often used by media members when interacting with sports PR professions (i.e., SIDs). SIDs historically came from the ranks of former journalists to work for a college, university, professional team, conference or sports organization. Increasingly, though, more are now receiving direct classroom training in communications/ journalism and/or sports management programs, while working their entire careers in sports information/media relations. They usually start as college students who work for their universities' athletics departments as volunteers or interns. Under the umbrella of sports information, SIDs have several jobs — providing information, writing copy, establishing and maintaining media contacts, credentialing, communicating within the organization and, as we have seen, crisis management. We can loosely call these functions creating, disseminating, networking and strategizing (Figure 7.2).

Creating refers to content creation, and this is a major component of the job. The SID must make a constant flow of information — statistics, player and coach biographies, schedules and the like — available to the media and other constituencies. Working alone or with assistants, the SID is constantly writing and organizing this material for distribution. Some of it is done for the long term, such as a media guide to the entire season, while other information is produced daily, like news releases and statistical updates.

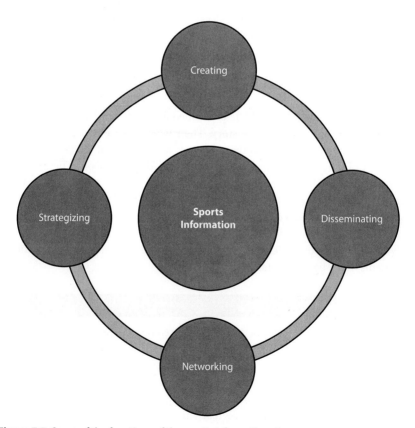

Figure 7.2 Some of the functions of the sports information director.
No matter the organization, the sports information director has essentially the same responsibilities.

News releases should be written to help the reader understand the 5Ws — who, what, where, why and when. The information should fit on one page so it doesn't overwhelm readers with information, and should be both visually appealing and understandable at a quick glance. Do not make the reader hunt for important information. In this regard, writing news releases is very similar to traditional AP-style newspaper reporting, at least in terms of the inverted-pyramid style and clarity of writing. The release should also include the SID's contact information in case the reader has any questions or needs more details (Figure 7.3).

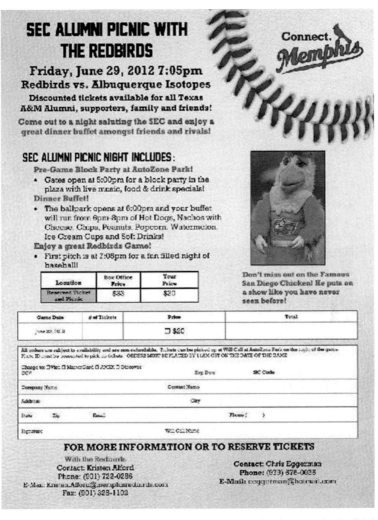

Figure 7.3 A typical release, this one for a promotional event by the Memphis Redbirds baseball team. SIDs must create and release information on a daily basis. Some of this information is promotional material, such as this release from the minor league baseball team Memphis Redbirds. Notice how this release makes all the important 5W information easily accessible, and includes contact information.

Courtesy of the Memphis Redbirds

Almost all colleges and universities also publish media guides for their different sports. The term media guide is somewhat misleading because schools now use the publication as a recruiting tool to entice prospective athletes with flashy graphics and high production values. But its main function is still as a resource book for media members, and as such it contains reams of information on player and coach biographies, schedules, statistics and team records and history. Because they contain so much information media guides can be quite bulky, but many schools have eliminated this problem through electronic distribution (Figure 7.4).

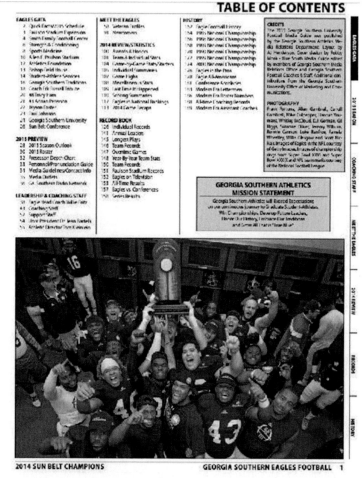

Figure 7.4 A media guide cover for the Georgia Southern University football team. Georgia Southern University is among the hundreds of schools that produce athletic media guides. Because these guides contain so much information, a good table of contents is essential to help the reader. You can see just from the length of the table of contents how much material is in the guide, which in this particular year ran to nearly 200 pages. Thanks to electronic and digital publishing, schools have been able to greatly reduce the cost of their media guides without having to sacrifice size or length.
Courtesy of Georgia Southern University/AJ Henderson

Depending on the size of the organization, an SID may have other staff responsible for churning out the media guides and daily news releases. At a large university, for example, this job may fall to any number of assistants, while at a small school one person is often in charge of everything. Regardless of the size of the staff or its resources, content creation is the primary job of the SID.

Once that content has been created it needs to get into the hands of the media or other audiences. *Disseminating* this material depends largely on the technology available, and today's sports information is usually distributed instantaneously. This is accomplished through such tools as cell phones, social media and the Internet, and is a great improvement over sending information by mail and fax machines. For example, if the SID wants to announce an unscheduled news conference, it can be done quickly and easily through email, text messaging and social media. Certainly, some information is still sent the old-fashioned way, but the overwhelming majority of sports information today, including media guides, is sent electronically and made available through the Web to all media members, and occasionally to everyone who logs onto to those pages.

This makes the job of the SID much more demanding and requires an ability to work, schedule and organize in a much shorter time frame. The speed of dissemination has made it easier and faster to get information out, but has reduced the time for consideration, introspection and vetting of such material. "The Internet and social media have impacted almost every part of our jobs," said Claude Felton, who has directed the University of Georgia's Sports Communication Office (i.e., previously called the UGA Sports Information Department) since 1979 (personal communication, 2015). For example, in 2015 the University of Nebraska fired stadium announcer Jon Schuetz less than a week after he got the job. The reason was the discovery of an old Facebook post in which Schuetz criticized the school's administration over the firing of a football coach the previous winter. "If I were in their shoes, I would've done the same thing," Schuetz lamented of his firing. "I've hired people. I get it. If you say something about a prospective future employer, it's legitimate to say, 'If you're not on board with what we do here, maybe you shouldn't be here'" (Chatelain, 2015, ¶ 9).

The Schuetz situation shows just how difficult it is for an organization to maintain a consistent message and fully monitor the social media postings of its employees. It also points out the dangers of personal social media use in professional situations, and the consequences of ignoring the permanence of the medium. The SID bears no particular responsibility in this situation, but as someone in charge of the organization's public profile, more proactive strategies — including a social media policy — might have helped. The university has specific social media policies in place for its student athletes, but many need clearer guidelines for employees. Accordingly, many athletic departments are now contracting with external agencies for social-media training or, in some cases, monitoring. "Too many coaches or athletics directors think they can fix this problem by just banning social media, which incidentally restricts First Amendment rights," said Kevin DeShazo, founder and CEO of Fieldhouse Media, which addresses social media education, strategy and monitoring and has contracted with more than 70 college athletics departments. "Our goal is to teach you how to use social media wisely to advance your team, organization or career. It can be a great tool for spreading positive messages" (personal communication, 2015).

Networking is just another way of saying that the SID needs to work with a variety of stakeholders, most especially the media. We have already seen how the SID continually creates and distributes information that the media need. Certain situations will also require direct interaction with media members, such as covering a game or event. The SID is in charge of credentialing — determining who gets official access to games, interviews and the like — as well as maintaining standards and expectations of media behavior. SIDs decide who sits where in the press box, who gets sideline access and which players will be available for interviews after the game (although media requests for specific players and which players coaches want to send out to media also play a large part in the selection of players for interviews). In addition to these official rules, SIDs also enforce unwritten guidelines such as the long-standing admonition of "no cheering in the press box," which means media members should not outwardly show favoritism during games.

All of this interaction suggests that SIDs must have good working relationships with members of the media. Cultivating these relationships ahead of time can help when problems do arise, such as the need to say no to an interview request or to reduce the number of credentials issued for a particular game. This is not to say that SIDs should be excessively friendly with media members, because that may raise issues of conflict of interest. But a professional relationship in which the expectations of both sides are clearly understood is essential.

We have already talked about the role of agenda in sports communication, and SIDs represent the agenda of the school or organization that employs them. Accordingly, SIDs work to maintain the reputation of the organization and to put it in the best possible light. Part of an SID's job is to *strategize* how to best support this agenda, and this means regular meetings with organizational administration to design and review agenda strategies. An SID also meets with sports information personnel to implement these strategies. What players or coaches merit special emphasis? Is there a record about to be broken? Perhaps a promotional campaign can be tied in with a game or event.

It is interesting to see how SIDs strategize when their schools have a Heisman Trophy candidate. This is sports public relations in its purest form — trying to create favorable public impressions through a media blitz in newspapers, television and the Internet. When football quarterback Joey Harrington was a Heisman candidate in 2001, the University of Oregon emphasized his campaign with a huge billboard attached to an office building in New York City. Oregon's campaign for Joey Harrington didn't succeed as the quarterback finished fourth in the voting in 2001. But SIDs continue to try innovating campaigns to get their Heisman candidate noticed among the nation's sports writers who vote on the award (Table 7.2).

Social media and the Internet have not only changed the role of the SID, they have also empowered those outside the traditional sports public relations system. Athletes and coaches are now using new technologies to communicate directly

TABLE 7.2   Notable Heisman Campaigns

Player	Year	Campaign	Result
Ty Detmer BYU	1990	Cardboard ties mailed to voters	won
Ryan Leaf Washington State	1997	Staffers raked leaves on campus and sent a single leaf to each voter	third
Michael Turner Northern Illinios	2003	"Turner the Burner" hot sauce bottled in Turner's honor	out of top 10
Dan Persa Northwestern	2011	Seven-pound dumbbells (representing Persa's #7) sent to voters	out of top 10
Matt Barkley USC	2012	A free mobile app to track Barkley and other USC award candidates	out of top 10
Jordan Lynch	2013	"Lunch with Lynch"	
Northern Illinois		Lunch bags sent to voters	7th

Source: Athleticbusiness.com

with audiences and, in a sense, become their own public relations managers. Athletes have especially taken to Twitter, which delivers them the opportunity to craft their own messages directly to audiences of millions, which includes sports journalists who now often quote athletes directly from their social media posts (Table 7.3).

Photo 7.1 Part of Northern Illinois University's "Lunch with Lynch" Heisman campaign for Jordan Lynch. Jordan Lynch of Northern Illinois University didn't win the Heisman Trophy in 2013, but not for lack of a media campaign. The university created a "Lunch with Lynch" promotion that appeared on lunch boxes as well as social media.
Courtesy of Northern Illinois University

TABLE 7.3   Athletes with the Most Twitter Followers, 2017

Athlete	Sport	Twitter Audience (in millions)
Cristian Ronaldo	Soccer	53.7
LeBron James	Basketball	37.0
Neymar Junior	Soccer	29.8
Kaká	Soccer	27.2
Sachin Tendulkar	Soccer	16.8

Source: https://twittercounter.com/pages/100/sports-athlete

Athletes can use Twitter to give a glimpse into their private lives, discuss particular issues, or give their opinion about the big game. No matter what the topic, the platform allows athletes and coaches to bypass the mainstream media and talk directly with huge sports audiences.

Athletes are just beginning to realize the public relations potential of social media. When longtime Yankees' star Derek Jeter announced his retirement in 2014, he did so on Facebook rather than through the traditional outlets. This allowed him to create and present his own message without having to answer a lot of questions from reporters. Similarly, NBA star Shaquille O'Neal announced his retirement from the NBA in 2011 on the social media platform Tout. "He had full control of when, where and how he wanted to make that announcement," said social media advisor Amy Jo Martin. "No press releases needed. It was about him using this influence he had built to communicate directly with his fans" (Ortiz, 2011, ¶ 20).

Sports public relations officials must deal with these empowered athletes and try to keep them "on message" and out of trouble. Colleges and universities typically have social media rules in place, but even that has not prevented athletes from posting comments that have led to suspensions or even dismissal. In addition to guidelines, many schools now have mandatory workshops to help their athletes better understand the issues involved.

Add on top of this that fans are now using social media to take part in the process. One photo of a coach or athlete caught in a compromising situation and posted to social media can quickly undo any positive public relations efforts. In 2008, Josh Howard of the NBA's Dallas Mavericks was attending a charity football game when a fan shot video of him disrespecting the National Anthem. "The Star Spangled Banner's going on right now and I don't celebrate that s***," Howard said. "I'm black" (Chandler, 2008, ¶ 2). The video went to YouTube, piled up hundreds of thousands of views, and created a negative backlash that forced Howard to publicly apologize.

FINAL THOUGHTS

You can see that managing sports public opinion has become much more complicated in recent years. Primarily, that is due to the technology that makes it harder for the public relations professional to shape and control the message. Today, athletes, coaches and fans have the ability to create and disseminate their own content, and thus all take part in the public relations process. A successful SID or public relations practitioner must accept these new realities and work within a quickly changing environment. Those who understand the role of agenda, and can formulate effective strategies that incorporate the role of new technologies, will be successful in the evolving sports public relations field.

FEATURE INTERVIEW

WILLIAM D. COHAN

Journalist and Author

THE PRICE OF SILENCE

WILLIAM D. COHAN

Five years before the Penn State–Jerry Sandusky scandal broke, Duke University went through its own public relations nightmare. In 2006, a female stripper hired for a party held by the men's lacrosse team filed rape charges against three of the players. The accusations made national headlines and threw the campus into turmoil. Shortly after the incident, Duke alumnus, journalist and author William D. Cohan received a routine call from the school asking for donations. "I gave them some free advice," Cohan remembers. "I told them to get their hands around this thing and get a crisis manager. Instead, they 'lawyered up,' and everything got scripted."

Photo 7.2   Photo courtesy of William Cohan/Joy Harris Literary Agency

The result, according to Cohan, was a "PR nightmare," as the university essentially went on communications lockdown. Following the story in *The New York Times*, Cohan noted that at first "the feeling was that the kids were guilty and needed to be punished. But then the narrative changed. The DNA tests came back negative. The stripper turned out to be something of a loose cannon; the district attorney prosecuting the case was ambitious and out of control." The story seemed to be shifting almost daily, and the university appeared unable to keep up.

Cohan, himself a veteran investigative reporter with stints at *Vanity Fair* and *Fortune*, decided he needed to find out what happened for himself. He spent two years investigating the lacrosse story with little or no help from officials at Duke. "I knew Duke President Dick Brodhead and wanted to interview him, but he wouldn't talk to me," says Cohan. "Coaches, public relations officials, no one in the Duke administration would talk and a lot of them tried to shut me down. They didn't realize that so much of the story was already public information." Cohan pressed forward and in 2014 published his account of the crisis — *The Price of Silence*.

continued

More than ten years have passed since the incident at Duke, and the school has instituted a crisis communications policy to help it deal with future situations (see Breakout Box). But in other areas, change has come slowly. The university's president and judicial affairs staff remains the same as it was in 2006. Duke lacrosse coach Mike Pressler, fired during the investigation, sued the school's senior public relations officer John Burness for slander and eventually settled out of court. Burness retired, only to be brought back to Duke as a professor of public policy. "They brought him back to keep him quiet," says Cohan. "Keep your friends close and your enemies closer. That so many people who were there during the crisis still have their jobs is astounding to me."

Charges against the lacrosse players were eventually dropped and the only person to spend any time in jail was the district attorney, Mike Nifong. Cohan estimates that between legal fees, settlements and other public relations fees, the incident likely cost Duke close to $100 million. The damage to its reputation is incalculable. "The university was on a path of soul-searching," says Cohan, "but that eventually dissipated. This was a different situation than at Penn State. We pretty much know what happened there. At Duke, we don't know and we'll likely never know."

You can find more information about William D. Cohan and *The Price of Silence* at http://williamcohan.com/

BREAKOUT BOX

In 2007, a year after the lacrosse scandal, Duke University instituted a new crisis communications plan. Among other things, the plan:

- Created and defined a crisis communications team that was empowered to control communication efforts
- Determined who will act as the primary spokesperson
- Described how to carry out a Web response
- Called for a media center to determine if/when news conferences need to be held
- Called for media training and annual emergency drills to test the plan
- Determined when the crisis ends and normal communications can resume

The plan acknowledges that "Our efforts to be simultaneously accurate and quick may mean that some communications are incomplete. We accept this, knowing that how we communicate in an emergency or a crisis will affect public perceptions of the university. Honesty and speed are the most effective means to avoid lasting damage to the institution and widespread second-guessing by the public, which expects immediate access to accurate information. A good offense is the best defense."

While Duke and Penn State were somewhat late in coming to the party, their well-publicized incidents have convinced almost all schools to create a crisis communications plan. In his study of such plans, Matthew Seeger developed a list of 10 best practices in crisis communications:

1. Communication strategies should be fully integrated into the decision-making process.
2. Plan ahead of time before the crisis begins.
3. Partner with the public in the communication process.
4. Listen to the public's concerns and understand the audience.
5. Practice honesty, candor and openness to build credibility and trust.
6. Collaborate and coordinate with credible sources.
7. Meet the needs of the media and remain accessible.
8. Communicate with compassion, concern and empathy.
9. Accept uncertainty and ambiguity.
10. Create messages to help the public reduce harm created by the crisis.

Courtesy of Duke University (http://emergency.duke.edu/plan/); Seeger (2006).

CHAPTER WRAP-UP

Sports public relations is dominated by competing agendas, usually among the media, athletes, organizations and audience. Each of these groups has a different agenda in terms of handling information, as was vividly demonstrated during the Ray Rice situation in 2014. Each stakeholder in that situation was trying to shape the information for a specific purpose.

The Ray Rice episode also serves as an example of crisis communications. Organizations and athletes can have a variety of responses to a public relations crisis ranging from total openness (typically very rare) to complete silence (called stonewalling). It is important for organizations to have a communications plan established before a crisis happens. If not, as was the case with the Penn State football scandal, the results can be disastrous.

Sports information directors (SIDs) who work at schools or other organizations have a variety of functions including creating and disseminating information, networking and strategizing. Creating effective messages that conform to the organization's goals and agenda is an essential part of the job.

REVIEW QUESTIONS

1. How can the media, athletes and audiences all have a different agenda on the same issue? For example, if a popular local football player is arrested for DUI, how might the agenda differ among those three groups?
2. What impact are new technologies having in regard to sports public relations? Does this make it easier or harder for the media and athletes to control and shape information?
3. What are the drawbacks of using the stonewalling strategy during a crisis? Can you think of any benefits of such a strategy?
4. Both Penn State and the University of North Carolina have gone through public relations issues in the past few years that have severely damaged their images. What did the schools do wrong and what could they have done to minimize the damage?
5. Of all the functions of the sports information director (creating and disseminating information, networking and strategizing), which do you think is the most important and why?

GROUP ACTIVITIES

1. It is not hard to find a controversy in sports media. Within your group, select a current situation and discuss it in terms of the media, the athlete/organization and the audience. In terms of agendas, do these groups have any overlapping similarities? How are they different?
2. Develop hypothetical crisis scenarios for each member of the group. Have each group member research and develop a scenario, and then have that person present a mock news conference to the group with the other members acting as reporters. Observe how the strategies differ according to which role is portrayed.
3. Given these same hypothetical scenarios, have each member of the group select and defend a specific response strategy (stonewalling, avoidance, blame shifting, defensibility, good intention, etc.). How can each of these strategies be utilized for the given scenario?
4. Work together to develop a crisis communications plan. What specific strategies are most important for the plan? What specific media platforms are involved and how do you incorporate social media?

CHAPTER 8

Television Sports Broadcasting

An argument can be made that there is no more powerful force in sports today than broadcasting. The delivery of events, news and information through radio, television and now the Internet has fundamentally transformed the sports industry. This transformation has taken place in all facets of sports, most notably in economics and technology.

From an economic perspective, broadcasting has been primarily responsible in transforming sports from geographically isolated pastimes into global multibillion-dollar enterprises. The money comes from audiences willing to pay money to access sports content and from advertisers willing to pay huge sums to reach those audiences. The system depends on large audiences that are attractive to advertisers, which is where the "broad" in broadcasting comes in. Broad, mass audiences for events like the Super Bowl or Olympics are perfect vehicles for companies to sell products, and as those audiences have grown, so has the ad revenue (Table 8.1).

In terms of total audience watching, Super Bowls account for the 21 most-watched television shows in U.S. history. Super Bowl XLIX in February 2015 reached a record 168 million viewers. It's no wonder that the cost of reaching that audience through advertising has increased so dramatically.

The networks and content providers reap the benefits of this ad revenue, but they must pay for the rights to broadcast the event. These rights fees go to the owners of the sports content — professional leagues such as the NFL, NBA and NHL and separate organizations such as the International Olympic Committee and FIFA, which broadcasts the immensely popular World Cup soccer tournament every four years. As with ad revenue, these rights fees have increased dramatically over the years, pumping billions more dollars into the system (Table 8.2).

Networks like CBS, NBC and ABC make millions on advertising, but they in turn pay huge fees to the professional leagues and organizations for the rights to carry the events. All rights fees have increased dramatically over the years, but the Olympics particularly highlight how much more money is now involved.

All of that money has made those responsible for sports content — primarily team owners and athletes — incredibly rich. *Forbes* magazine annually ranks the top 50 sports organizations in the world, each of which now has a valuation of more than $1 billion (Badenhausen, 2015). That money has passed along to individual athletes, many of whom make annual salaries in the tens of millions of dollars.

TABLE 8.1   An Expensive 30 Seconds

Super Bowl/Year	Cost of 30-second commercial
1967/Super Bowl I	$40,000
1985/Super Bowl XX	$500,000
1995/Super Bowl XXX	$1,000,000
2005/Super Bowl LX	$2.4 million
2015/Super Bowl XLIX	$4.5 million
2016/Super Bowl L	$5.0 million

Sources: Boyd, 2015; Groden, 2015.

TABLE 8.2   Faster, Higher . . . More Expensive

Olympics/Location	Network	Rights Fees Paid
1960/Rome	CBS	$390,000
1972/Munich	ABC	$7.5 million
1984/Los Angeles	ABC	$225 million
2012/London	NBC	$1.18 billion
2032/TBA	NBC	$2.6 billion

Source: Fang, 2014.

It is a system that has worked well now for decades, but there are also signs that it may be changing. The change is coming from new technology, particularly digital technology and distribution. The ability to stream content over the Internet, the growth of home satellite systems, and the emergence of social media have greatly empowered the sports consumer. Audiences, for years confined by the limits of broadcast signal range and spectrum space, can now choose from an almost endless list of program options delivered on a variety of platforms. Sports audiences have clearly demonstrated a willingness to pay for this convenience in the form of pay-per-view events and special subscription packages. For example, DirecTV, which owns the NFL's Sunday Ticket package, has more than two million subscribers, each paying around $300 every year for the service.

Thus, while mass audiences are still important in sports broadcasting, technology has created a diverse set of niche audiences that can pick and choose what content to consume. There are now dedicated channels for specific sports (MLB Network, NFL Network, etc.), specific organizations (Big Ten Network, SEC Network, etc.), and those that cater to one single team (YES Network, SNY, etc.). This new approach to broadcasting has been called "narrowcasting" in that it targets specific segments within the audience rather than the audience as a whole.

Technology has also allowed the audience to be more active in the sports broadcasting experience. In former days, watching or listening to a sports event was a totally passive experience that was unidirectional — broadcasters sent out the program and audiences consumed it. Today, the experience is multidirectional in that audiences can communicate with the content providers and even each other through such tools as blogging and social media. Recognizing the importance of cultivating audiences, sports content providers now encourage this form of participation in the broadcast process.

Today's sports broadcaster must be aware of these new realities, but at the same time have adequate training and background in the traditional practices of the industry. These realities also demand that those creating the sports broadcasting content — especially anchors, play-by-play and color commentators — exhibit a level of professionalism that creates audience demand and justifies the associated expense.

ANCHORING

The term "anchoring" itself comes from the notion that the person will "anchor" the television sports desk. "Anchor" is also a good word in that it suggests steadiness, dependability and strength. A good anchor combines all of these qualities, and many more, in the process of delivering a sports presentation.

On one level, anchoring seems quite simple. A person delivers sports material on the air, which suggests little in the way of skill other than the ability to read. This process is made even easier through the use of a teleprompter, a device that scrolls the material through the camera at eye level.

Photo 8.1 All anchors use a teleprompter, but its use does have both drawbacks and limitations. Teleprompters make it very easy for an anchor to read material, which scrolls directly through the camera, but good anchoring is much more than just reading. The reality is that good anchoring requires a variety of skills, many of which are learned only through years of study and practice.

Working Under Pressure

Sports anchoring and reporting is a deadline business where success is often measured in minutes and seconds, not hours. When deadline hits and the program needs to be on the air, the anchor has to be ready. This includes preparing all facets of the program, including copy to be read, taped material to be aired and a rundown that includes the order of the material. In some cases, producers help in these areas, but the bottom line is that the anchor is the face and voice of the program. Whether the presentation is good, bad or in-between, the anchor will get the credit or the blame.

Thinking on Your Feet

An anchor must be able to think quickly and adapt to ever-changing situations. Much of sports anchoring is "live" reporting, whether on a set where the conditions are somewhat controlled or out in the field where there is a greater sense of unpredictability. Because the industry is so dependent on technology, all kinds of unforeseen things can happen — cameras and microphones can go dead, cables can become unplugged and satellite signals can get lost, just to name a few possibilities. An anchor must expect the unexpected and be able to deal with any situation. This suggests that the anchor must be able to ad-lib — that is, come up with unscripted commentary depending on the needs of the situation. Sometimes the anchor will have to "stretch" and give additional material to fill time, while other situations might require cutting or condensing material when time is short.

When to stretch or condense is usually a decision made by the producer or other technical crew associated with the program. Such personnel are in constant contact with the anchor to give updates on timing, changes in the show and other necessary information. Anchors usually wear an IFB (short for interruptible feedback) earpiece that allows them to hear instructions and discussions from the control room. In the control room, producers and technical crew punch the buttons that get the program on the air. While it is an essential benefit for the anchor to be able to hear from the producer, it can also be distracting. Many anchors find it difficult to concentrate on what to say when they are hearing a constant stream of chatter in their ear.

Good Writing and Storytelling

Good writing is an often undervalued or ignored part of the anchoring process. So much emphasis is put on the presentation that we tend to forget the importance of what is actually said and written. But good writing is essential in any form of communication, and sports is no exception.

The best writing in sports is usually storytelling. Sports are about stories. Sometimes these stories are very simple, such as who won, how they won and who starred in the game, but other times the stories are more complex. Programs such as ESPN's "Outside the Lines" and "30 for 30" documentary series investigate a singular topic on a variety of levels. The bottom line is that the anchor should have a well-written story to tell, and many times the writing gets lost in the push to engage the audience.

There has been a movement in recent years to simply show video for the sake of video. The "hey, look at this interesting video" movement is an outgrowth of the YouTube generation, which emphasizes the fleeting visual moment as a way of increasing audience traffic. Cats playing ping pong may get millions of hits on the

Internet, but remember that broadcast time is finite and limited, whereas the Internet is not. What draws people to the broadcast are compelling stories, for which most Internet users don't have the time or interest. Use your broadcast time to tell a good story and leave the cats to YouTube.

Audience Interaction

We have already noted how technology has empowered the audience and made the sports communication process more multidirectional. As a result, anchors today must engage audience members in an ongoing conversation. Historically, this was handled through such things as talk radio, which is still a very powerful force in sports broadcasting. Fans love the opportunity to have their opinions heard, and radio personalities such as Jim Rome and Dan Patrick command huge audiences.

There is even more opportunity for interaction today, even within the context of a live sports presentation. Even if the sports anchor does not take live phone calls, he or she can incorporate audience tweets as part of the content. The anchor can also use Twitter, Facebook and other social media platforms to communicate directly with audiences. This communication can take the form of breaking sports stories, promoting

Photo 8.2 Carrie Anderson of WMC-TV in Memphis shows how today's sports reporters must interact with audiences. Sports anchors and reporters today must engage their audiences through such platforms as social media. Almost all of them have a Twitter or Facebook page with which they post breaking news or simply talk to fans. Neither the station nor the anchor make any money from it, but the idea is to get as many followers as possible in hopes that they migrate over to the broadcast content. Carrie Anderson spent 16 years with WMC-TV in Memphis, Tennessee.

Photo courtesy of Carrie Anderson/WMC

material on the broadcast platform ("Be sure to watch my sports segment tonight at 6 to get an update on Steph Curry"), or simply to answer fans' questions or comments.

Such audience interaction is usually a combination of news, self-promotion and commentary, and on that last point anchors need to be extremely careful. Fans love to hear strong opinions, but the ethical boundaries are not well established and many anchors and reporters have gotten into serious trouble. As one example, in 2015 broadcaster Curt Schilling was suspended by ESPN for a tweet in which he compared Islamic extremists to Nazis (Almasy, 2015). Almost all media outlets now have policies in place to help employees in this area.

Looks and Personality

The dirty not-so-secret part of the broadcast industry is that it favors the young and attractive, especially in television, less so in radio. Typically, anchors must look and sound a certain way to be appealing to audiences. In an age where there are so many different channels and viewing options, it is mainly the looks and performance of the anchor that causes audiences to watch one program over another.

This is a continuing source of frustration for many aspiring journalists and anchors. They spend at least four years in training at a journalism school or a university, learn essential skills and undertake valuable internships, only to find entry into the field difficult if not impossible. It's not that they have done anything wrong; rather, they have just run up against the first and oldest commandment of the broadcast industry: Thou shalt look and sound a certain way.

But it also raises issues of age and gender discrimination. How old is too old? How pretty is not pretty enough? A Kansas City news anchor named Christine Craft asked those same questions. In the early 1980s, Craft was demoted from her anchor spot at KMBC after a focus group determined that she was "too old, too unattractive and wouldn't defer to men" (Willis, 2010, p. 114). Craft sued the station and won two jury trials, but the verdicts were eventually thrown out. Craft went on to write a book entitled *Too Old, Too Ugly, Not Deferential to Men*. Christine Craft was not an isolated case, and the same standards still apply in the industry today. As unfair and borderline illegal as it seems, looks and personality are basic standards for work as an anchor.

Be Yourself

An engaging personality is a big reason why some broadcasters become so successful. John Madden, Howard Cosell and Jim Rome became household names because their personalities resonated with audiences — Madden the blustering favorite uncle type, Cosell the bombastic elitist and Rome the snarky provocateur. Unfortunately, they spawned numerous copycats who figured imitation was the surest way to fame and fortune.

There's always room in broadcasting for interesting personalities, as long as the personality is unique to you. If being showy and over-the-top is your personality, then fine, go with it, but don't try to copy that style. A few years ago, an anchor in Louisville, Kentucky, did the entire sportscast in "Seinfeld" references; around the same time another anchor in Boise, Idaho, did his show entirely as fictional newsman Ron Burgundy. Such efforts are good for a few laughs and some hits on YouTube, but such gags are often quickly forgotten. What is going to get you noticed is solid anchoring and reporting, professionalism and an ability to connect with audiences by being yourself.

Personal Branding

This last point isn't so much a requirement as a very strong suggestion. Given the emphasis on an anchor's looks and personality, the strong attachments audiences have to certain anchors and the relationships that can develop through social media, there exists the possibility of anchors and reporters developing their own personal brand.

The concept of a personal brand simply means that the audience has more attachment to the anchor than the outlet. That is, if John Jones is working at Channel 2, audiences are watching because it's John Jones, not because it's Channel 2. If Jones leaves to go to another station, audiences will follow.

Perhaps the best example is Bill Simmons. Unemployed and nearly broke in 1997, Simmons decided to create his own sports website, BostonSportsGuy.com. The site became an immediate hit, and eventually caught the eye of ESPN, which hired Simmons in 2001. Before his unexpected departure from the network in 2015, Simmons served as its basketball analyst, created and edited the online Grantland sports magazine, authored a *New York Times* bestseller and grew a Twitter audience of nearly 5 million. Jim Rome and Dan Patrick have similarly created personal brands independent of a specific media outlet.

There are obvious advantages to such branding. When ESPN finally decided to part company with Simmons over some of his outrageous and controversial comments, Simmons had developed such a loyal audience that the move barely fazed him. He was quickly picked up by HBO, but his show on that network was cancelled after only four months.

REPORTING AND PACKAGES

Anchoring jobs, especially in sports, are highly coveted and few in number. Compared to anchors, there are many more sports reporters whose main job is to create stories or packages on a regular basis. The term "package" comes from the fact that broadcast stories are a complete package that includes video, sound and reporter narration.

Creating a package is a process that can include a crew of several people — reporter, videographer, producer, sound person, for example — or just the reporter working as a "one-man band" and responsible for doing everything. Larger markets usually have larger crews, although because the one-man band is economically efficient, it is becoming more common at all levels.

The process begins with the story idea. It is something that catches the reporter's attention that could possibly be turned into a developed story. For example, the reporter might go to the local gym and see a crowd around a woman lifting weights. Getting closer, he notices the woman is lifting an incredible amount of weight. This leads to a possible story idea — "woman weight lifter."

The story idea then needs to be developed into a theme, or in other words, what the reporter wants to say about the woman weightlifter. You can't just have a story that says "woman weightlifter." Doing some investigative work, he finds out that the woman often beats men in weightlifting competitions and has won several trophies. Now the theme becomes clearer: "Woman weightlifter breaks stereotypes to succeed in what's considered a man's sport."

Once the theme has been established, material must be gathered for the package. This primarily includes video, interviews (with the woman and others) and natural sound (the sound that takes place at the scene of the story, such as the woman straining to lift a weight). All of the material should support the theme. That is, you would not get an interview with the woman talking about her home life. She needs to talk about what it's like to compete with men and beat them. Other interviews could be with men who can talk about how tough a competitor she is.

The reporter then looks at the material that has been shot and figures out what to use. There are no set rules for this, except that it should be the material that best supports the theme and tells a compelling story. Certainly, any dramatic or exceptional video and sound should be included.

Once the decision has been made on what material to use, the reporter then begins to think about writing. One good rule to keep in mind is that the stronger the video and sound, the less you have to write. Think of the words as merely the glue that holds these elements together. Sometimes you need more glue when the pictures aren't very good, and sometimes you need less when they are better. In some cases where the video and sound are especially dramatic, you may not use any narration at all, and edit the package without your voice.

The final part of the process is editing, in which the reporter arranges the elements (video, sound and writing) in the most compelling fashion. There are two main goals in the editing process:

1. The finished story should support the theme and be easily understood by the audience. That is, someone can walk away from the story and say, "I get it. This woman is really good and often beats the guys." They may not agree with the point of the story, but they should at least understand it.
2. The story should engage the audience in some way. In other words, they should find it interesting and worth watching, or they will simply change the channel. This can be accomplished through effective use of video, interviews, natural sound and editing. A big part of engagement is personalization. Focus your stories on people rather than events, because people find other people fascinating. The whole concept of reality television is built around the idea that very few people care about the contest or game involved; what keeps them interested are the characters.

Certainly, a report on the big game needs to include the basics of what happened and why. But even then you can zero in on a particular character in the game who stood out, such as the player who came off the bench to get the winning hit. If you're not doing a game story, you should try to find those interesting characters — the 90-year-old man training for the Boston Marathon, the fan who hasn't missed a home game in 40 years, the wrestler who overcame personal tragedy to win the title — that make for compelling sports reporting.

Aspiring sports reporters should learn all parts of the process from shooting to editing. In fact, some of the best stories come from the one-man band because it's much easier for one person to develop and execute a specific vision from start to finish. Involving more people in the process can get things off track. Even when reporters are responsible only for one part of the process, their knowledge in the other areas can help make for a better final product.

Sports reporting and creating effective packages is really an art form that allows the reporter to demonstrate his or her creativity. The emphasis today in broadcast reporting is on good storytelling, and how the story is told depends a great deal on the individual reporter.

PLAY-BY-PLAY

Perhaps no part of the sports broadcasting business is as mythologized as play-by-play. Those with the ability to describe a game on the air have become larger-than-life figures with national, and even international, reputations. Starting with the pioneers in radio — Graham McNamee, Ted Husing and Bill Stern — through the modern era with men like Bob Costas, Pat Summerall and Jim Nantz, the play-by-play announcer has become the face of the sports broadcasting industry.

Before the Game

Much like anchoring, play-by-play is a seemingly simple activity — describing the live action of a game on the air — that is actually very complex. There are hours of preparation involved before the play-by-play person even gets to the announcer's booth. He or she must read volumes of material related to the teams and the players, record interviews with players and coaches to run during the game and coordinate with technical crew to make sure everything runs smoothly.

SCHEDULE FOR A PLAY-BY-PLAY ANNOUNCER

As an example of how all this works, consider a typical college football game that will kick off on Saturday night. The schedule for the television play-by-play announcer begins the previous Monday:

Monday and Tuesday:	Read media guides, statistical information and news stories on the two teams
Wednesday:	Conference calls with the coaches and players from both teams

continued

Thursday:	Travel to game site
	Visit home team practice
	Stadium technical walk-through
	P.M. production meeting
Friday:	Crew call
	Meet with school sports information directors
	Meet with coaches and players for taped interviews
	Film session with game analyst
	P.M. production meeting
Saturday:	A.M. production meeting
	Arrival at stadium (three hours before kickoff)
	Rehearse promos and lineups
	Check communication and technical setup
	Record opening segments
	Kickoff and game
	Press conferences after game

The schedule is somewhat similar for radio broadcasters, although the technology requirements are not quite as involved. All of the preparation leads to the on-air performance, which is, of course, all the audience sees or cares about.

During the Game

While the game is in progress, the play-by-play person has to juggle different communication responsibilities simultaneously. This includes receiving communication from the technical crew and producer, and interacting with those in the broadcast booth and the sideline, all of which is done while describing the action.

Throughout the game, those in the control room will constantly be talking to the play-by-play person through an IFB. They are there to provide timing cues, indicate what particular replay or segment is coming up next, and update on changes or problems in the broadcast. While essential, this talk can be quite disconcerting. "Talk continuously for one possession in a football game," says NBC sports anchor and play-by-play man Bob Costas, "and just see if what comes out of your mouth even rises to the level of gibberish" ("The sportscasters," 2000).

While all this is going on, the play-by-play person must also constantly be processing information in the broadcast booth. Some of this information will come from a spotting board, a large paper or poster that contains player names, numbers and statistics that the play-by-play person can access at a glance. In some situations, there is a spotter to help in this process. The spotter is never seen or heard on air, but stands next to the play-by-play broadcaster to give names, numbers, statistics and other information.

Undoubtedly, the most important person in the booth for the play-by-play person is the color commentator. The two are in direct communication with each other before, during and after the game, and their relationship, both on and off air, is an essential element in the success or failure of the broadcast. Ideally, the two should at best like each other, and at worst get along amicably. The best broadcast teams — Pat Summerall and John Madden in football; Dick Enberg, Al

Photo 8.3 A small portion of the information that play-by-play announcers deal with during a game. The play-by-play person must constantly be processing information during the game, much of which is available for instant access. Networks usually include a spotter to help with this, but local broadcasters often have to do it alone.

Photo 8.4 A play-by-play person and color analyst prepare for a live broadcast. The relationship between the play-by-play person and the color commentator is essential to the success of a sports broadcast.

McGuire and Billy Packer in basketball; Vin Scully and Joe Garagiola in baseball — genuinely liked each other, and that chemistry was appealing to audiences.

Harmony, though, can be difficult to achieve, especially if there are egos involved as the broadcasters compete for air time and attention. It was just such a clash of egos between Howard Cosell and Don Meredith that prompted Meredith to leave the incredibly popular "Monday Night Football" telecasts in the 1970s. Mike Francesa and Chris Russo dominated sports talk radio for 19 years on WFAN in New York, until a rift ended the relationship in 2008.

The ideal situation is that both broadcasters complement each other and play to one another's strengths. That is, the color commentator should not step on the play-by-play person in the midst of describing the action, while the play-by-play person should set up the commentator for analysis and perspective. At the most basic level, the play-by-play person should give four of the 5Ws of the action — what happened, who was involved, and where and when it happened. The other W — why — should be left to the color commentator. "When I'm doing television it's more of a vehicle to set up the color analyst," says longtime broadcaster Marv Albert. "It's extremely important to have the proper rapport with whomever you're working with" ("The sportscasters," 2000).

This process is different on radio than it is on television. In television, the broadcaster should let the pictures do the talking and only fill in enough detail to help the audience understand what is being seen. It is a minimalist approach that recognizes that saying too much can often ruin the impact of compelling visuals. At the conclusion of a dramatic play or moment in the game, experienced play-by-play people will stop talking and let the sound and visuals carry the moment.

In contrast, the radio broadcaster has to work much harder. Because the listener can't see what's going on, it's important to create an image of the event in the listener's mind through vivid description and detail. The radio broadcaster can't take long pauses like the television broadcaster because the audience would get lost. "Radio is where you are painting the picture," says Los Angeles Dodgers broadcaster Charley Steiner. "You are watching the game for millions of people. It's your eyes, your experience, your use of voice and the ability to paint that picture and tell the story" ("Careers in," 1999; see Table 8.3).

Beyond describing the action, the play-by-play person should help set the scene for the audience and "bring the game" to them. That is, that person should describe the events in such a way that the audience feels as though they are a part of the game, and a part of the broadcast. Ideally, audiences should think of the play-by-play person as a trusted friend invited into their living rooms. Developing a conversational yet professional style takes years of practice.

In some circumstances, especially at the local or high school level, the play-by-play man will be the only one in the booth. In that case, he or she will have to both describe and analyze the game, which while not necessarily difficult, is not as rewarding for audiences that like to hear the interplay between different voices. The standard today remains a play-by-play person and color commentator in the booth, with occasional input from a sideline reporter.

TABLE 8.3   Radio versus Television

The role of the play-by-play person is vastly different on radio as compared to television. Consider how a broadcaster might describe the same event on the different media. Notice also the importance of regularly announcing the score on radio. Television broadcasts superimpose the score and more information throughout the broadcast.

Radio Broadcaster	Television Broadcaster
We'll start the bottom of the eighth with Kelvin Johnson. Johnson steps into the batter's box, and even with glasses on he has to shield his eyes from a glaring sun. It is a hot one today and beads of perspiration are pouring down his face after a day behind the plate.	Kelvin Johnson to lead off for the Tornadoes in the bottom of the eighth. The catcher 0-for-3 today with a couple of strikeouts.
Wagner gets the sign, kicks and delivers, and it's low and away, ball one.	He takes low and away, ball one.
The infield guarding the lines here with a 2-0 Metros lead in the eighth. Huston is only a couple of steps off the bag at first, and Tyler is practically standing on the bag at third. I'm not sure you could fit a sheet of paper between him and the line as he guards against the extra base hit.	
Wagner has called time to go over signals, so there's another conference on the mound. That's about the fourth time Wagner and Boyd have had to meet, and the home fans are getting a bit restless. You can feel the agitation in the stands, both at the score and the delays. Finally, umpire Augie Campella walks out and tells them it's time to break it up and get back to business . . . and a mock cheer breaks out.	Wagner and Boyd have had trouble communicating all afternoon, and here we go with another meeting on the mound. Boyd might have been crossed up on that last pitch. Home crowd doesn't like it, and here comes Campella to break it up.
Boyd crouches back down behind the plate and we're ready to go with the 1-0 pitch . . .	

COLOR COMMENTARY

There isn't much more to say about the color commentator, mainly because the field is almost entirely shut off to young sports journalists. Color commentators are there to add expertise and analysis to the broadcast, and thus they almost always come from the ranks of former players.

We have already made some general observations about color commentators, but we should also state the obvious — that they should bring something to the broadcast that is different from the play-by-play. "What I say to my analyst is 'take me beyond,'" says ABC broadcaster Al Michaels. "You go someplace new; go someplace where guys haven't gone before" ("The sportscasters," 2000).

Audiences seem to respond to color commentators who are honest and direct. This is something of a change from the style in the 1960s and '70s, in which the commentators were fairly reserved types who spoke only infrequently. All that changed when coaches like Al McGuire and John Madden retired and went into broadcasting. Both men, especially Madden, did not try to fit into the traditional pattern of a color analyst, but instead brought their unique personalities to the air. "Sometimes, I just blurt out," he said. "'Holy, moley! Did you see that?' That type of thing" ("The sportscasters," 2000).

SIDELINE REPORTER

Sideline reporting is a somewhat recent development in the live event broadcast. For years, only the play-by-play person and the color commentator had an on-air role, and even after sideline (also called courtside, rinkside, etc.) reporting began to develop, the segments were very short and limited to injury updates. Today, that role has expanded to include in-game interviews, the introduction of taped segments and other types of reporting.

Having someone down on ground level gives the advantage of accessing and reporting information that is not directly obvious simply by watching the game. The play-by-play person and color commentator can see the player carried off the field, but after that they return their focus to calling the game. The sideline reporter can follow up and find out what kind of treatment the player is receiving and how he or she is responding, and can talk to team officials about the player's status for the rest of the game. This level of access applies not only to injuries, but to situations outside the playing area, such as disturbances in the stands, or something the coach might say or do off camera.

The visibility of the sideline reporter has increased dramatically in recent years. Part of this is due to the growing demand for instant access to information on the part of sophisticated audiences. Several years ago, an injured player might rate a short mention from the play-by-play person; today, the sideline reporter will give full details as soon as practical after the injury has occurred.

Another reason for the increased visibility of the sideline reporter is more controversial. Women have greatly expanded their role in the sports broadcasting field, especially as sideline reporters. That many of these female reporters are also extremely attractive has led to charges of pandering and sexual objectification. Erin Andrews became a media sensation as a sideline reporter for ESPN, as did Ines Sainz for Azteca Deportes. In fact, Sainz used her notoriety to launch a successful career as a model (see Chapter 2).

On the other side, women sports journalists resent the implication that they are only there because of their attractiveness, or that looks are more of a prerequisite for the job than good journalism. There are also multiple stories of sexual harassment, including a notable incident in 2003 where an inebriated Joe Namath tried to kiss sideline reporter Suzy Kolber during a live report.

Despite the abundance of female sideline reporters, there are still plenty of men in the position. Many of them succeed as "information men"— those who have the inside scoop based on solid reporting and a network of sources. Ken Rosenthal at Fox Sports and Jim Gray, who currently reports for multiple outlets, have developed such reputations. Gray also practices a no-nonsense, take-no-prisoners style that is in sharp contrast to much of the fluff sideline reporting today. His most famous sideline interview, with Pete Rose before a World Series game in 1999, became a heated exchange in which Gray tried to get Rose to admit his gambling problem, with Rose countering that he felt like he was being ambushed by a prosecuting attorney.

But these are exceptions rather than the rule, and for the most part, sideline reporting is innocuous bordering on vapid. Most on-field interviews with coaches, now standard practice before games, during halftime and immediately after games, are derided for their lack of interesting information and spontaneity. On some occasions, live reports have raised ethical issues after athletes have said or done something inappropriate on the air.

For the most part, sideline reporting is here to stay. The networks believe they add an extra dimension to the broadcast, and there is always that segment of the population that will tune in simply for the sexual edge of the reporting. As with anchors, looks and personality are undeniably important qualities. It is also important to have the ability to ad-lib, as most material is delivered without a script or teleprompter. The role also demands the ability to interview and to dig out and communicate information quickly.

STRATEGIES FOR SUCCESS

How can aspiring sports broadcasters learn the skills they need? Certainly, your education in journalism or communication school will help. You will develop critical thinking skills that any good journalist should have, including those that areas that relate to sports. These include such things as ethics, law, diversity and other areas covered elsewhere in this book. But much of your success depends on what you can do outside the classroom. Primarily, this means getting practical experience through working in student media and internships.

If your school has a student media department, such as a radio or television station, you should engage yourself as much as possible. You will learn practical skills in an atmosphere designed more for learning than the cutthroat competition of the professional broadcast industry. Charley Steiner, who spent several years at ESPN before moving on to do baseball play-by-play work for the Los Angeles Dodgers, believes his college media experience played a big role in his career. "When I arrived at Bradley University, the first thing I did was go to the radio station and say, 'Folks, you better get used to me because you're going to see a lot of me over the next four years,'" said Steiner. "I played records, read news, did play-by-play and managed the station" ("Careers in," 1999).

Internships are valuable for many reasons. They certainly help you learn basic broadcast skills, and by working in a professional broadcast environment, you quickly learn the demands and expectations of the profession. Internships are also great networking opportunities. Working with those already in the industry gives you important connections, and many temporary internships have turned into

Photo 8.5 A student sports journalist at the University of Mississippi interviews a local high school football coach. Student-run radio and television stations are excellent places to learn the basic skills of the industry.

future permanent jobs. Additionally, many students use their internship opportunity to collect material for their résumé reel. Using superior equipment in anchoring or reporting, even if the material never makes it to air, can give the broadcast résumé a more polished and professional look.

While internships and student media experience are highly encouraged, not all students will have these opportunities. In such cases, practice as much as you can on your own. For anchors, prepare and read copy into a mirror. If you want to do play-by-play, take a recorder up into the stands and do a game on your own. Volunteer to work at local radio or television stations, even if it's unpaid or it means stringing cable and hauling equipment. There is still room in the industry for people willing to start at the bottom and work their way up.

This is especially true for play-by-play students, as the internship and job opportunities in that field are severely limited. Most of the well-known play-by-play people today started out calling high school or other local games. They did it for next to nothing in salary, or in some cases for free, and often worked by themselves as one-man operations — hauling and setting up equipment, doing their own spotting and conducting postgame interviews. This type of work allowed them to create demo reels with which they could try to move up to the next rung on the broadcasting ladder. For anchors or play-by-play people, employers are looking for the three Ps — poise, professionalism and past experience. The best way to get there is through a fourth P — practice.

FEATURE INTERVIEW

NORMAN SEAWRIGHT III

WOWK-TV

Norman Seawright III is an example of the new breed of "millennial" sports broadcasters — those just coming into

Photo 8.6   Photo courtesy of Norman Seawright III

the industry who have grown up with YouTube, social media and hundreds of sports channels on television. But upon entering the field, he discovered that in some respects things had not changed all that much.

"The pay is generally lower, resources may not be directed to sports departments as readily, and the sports broadcaster may tend to feel overworked," says Seawright. "Even more disheartening is the tendency for producers to cut time from sports to balance out a show that is running longer than the allotted time slot. The aspiring sports broadcaster may be unaware of prevailing attitudes toward sports personnel in a traditional newsroom setting."

Still, he says, "True passion for this career path is loving what you do," and Seawright has had a passion for sports broadcasting from a young age. After an undergraduate degree at the University of Mississippi and a master's degree from Syracuse, Seawright began his sports broadcasting career like so many others — at a small-market station in Duluth, Minnesota. Two years there led him to the sports director position at WOWK-TV in Charleston, West Virginia. "The most immediate challenge facing someone just entering the sports broadcasting industry is the demand," he says. "There are significantly more general news reporting jobs than there are sports, so the aspiring sports broadcaster faces an uphill battle. Internships, chance encounters, and making direct contact go a long way toward putting a candidate in position to land the first job."

Seawright says his undergraduate degree taught him the basics of broadcasting, while his graduate work introduced him to the rigors of daily work in a newsroom. Some things, however, he could only learn after getting his first job. "The most important thing I learned about sports broadcasting is that the broadcaster's role is to lighten the mood. Sports should be fun. Carrying a certain lively energy as a sportscaster, without going over the top, serves as a welcome break from hard news."

With thousands of aspiring sports broadcasters graduating from colleges every year, the pressure to find that first job is intense. Internships, working in student media and creating a website to display resume material are all important strategies.* So too is networking and making contact with

continued

those in the industry. But if he had to give only one piece of advice, Seawright says it would be about style.

"Find a way to stand out from the crowd," he says. "Anyone can read highlights and recap a game; your delivery, tempered excitement, and even a little humor can make you the type of broadcaster that makes an impact in a television market. Above all, understand that not everyone will like your style. It's yours, and as long as you commit to improving it, you will find a place to fit in; furthermore, ignore the naysayers. Unless the criticism you receive has an element to it that helps you improve, don't waste your time or emotions dealing with it."

You can see Seawright's personal resume and professional page at http://www.seawrightsays.com/

CHAPTER WRAP-UP

Sports broadcasting is an economic giant that brings billions of dollars into the industry through advertising revenue and rights fees. The sports fan who consumes all this media has become much more empowered in recent years thanks to technical breakthroughs in content access and distribution. In many ways, today's broadcasters are actually "narrowcasters" targeting a specific segment of the sports audience.

Anchoring a television or radio sports segment remains popular, but by far the most popular and lucrative sports content remains the live event. Play-by-play announcers, color commentators and sideline reporters are extremely important in these events and have become media stars in their own right. Women have had more difficulty breaking into these roles for several reasons, but in recent years have started to develop a stronger presence, especially as sideline reporters.

REVIEW QUESTIONS

1. Given the economic success of sports broadcasting, where does all the money come from? Do you see this changing in the near future or not?
2. How are today's sports consumers more empowered than those of just a few years ago? What is driving this new empowerment?
3. Beyond the ability to simply read words on a screen, what are some key qualities a successful sports anchor must have?
4. How would you explain the differences between doing play-by-play on radio compared to doing it on television? What are the similarities?
5. What are some of the issues and challenges facing women seeking to get into the sports broadcasting field today? Do these issues seem to be getting any easier or, perhaps, are they getting worse?

GROUP ACTIVITIES

1. Record both the radio and television versions of the same live sports event. One part of the group can analyze the radio version, while the other looks at the television version. Compare and contrast how the media differ in terms of style, presentation and approach.

2. Write some sports material for on-air television delivery. Have students take turns delivering the copy on the anchor desk; other students can evaluate and critique the performances. (If a studio or anchor desk isn't available, this can still be done fairly easily in a classroom setting.)

3. Have students work together to conceptualize a good local story that would make a compelling sports package. The group can work to identify the story idea, theme, accompanying elements and other parts of the process. (If equipment is available, the concept can be carried through to actual execution.)

4. Perform a content analysis of social media content for various figures in sports broadcasting. For example, the Facebook, Twitter and Instagram posts of selected sports anchors, commentators and play-by-play people could be analyzed for a certain period of time (such as a week). The group can discuss the content, differences, approaches and styles of the posts.

CHAPTER 9

Sports Radio and Online Sportscasting

Sports radio is an important part of sports coverage, and has been since the early 20th century. Whether it is radio play-by-play coverage of games, sports talk shows or news and updates relating to sports, sports radio makes a key contribution to the way fans consume the sports product.

This chapter covers a lot of ground, focusing on both the traditional realm of sports radio and the new media realm of online sportscasting. The purpose of the chapter is to expose you to the ideas and concepts behind these types of sports broadcasting, providing you with conceptual, technical and practical information on how to build skills in each of these areas.

PLAY-BY-PLAY BROADCASTING

Play-by-play coverage of games has been a constant feature of sports broadcasting since the dawn of radio in the early 1900s. For decades, audiences have listened to broadcasters describing the action of their favorite teams, and the characters on many play-by-play radio broadcasts have achieved almost familial status among

Photo 9.1 Play-by-play broadcasters report in real-time on games.
Photo courtesy of Edward Koton

certain fan bases. The early days of play-by-play didn't even feature a broadcaster at the game. Due to technical limitations, radio stations were forced to re-create game descriptions based on phone calls and reports from people at the stadium. Gradually, radio stations started sending on-site broadcasters to stadiums, and broadcasts of games became incredibly popular among audiences.

Radio play-by-play is among the most prevalent types of sports radio, with broadcasts featuring games from a variety of levels of sport, including high school, college and professional leagues. At the high school level, these broadcasts are generally produced by local radio stations. Collegiate athletics broadcasts are often produced by rights-holding companies such as ISP or Learfield that purchase the rights to radio broadcasts from school athletic departments and then provide the broadcasters and radio network upon which the broadcast is heard. At the professional level, individual teams often form their own broadcast networks and the broadcasters work as direct employees of the team. There are also national sports networks, such as Westwood One, ESPN and CBS, that produce and broadcast games nationwide on affiliate radio stations.

The traditional radio play-by-play broadcast contains two primary figures: the play-by-play broadcaster and the color commentator. Occasionally, broadcasts will also feature a sideline reporter. Each of these roles requires a different skill set, with workers in each position generally coming from different backgrounds.

The play-by-play broadcaster serves as the primary voice of the radio broadcast. This role is focused on providing a highly descriptive account of the on-field action as it takes place, while also integrating the other members of the broadcast team into the flow of the call, and making sure that the listener is provided with a comprehensive understanding of what is going on with the game. The play-by-play broadcaster ideally serves as the eyes of the broadcast for the listener, and the best in the business are able to "paint a picture" of the action that the people in the audience can envision in their minds. The play-by-play position is generally filled by a professional broadcaster, someone who has attended school for broadcasting and has worked in prior broadcasting jobs.

The color commentator, or analyst, serves a different role, that of providing context, background and humor into the call of the game. This position is almost always filled by someone with prior background in the game that's being called, such as a former player or coach. This person often doesn't have any professional broadcasting education.

Sideline reporters are generally featured only on national play-by-play broadcasts, providing on-field interviews and reports on player injuries. These roles are also generally filled by trained professional broadcasters, rather than former players or coaches. For more information on television play-by-play roles, see Chapter 8.

Careers in Play-by-Play

Students interested in a career in play-by-play broadcasting need to understand early on that practice and experience are the most important factors in being competitive for jobs in the field. Play-by-play is one of the most challenging jobs in

Photo 9.2 Keeping up with the action while at the same time checking on statistics and trends are just a couple of the jobs required in play-by-play broadcasting.
Photo courtesy of Edward Koton

all of broadcasting, due to its unscripted nature, need for immediate reaction to events and the necessity of doing tremendous amounts of preparatory work before each broadcast.

Fortunately for interested students, there are often opportunities in high school and college to gain hands-on experience doing radio play-by-play of sporting events. College radio stations often have access to athletic events for the purposes of broadcasting, and at many schools, there are only a small number of students interested in pursuing these opportunities.

The career path for radio play-by-play generally requires that aspiring broadcasters start working at the lowest levels of a sport. Minor league baseball, minor league hockey, small college sports, and high school sports are often the starting points for the young play-by-play voice. These jobs often involve other tasks, such as sales or media relations, and they are often located in less-than-glamorous parts of the country. However, the experience that you get as a broadcaster in these locations is invaluable because it allows you to accrue a huge number of hours on the microphone, developing your skills and working the kinks out of your delivery.

After a few years in the low minors, most broadcasters will have developed enough expertise to move up to a larger team in a better league. You should engage in a process of continual self-evaluation during this time period. Be sure to record every syllable you broadcast, and listen to recordings of your own broadcasts regularly. Ask for feedback from people you trust in the broadcasting field, but also trust your own instincts when it comes to your own style and approach to calling games.

BEST PRACTICES FOR PLAY-BY-PLAY BROADCASTING

Play-by-play broadcasting is perhaps the most demanding job in sports media. Here are some tips to make your calls more professional.

- Any good play-by-play broadcaster will tell you that preparation is the key to doing the job well. Start this process by reading as many pieces of information as you can find about both teams involved in the upcoming game. Watch highlights of games, most of which are readily available on the Internet. Learn how to pronounce players' names and practice those names until you don't have to think about them.
- Most play-by-play broadcasters use a spotting board, which is a card, sheet or folder full of information about both teams. The spotting board should contain the lineups for each team, information about each player, key statistical information about each team, and current standings and statistics for the league. Your spotting board should be cleanly written and easy to read, so that you can quickly use it during the broadcast.
- Radio play-by-play is different from television play-by-play because the radio broadcaster must paint a picture for the audience with his or her words. You should work on developing a fluid style of description where you provide the listener with context about the location of the players on the field, the location of the ball or puck, and the most important action elements that are happening at any given time.
- One of the biggest keys to successful play-by-play broadcasting is instilling your voice with confidence and energy. Confidence comes from knowing as much as you can about the game and the teams you are broadcasting. The most confident-sounding broadcasters are the ones who are never at a loss for something to say. Energy comes from proper broadcasting technique, including breathing from the diaphragm and sitting or standing with proper posture during the broadcast.
- Be sure to tape all of your broadcasts and listen to them regularly, taking notes on what you need to improve on. Create five- to 10-minute clips of your best play-by-play calls for use in demo reels. Contact professional play-by-play broadcasters and ask if they will critique your broadcasting style. You will find that many pro broadcasters are happy to help out young broadcasters who are polite and interested in improving themselves.

Photo 9.3 At its best, sports talk radio provides robust discussion of the major sports issues of the day.

SPORTS TALK RADIO

Even though it has only existed as a recognized radio format since the late 1980s, sports talk radio has become a key part of sports broadcasting. Radio stations across the country devote entire schedules to local and national radio shows featuring broadcasters talking about sports, taking phone calls from sports fans and interviewing athletes, coaches, and journalists about the sports world. Shows like "The Herd with Colin Cowherd," "Mike & Mike" and "The Dan Patrick Show" have become a part of the daily sports conversation. ESPN Audio, the division which oversees ESPN's sports talk radio wing, averages just over 20 million listeners per week (Deitsch, 2015).

Sports talk radio can generally be split into two categories, national and local. National shows are provided on major sports radio networks, such as ESPN Radio and Fox Sports Radio, and feature shows that concentrate on the major sports leagues in the United States, primarily the NFL, NBA, and Major League Baseball. Local shows are specific to one station, and are most prevalent in major media markets. These shows focus their attention on the most popular local teams and athletes, with some conversation about national issues included.

Most contemporary sports talk radio shows are set up in a similar format, with one or two hosts on a three-hour show that features on-air discussion about current sports topics, interviews with key figures in the worlds of sports and sports media, and phone calls from listeners. Most shows focus on broad issues and the most popular of sports teams, while at the same time avoiding niche sports and nuanced discussion. Shows that feature co-hosts often present these individuals as opposites, and all sports talk radio shows tend to use debate and contrarianism to attract and retain listeners.

Similar to television, sports talk radio is programmed into a series of segments that comprise each hour of broadcasting. Most sports stations sell between 12 and 20 minutes of commercial time per hour, spread over three or four scheduled breaks (Barrett Sports Media, 2015). This segmentation becomes part of how sports talk shows approach topics, with each segment focusing on a different area and segments rarely lasting longer than 15 minutes.

The current era of sports talk radio features two primary types of roles for aspiring sports media members. These are the *on-air* and *off-air* roles of sports broadcasting.

On-Air Roles

The most visible people in sports talk radio are those filling on-air roles, and the most prominent of these roles is the sports talk show host. The host is the star of the show, and sports talk shows often bear the name of the host or hosts. It is the job of the host(s) to propel the show for up to three hours with a mix of charisma, commentary, entertainment, humor and interviewing.

Most sports talk show hosts start out at the bottom of the broadcasting ladder, either as DJs in small-market radio or in off-air roles, and gradually work their way into hosting positions. Less-experienced hosts often start with once-a-week shows on the weekend and then gradually move into hosting roles during more popular time slots. Some sports talk show hosts come from the world of ex-athletes, such as ESPN's Mike Golic and WFAN's Boomer Esiason, but most hosts come from the world of professional broadcasting.

Hosts spend several hours before each show preparing material. This includes reading a wide variety of sports stories, selecting show topics that will appeal to the audience and working with their co-hosts and producer to ensure that the show will have a proper flow to it. Hosts are expected to maintain a deep level of knowledge and understanding of the sports world and, in particular, the areas of sports that are most important to their fan base.

During the show, hosts are expected to maintain a high level of energy, while presenting decisive takes on the topics of the day. The goal of sports talk radio is to get people to listen, and to keep them listening once they have started doing so. Therefore, sports talk radio hosts often try to focus on topics, opinions and guests that will be compelling to the audience. Hosts themselves must be compelling and willing to take controversial or unorthodox stances on certain topics at times.

Off-Air Roles

While sports talk show hosts receive most of the attention and glory, the support staff that helps the show go on the air play a tremendously important role in the success or failure of the show.

The primary off-air position for sports talk radio is the producer, whose job is to work with the host to ensure that the show operates smoothly throughout. This includes helping to produce show outlines, researching and booking show guests, organizing advertising live reads, developing content for the show, incorporating creative elements into the show and acting as a liaison between management and

BEST PRACTICES FOR SPORTS TALK RADIO

Sports talk radio has dominated the landscape of sports radio for decades now. Here are some ways to get your show up and running on a weekly basis.

- Sports talk radio is all about finding the topics that captivate your audience and then finding a debate point within that topic that causes your audience to have to choose a side. Even though entities such as ESPN have been criticized for the "embrace debate" credo that has ruled some of their television properties in recent years, the reality is that debate and argument work in radio because the audience finds it compelling. Hosts and producers must develop an eye for what stories are most appealing to the audience and then they must figure out what approach to that topic will generate the most interest.

- Remember that your audience is made up of "average" sports fans, most of whom have very clearly defined rooting interests in the most popular sports in your market. You should be able to figure out very quickly which teams are going to be the most interesting to your audience. Cultivating relationships with people connected to those teams, and being able to craft interesting takes on those teams' successes and failures, is a key part of building and maintaining an audience.

- Be cautious about introducing unorthodox sports or topics into your marketplace. Sports such as auto racing, soccer, and lacrosse probably aren't going to resonate in most markets on a daily basis. You may be a huge soccer fan, but if it doesn't resonate with your audience, it's not going to work on your show. You need to be willing to educate yourself on whatever interests in the sports world your audience has.

- Sports talk radio is perhaps the most personality-driven type of sports broadcasting that there is. You have to develop an on-air personality that audience members find compelling in some way. Being an effective sports talk radio host is very different from being an effective television sports anchor. Sports talk radio requires hours of audience contact per week, and your voice and personality are the only things carrying the show in many cases.

- How do you develop that personality? It's a matter of figuring out how to be yourself, how to be confident, and how to make people interested in what you have to say, day after day. If you think you might be interested, try to take work opportunities that give you the chance to speak to audiences by yourself. Live broadcasting on Facebook or Periscope can be a great way to help develop your abilities in this area. Try hosting a few sports-focused broadcasts and see how comfortable you feel talking out loud and carrying a topical conversation by yourself. Some people take to it naturally, while others are uncomfortable with the lack of immediate feedback.

talent. Producers must be very detail-oriented, keeping track of short- and long-term news trends within sports and understanding how those trends can be used to put on the best possible show.

Another off-air role is that of the call screener, who is responsible for filtering callers to the show and informing the host of the topics or opinions that the caller wishes to share. Producers often serve as call screeners in all but the largest and most popular sports talk shows.

PODCASTING

While play-by-play and sports talk radio are the traditional avenues of audio-based sports broadcasting, the emerging world of podcasting is becoming a major source of sports opinion and commentary. Podcasts, which are audio files delivered via Internet syndication to subscribers, have shown steady growth over the past five years and are poised to become a major part of sports media's online presence during the next decade.

Podcasting, which was originally referred to as audioblogging, has been around longer than Facebook, but struggled for many years to penetrate the sports marketplace. However, in 2005, Apple created a podcast directory on its popular iTunes music store, which aided users in searching for podcasts that matched their interests. Sports commentator Bill Simmons can be credited for helping to popularize the podcast in sports media. His original podcast for ESPN, named "The B.S. Report," started in 2007 and quickly became the most downloaded podcast at ESPN, averaging 2 million downloads a month (Fry, 2010). After leaving ESPN and starting the multimedia site The Ringer, Simmons noted that his new podcast on that website had exceeded 50 million downloads in an eight-month span (Glasspiegel, 2016).

Photo 9.4 Podcasts are a new and exciting way for young media members to talk about sports.

The growth of Simmons's sports podcasts mirrors the growth of podcasting in general. In 2010, only 12 percent of adults had listened to a podcast in the previous month, but by 2016, that number had grown to 21 percent (Barthel, 2016). It is estimated that 56 million Americans listen to podcasts each month (Garrubbo, 2016).

Sports podcasts may seem very similar to sports talk radio, but there are several differences that make podcasting its own unique part of sports broadcasting. Unlike the heavily segmented formatting prevalent in sports talk radio, podcasts are generally more free-flowing, allowing for real back-and-forth conversations to take place between host and guests. This allows for more nuanced conversations about sports topics, which is often appealing to more educated or hard-core audiences. Podcasts often spend far longer on individual topics, without having to arbitrarily stop the conversation because a segment is ending.

Podcasts are also great places for shows focusing on topics that wouldn't get discussed on a traditional sports talk radio show. Emerging sports interest areas in the United States such as soccer, MMA, and fantasy sports have struggled to penetrate major national sports talk radio, but podcasts on those topics are highly popular. A good example is the success of the "Men in Blazers," a soccer podcast featuring hosts Michael Davies and Roger Bennett that focuses on English Premier League, MLS, and U.S. Men's National Team play. The podcast, which originally launched as a part of ESPN's now-defunct Grantland website, averages about 300,000 listeners every week and served as the launching pad for both a television show and an international soccer convention (Jurgensen, 2015).

The success of "Men in Blazers" is illustrative of the sea change that podcasts represent in the sports world. The two hosts of the show are not professional broadcasters; Davies is a television producer and Bennett is a writer. The weekly podcast primarily features the two hosts sitting together and talking about soccer for 60 minutes or more, with humor, diatribes, obscure cultural references and social media feedback integrated into the show, all without commercial interruption and featuring only occasional sponsor advertising reads. Interviews are generally published separately, last more than 30 minutes and often feature individuals with no obvious tie to the world of soccer, such as Oakland Athletics manager Billy Beane, *The Fault in Our Stars* author John Green, and former Pavement singer Stephen Malkmus. The format of the show is antithetical to the traditional patterns of sports talk radio, and one could argue that's what makes it so successful.

Becoming a Podcaster

Creating a podcast is pretty easy these days, but it can seem daunting to those who haven't done it before. The first step in podcast creation is deciding on a good subject for your podcast. It's best to have a narrow scope because people are more likely to find your podcast and listen to it if they have some idea what it's about. The subject should also be something that *you* know about and are passionate about. It's hard to come up with interesting things to say about a topic about which you really don't care all that much! So make sure that whatever you're talking about is something that you have both knowledge and interest in.

Once you've selected a subject, it's time to think about your episodes. In many sports podcasts, these episodes will be end up being whatever is happening in the sport during a given week. For example, if you decide to do a podcast about Formula One racing, your episodes will likely be focused on the news and events that happened during the previous week of qualifying and racing. Be sure to keep your podcast issues timely and topical.

Next, you need to figure out where to host your podcast. There are a variety of options on the Internet for podcast hosting, ranging from free hosting and limited storage space to unlimited bandwidth and storage for a fee. Many podcasters choose to use their own website, and most Web hosting companies offer competitive rates on websites that are under $100 annually. There are also software solutions such as Soundcloud, an app which hosts audio files for a monthly fee.

Wherever you choose to host, you will need to take advantage of RSS, a syndication system that allows podcast listening software to detect and download your podcast. Most Web hosts offer access to the content management system Word-Press, and WordPress has plug-ins that will create an RSS feed for your podcast. This feed can then be submitted to sites such as iTunes for free, which then allows your podcast to be searched for and subscribed to by anyone using iTunes. Once iTunes has your podcast, it will automatically update those users when you create a new episode.

The last thing you need for a podcast is an actual audio file featuring your voice (and the voices of others) talking about the subjects you choose. There are a wide variety of technical options available, from simply recording an MP3 file on your phone all the way to buying hundreds of dollars of microphones and software and recording in a professional studio. Many podcasters will choose to purchase a decent USB microphone for each person on the podcast, which can cost between $50 and $150 per microphone. You can record your podcast directly onto your computer using a variety of different software options, including Audacity, a free software program that also allows for basic sound mixing and editing. Once you've recorded your podcast, you can save it as an MP3 file, upload it to your podcast hosting site, and voila! You're now a podcaster.

Promoting Your Podcast

Creating and recording a podcast is great, but what's the point if nobody listens? Effective podcasting requires you to also take steps to market your podcast to an interested audience. Fortunately, the social media age gives you ways to do exactly that.

Your first step should be marketing your podcast on your own social media networks, particularly Facebook and Twitter. The people who are most likely to start listening to you soon after you created your podcast are the people who know you already. This may seem like cheating, but it's not. If you can start to build a solid base of interested listeners, that will only help in the later spread of your podcast to a wider audience.

Be sure to put the URL to your podcast prominently in your Twitter bio, and feature it somewhere on your Facebook profile. Post messages after every new episode is posted, give people a link to iTunes, and invite them to subscribe to the podcast in iTunes. On Twitter, post the link to the podcast a few times a day when it is published, and occasionally post a link to the podcast page even on days when there are no new posts.

Your next step is to target fan communities who might be interested in your topic. Let's say you decided to start a podcast about the NHL's Chicago Black-hawks. You would then want to start letting Blackhawks fans and media know about your podcast. This can be accomplished by joining the fan communities that the Blackhawks have online. Facebook groups devoted to the Blackhawks, message boards focused on the Blackhawks and other online communities are ex-cellent locations at which to aim that type of promotion.

A word of caution, though: Don't just drop in on an online community, post a link to your podcast and never return. Fans of a team are more likely to give your podcast a chance if they view you as a part of the fan community. You should become active in these communities by commenting on others' posts, liking what other people do and interacting with other fans in these communities.

Twitter is similar. You would obviously use the team hashtag whenever you post a link to your podcast, but try to use the hashtag for other things as well. Engage fans and media in conversations around games. Express your opinion on things and interact with the opinions of others. Invite social media to get involved in your podcast! Post messages before you tape episodes and ask users to submit questions that you and your co-host can address on the podcast. Make sure to recognize users who have taken the time to submit questions, via both the podcast and social media.

Make every effort to have guests from the media that cover the team on your podcast. In our hypothetical Blackhawks podcast, it would be an accomplishment to bring the beat writer from the *Chicago Tribune* on to talk about the team, lend-ing credibility to your podcast in the eyes of listeners. Additionally, if you pro-mote the podcast on Twitter as having that writer as a host, there's a good chance that the writer may retweet you, thereby exposing your podcast to a much larger market of listeners who are probably interested in what the *Tribune* writer has to say. The same process works for bloggers and other Internet-based content sites that cover the team. Many of those sites have their own fan followings, and you can tap into those followings through this method.

Encourage your audience to rate your podcast on iTunes. Ratings do matter, and the more and better ratings you receive, the higher up the podcasting charts your podcast will go. A higher chart position lends itself to easier discovery through search, leading to more listeners. Be sure to encourage ratings on iTunes both on the podcast itself and in your social media promotion.

TIPS AND TRICKS FOR SUCCESSFUL SPORTS PODCASTING

Sports podcasting is the newest form of sports broadcasting, and it has its own special concepts and techniques. Here are some good pieces of advice for aspiring sports podcasters.

- Remember that even though podcasting has many differences from sports talk radio, it also has many similarities, particularly when it comes to maintaining energy and personality during the podcast. You can "be yourself" a lot more on podcasts, but you should still be enthusiastic and easy to listen to.
- Preparation is just as much of a key to successful podcasting as it is with other forms of sports broadcasting. Even though podcasts aren't as segmented as sports talk radio, you still need to research your topics thoroughly and have an idea of the order in which they will appear on the show. The more you research your topics, the more confident you will sound in talking about them.
- Don't create a podcast with someone you agree with all the time. It might be great for your ego, but it won't be great for the audience. Listeners love to hear organic disagreement at times, particularly when it's from two people who really know what they're talking about but just have different opinions on things.
- Have guests on your podcast! A good guest who ties in to your subject area can increase people's interest in your podcast and can make them interested in subscribing to you on iTunes. If you can get a guest to come in and talk to you in person, then great. If you can't, there are ways of interviewing guests on Skype or other VoIP services and recording those conversations. As of the time of this writing, a free plugin for Skype called Callnote can be used to record conversations, and the audio quality is generally quite good.
- Take the time to learn some basic audio production skills because such skills will really help the overall quality of your podcast. Learn to set proper vocal levels when you are recording the show. Use multitrack audio mixing software such as Adobe Audition to edit your audio files, taking out awkward pauses or segments that don't flow. Use "hard limiting" to give your podcast a more consistent volume throughout, as this process amplifies quiet noises while keeping loud noises as they were. This is very useful when you have two voices on the podcast with markedly different natural speaking volumes.
- Mix in some theme music to your podcast — but make sure the music doesn't require royalty payments! Fortunately there are websites on the Internet devoted to providing royalty-free music for the creative process.

PERISCOPE, FACEBOOK LIVE AND LIVE INTERNET STREAMING VIDEO

Live streaming video on social media is one of the newest sports broadcasting formats and there is tremendous potential in its use for the sports media world. Streaming video normally requires that the broadcaster utilize a mobile phone as the broadcasting unit, with a link to the broadcast being sent out to followers on social media. Those followers can choose to simply watch the streaming broadcast, or to participate by commenting on or "liking" the broadcast.

The two primary streaming video providers are Periscope and Facebook Live. Periscope integrates seamlessly with the Twitter social media platform, allowing broadcasters to notify their Twitter followers of a new stream. Their audience can watch an archived version of the broadcast within 24 hours of the original stream. Starting a Periscope stream is as simple as opening the app on your phone, giving the stream a title, and hitting a button. Facebook Live works in a similar manner, but utilizes the Facebook platform. Facebook Live streams appear in the broadcaster's timeline, and friends or followers can access, like, and comment on the stream as they would any other Facebook timeline post.

Unlike sports television, most live streaming sports video is relatively low quality. It is not shot in a studio and does not use professional lights and microphones. Often live streaming is just a phone, a couple of people and their thoughts and ideas. Live streaming video is a great choice for bringing your audience behind-the-scenes footage of a sports or media venue, some spur-of-the-moment thoughts after the game or live footage of a press conference or media availability.

Live streaming video is also a great way to practice your broadcasting talents in front of a live audience without the risk that comes with being on live television. Early on in a broadcasting career, it is beneficial to get a lot of repetitions on air without having many viewers. If you mess up, or say something you're not supposed to, the overall damage done is minimal and you can chalk it up to a learning experience. Smaller audiences also allow you to be experimental with what you say and how you say it, giving you valuable insights into what works and what doesn't work with your delivery.

Another option for live streaming video is Google Hangouts, an online-only service to Google members, which allow users the opportunity to broadcast live to an audience through their free "Hangouts On Air" feature. Broadcasters can use the software to do live shows featuring multiple co-hosts and guests, using nothing more than webcams on each user's computer. These on-air hangouts are viewable on YouTube, both live and later in archived format.

WOMEN IN SPORTS AUDIO BROADCASTING

Sports audio broadcasting is a field historically dominated by males, both in hosting roles and in terms of audience. ESPN Audio's Traug Keller estimated in 2015 that the audience for their programming was 80 percent male (Deitsch, 2015). Barrett Sports Media performs a yearly rating of the top 20 national sports talk shows that is based on track record and content delivery, as well as other factors, and in 2016 it found that none of the top 20 shows featured even a single female host (Barrett Sports Media, 2016). In the top 20 sports media markets, which feature about 200 total sports talk radio hosts, only seven women are featured as hosts during weekdays (Ryan, 2016). The field of game broadcasting isn't any better. New York Yankees color commentator Suzyn Waldman is the only female radio broadcaster for a professional sports team. The lack of gender diversity in sports talk radio comes down to the decisions of management, according to Cheryl Raye-Stout of WBEZ in Chicago. "It's the management that has to decide who's going to be on the radio and who's not going to be on the radio," said Raye-Stout, "I don't see any of it changing unless it's forced" (Ryan, 2016).

However, sports radio is starting to see more females enter the broadcast arena, with ESPN Audio in particular giving women the opportunity to host their own shows. The recent launch of "The Trifecta" radio program with female co-hosts Kate Fagan, Jane McManus and Sarah Spain has a home on national radio, as does the show "TMI" with Michelle Beadle and Ramona Shelburne.

The podcast field is also ripe for the integration of female-hosted shows. Some podcasts, such as FiveThirtyEight's "Hot Takedown," already include multiple females as regular co-hosts and panelists.

The integration of female broadcasters into the radio booth is an important next step for radio programmers, as the female demographic is largely untapped for sports talk radio and podcasts. As sports broadcasting continues to enlarge its footprint, the expansion of the marketplace to include women is a logical next step for media managers.

FEATURE INTERVIEW

TOM ACKERMAN

Sports Director, KMOX-AM Radio, St. Louis, Missouri

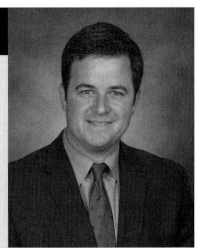

Tom Ackerman is a veteran of nearly 20 years in the sports radio business. A native son of St. Louis, Tom serves as the sports director at KMOX, in a city where almost the whole population is in love with sports. The city boasts two very successful franchises in MLB's St. Louis Cardinals and the NHL's St. Louis

Photo 9.5   Photo courtesy of Tom Ackerman

Blues, and Ackerman's station serves as the flagship for both of those teams.

continued

The sports radio business has changed since Ackerman started, and much of that change has been due to the changing concept of the news cycle.

"I started in 1997 at KMOX, which is a news/talk station that also provides sports talk," he says. "We have extended pregame and postgame shows, and we also have "Sports Open Line," the longest-running sports talk show in America, which runs four hours on nongame nights."

"The biggest difference from when I started to where we are now is that sports talk radio is now 24 hours. There are 24-hour sports TV networks. Sports content is available online and on-demand 24 hours a day. So, there's a lot more competition."

Ackerman says that it's not just the news cycle that's changed in sports radio, but also the demographics of the core audience. Sports isn't just a "guy thing" anymore.

"Sports talk radio audiences have historically been men aged 25–54," says Ackerman, "but the growing business of sports has certainly seen a rise in women as fans and consumers, particularly in the NFL. Locally, the Cardinals and Blues are popular among women. So, it's important to recognize that trend and adjust accordingly."

Technological change has also played a big part in the evolution of sports talk radio. Ackerman says that podcasts and online broadcasting aren't a threat to traditional radio stations, but instead should be looked at as tools.

"[Online broadcasting] has allowed us to be diligent in providing our shows, interviews, and features online as soon as they are available," he says. "We are quickly moving into an 'on-demand' lifestyle. Listeners want their content when it's convenient for them. We make sure we deliver that content."

Ackerman's advice to students who are looking to get involved in the field? Work on your core skills, and learn to be innovative.

"Versatility is key — the ability to deliver content in multiple forms and on multiple platforms. Creativity is also important. You have to always find new ways to attract listeners and be less predictable to your loyal audience."

Another important skill for young broadcasters, and one that often gets lost in the shuffle, is the ability to write.

"Writing skills are essential, whether it's for broadcast, online content, marketing, or advertising," says Ackerman. "Writing is the most underrated skill in broadcast media. Those who possess it have a clear advantage."

CHAPTER WRAP-UP

Sports audio broadcasting is one of the oldest fields of sports journalism, and has provided an important service to sports fans for decades. Sports radio play-by-play is one of the purest forms of sports journalism, since it involves a live, direct description of sports events as they happen. Sports talk radio allows audiences to hear regular analysis of their favorite sports in a portable format. And online sports audio broadcasting such as podcasts and live video are changing the norms of content within the field.

The traditional methods of sports audio broadcasting — play-by-play and sports talk radio — tend to have high barriers of entry, both due to the popularity of those jobs and the scarcity of radio stations that offer these formats. Podcasts, on the other hand, are accessible by anyone who wants to start a show, and are often a great launching pad for skills development or brand extension.

In any of the subfields of sports audio broadcasting, practice is key. Broadcasters must learn how to speak confidently on air, how to present things in an entertaining manner and how to write audio copy. Hands-on experience is the key factor for most people in developing these sorts of skills, and you can find that type of experience on most college campuses today. Student radio stations, podcast opportunities, and the ability to broadcast live sporting events on streaming video allow college students on many campuses the chance to develop their broadcasting chops before entering the industry.

REVIEW QUESTIONS

1. What are the differences in the roles of the play-by-play broadcaster and the color commentator?
2. What are some of the duties of a producer in sports talk radio?
3. What does a sports talk radio host have to do in order to put on a successful show?
4. What's the first thing you need to do when starting a podcast?
5. How do live streaming video productions differ from traditional television productions?

GROUP ACTIVITIES

1. Play-by-play preparation exercise: Have each group select a professional sporting event, and have the members work together to create a spotting board for a broadcast, using the elements mentioned in the chapter.
2. Sports talk radio exercise: Using current events in sports, and based upon your sports market, have each group create a show rundown for a hypothetical sports talk radio show in your area. Have each group place the segments in order of perceived importance, and have them include potential guests for interviews.
3. Podcasting exercise: Have each group create a plan for a new podcast, focusing on a topic of their choice. Have each group provide justification for the topic, the intended target audience and a tentative outline of the first three podcast episodes.

CHAPTER 10

Sports Video Production and Sports Photo Journalism

New technology has greatly improved sports video production and sports photojournalism. Sports enthusiasts now have access to professional equipment at a relatively low cost, while the opportunity to become a freelance sports videographer/photographer has improved. In this competitive world of sports video and images, the quality of work makes all the difference in gaining and maintaining a job. Knowing camera equipment (especially type of lens, apertures and shutter speed) and choosing the right editing software are essential to producing professional sports images. This chapter will cover these basic elements, and provide the necessary tools to produce quality sports images and videos.

Most if not all sports photography/video is shot digitally. Although there are some similarities in shooting sport stills and in shooting video, there are also substantial differences. These will be covered separately to better explain each realm. At this point you are probably asking how you can get started and how you can make your action sports images/video stand out. We will begin with the basics that apply to both styles.

BASIC SHOOTING TIPS FOR BOTH VIDEO AND STILL IMAGES

The first tip is: Be there for the action. This simply means always keeping the action in front of the lens. Being far removed from the action severely increases the chances of not being able to capture the moment and not drawing the viewers into your shot. It is more thrilling for the viewers if the action is coming at them rather than moving away. It helps to familiarize yourself with any sporting event you cover, so do advance research. Knowledge of the game allows the videographer/photographer to *anticipate* potential hot play areas and key players. There is always the chance the momentum and action will shift when a sure score is blocked or intercepted (in this case a 10X optical zoom and a tripod are necessary), but regardless, the key is to stay in front of the action.

Location

This leads to the second tip, location. Again, anticipating the action will help determine where the camera should be located. Here, too, familiarization with coaching strategies and the players will help videographers/photographers anticipate the action, and so be able to place the camera to capture the moment. The videographer/photographer must be able to get close to the action in order to record/ shoot the action. Also, being close to the action results in better images, and it increases your depth of field and thus enriches the overall image. Available placement on the field depends on the type of sport. For instance, in NCAA Division I football games, the media are restricted from shooting in the area between the two 35-yard markers. (This area is reserved for the players, coaches and athletics staff, allowing them to stand on the sideline.)

Being in the right location will also help with the next several tips, but first we will focus on *framing* and *angles*. How a photographer frames the shot has an enormous impact on how viewers perceive the action or how they see the human drama that unfolds. It is the human drama that draws fans and viewers to watch sports, so catching that pivotal moment is crucial to a videographer's/photographer's success. This element is so prevalent in sports media that ABC's classic sport program "Wide World of Sports" highlighted it in the opening title, "…The thrill of victory and the agony of defeat. The human drama of athletic competition…." To explain this tip further, examine Photo 10.1. In the image on the left the videographer/photographer only framed the Washington Redskins defensive player, which shows emotion but doesn't convey the entire story. In the second image, however, the frame includes the defeated kicker along with triumphant defensive players. In this image we see the agony of the second place finisher and can grasp a larger part of the story.

Most videographers start wide and then zoom in on the action. Even this approach, however, requires anticipating where the action will end. Any regular sports television viewer has seen plays that occasionally trick even the most talented and experienced videographers. If this happens, shake it off and continue shooting, but remember what happened so it is not repeated in the

Photo 10.1a and 10.1b These images show the importance of framing and editing your sports images. The image on the left is cropped and thus omits the greater context of the story behind the images.

Photos courtesy of Chuck Cook

future. Starting wide is the best approach, because as the action moves toward the camera the less likely the zoom will be used to its maximum. This is a good approach for several reasons. First, the slightest camera movement is over-exaggerated when using close-ups (or zoomed all the way in), so a novice cameraperson must be cautious when filming tight shots. The second reason again pertains to the depth of field. As the objects move closer to the camera, the background moves farther away, which increases the depth of field, thus creating a richer, more three-dimensional image. In contrast, tightening the frame by zooming the background results in images that appear flat or two-dimensional.

A good photographer/videographer looks for unusual *angles*, especially in regard to *cut-away* shots. These are typically short, nonaction shots used to help tell the story or cover the game, and to fill time between edited plays. These include shots of fans, cheerleaders, the scoreboard, coaches — any image that is away from the field or court. Cut-aways are an excellent way to add a sense of drama to the story or game. Be sure to get your cut-aways during lulls in the action; you wouldn't want to miss an action shot because you were busy shooting the cheerleaders. Another helpful tip is to shoot reaction shots before and after a big play. For example, during the last seconds in a tied basketball game, camerapersons try to get shots of fans, coaches, the scoreboard and players before that last-second shot is taken, and then get the reaction shots from the same list of elements after action on the court is stopped.

Timing and Reacting

The next two tips, timing and reacting, build from previous ones. As previously mentioned, location or being in the right place at the right time is crucial to getting that great shot or video. There are predictable moments in each sport, and knowing them will help in terms of timing. Knowing how long a field goal or a lay-up will take enables you to know how much time you have to frame and follow the action while obtaining usable video/photos. Knowing the "timing" will help capture those pinnacle or climatic moments (also known as the money shots) that is the goal of every cameraperson.

Timing is especially crucial when shooting still images because you can anticipate the action. This knowledge helps in focusing and clicking the shutter at the right moment. While video can roll constantly, a still camera is limited to capturing so many frames per second. If an inexperienced photographer snaps the shot too soon, the peak action moment might be missed. Sports photographer Chuck Cook has worked as an Associated Press (AP) freelancer for more than 20 years. According to Cook, "It takes the shutter a moment or two to open and close, and knowing this delay is the difference between missing the shot and capturing it" (personal communication, 2016). It takes time to truly learn your camera/equipment. Cook recommends a lot of practice.

Do not cross the 180-line (also known as the axis line). This rule holds true for all forms of sports images. Crossing the line disrupts the action and confuses

Photo 10.2 "The It Moment."
This image provides an example of capturing the "it moment" of a game. Pay attention to the detail and the rich depth of field.
Photo courtesy of Chuck Cook

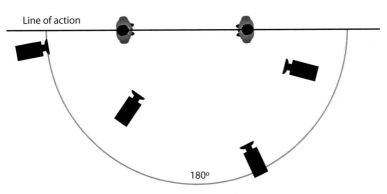

Figure 10.1 Axis 180-line.
This image illustrates the imaginary axis line that guides the on-screen spatial relationship between characters.

viewers. The 180-line is an imaginary line that runs in front of the camera's position (see Figure 10.1). It guides the on-screen spatial relationship between characters. Character one (or Team A) is to the left of character two (or Team B). Crossing the axis reverses the camera shot, or, in other words, the image is from the other side of the field, facing back toward the original position. Direction is a critical element in shooting sports. In football, Team A starts in the left end zone and moves across the field to the right as it tries to score a touchdown. If we begin shooting from one side of the axis and then jump to the other it would appear as if Team A is moving in two different directions. Not crossing the 180-line also makes editing easier, so stay on the same side of the field. Remember to factor in the sun when choosing which side of the line to shoot. You may start the game without the sun in your eyes, but by the end of the game you could be shooting straight into it. It's always recommended to have the sun, or other dominant light source, behind the camera. It is possible, however, to cross the line without confusing the viewers. It requires a cut-away or a neutral shot that will then allow the cameraperson to re-establish the line.

Beginning photographers often make the mistake of viewing the game only through the viewfinder; this is extremely shortsighted. You should pay attention to all aspects of the game. This includes fans, coaches and other elements that contribute to the overall feel of the action. Looking only through the viewfinder would likely result in missing these other vital components. Finally, keep an eye open for your own protection. You must stay alert at all times during the action, because you never know when a loose ball or player maybe headed right toward you.

Weather and Respect

Be prepared for all types of weather. Shooting sports may mean shooting outdoors. Weather can be unpredictable, so if there is even a slight chance of rain, bring raingear. Many professional sports photographers also bring a second set of clothes. Imagine having to shoot a football game in wet clothes with the temperature dropping below freezing; the ability to change clothes at half time is more than a luxury. Depending on the sport, wearing kneepads may also become necessary. For example, there are numerous football stadiums with spectator seats close to eye-level, which require sports photographers/reporters to cover the games on their knees. At first, this may not sound very difficult, but after a few hours in this position the padding for your knees will become much appreciated.

Lastly, respect the equipment. Mishandling the equipment will cause it to break. Broken equipment means no captured images.

Depending on the media outlet and owner, the approach to shooting a game will differ. Generally, working for local newspaper or TV station means covering the home team, while working for a major organization like *USA Today* or a major network means shooting the game without focusing on one team. Patrick Hartney is a veteran videographer in the extremely competitive market of Chicago, Illinois, at WBBM-TV. Both Hartney and sports photographer Chuck Cook use a "checklist" approach to shooting a game. The list includes the following basic shots: coaches, action shots of each team (this keeps you unbiased), scoreboard (after each score and at the end of a quarter/period/inning, etc.), game officials, fans and star player(s). Cook noted that with still photography he tries to "shoot one series from each team from the sidelines early in the game" (personal communication, 2016).

BASIC SHOOTING TIPS FOR BOTH VIDEO AND STILL IMAGES

- Be there for the action. Accomplish this by keeping the action in front of you. Some sports are predictable. Knowing them will help with timing your shots properly.
- Set up is crucial — it is all about location, location, location. Knowledge of the game and coaching strategies will help you anticipate the action, and thus know where to locate your camera.
- The basics matter, so be sure to be focused. Moreover, look for unique angles, especially for cut-aways.
- Cut-away shots can include shots of fans, coaches, players and the scoreboard. Cut-aways are a good opportunity to capture emotional images that help tell the story of the game.
- Do not cross the axis line. You confuse the viewers/audience when you cross this line. Be very conscious of not reversing your camera shots (e.g., if Team A is left of frame, do not flip sides and make it framed right).
- View the game through both eyes. In other words, do not get lost in the viewfinder.
- Be conscious of the weather and your surrounding environment.
- Last but not least, respect, value and protect your equipment.

CAMERA PLACEMENT OR BEST ADVANTAGE SPOTS

When obtaining sports images for events that are not being transmitted live, the photographer has complete control over which shots to obtain. Since the photographer usually works alone this requires a lot of hustle and foresight. Depending on the sport, a freelance photographer and/or sports videographer will frantically move up and down the field or court to stay with (or ahead of) the action. AP sports photographer Chuck Cook put it this way: "I rarely sit in one position for a long time and I tend to move around a lot — even at basketball games." Cook says the key is to "look for different angles while staying out of the way of the referees" (personal communication, 2016). Videographer Patrick Hartney added, "It helps to be in good shape — the equipment is heavy and you have to move up and down the field" (personal communication, 2016). The following shooting tips will help you develop the proper skills needed to become a professional sports videographer.

Football
Covering football is one of those sports that requires a lot of movement by the photographer. There are three basic positions for shooting football (see Figure 10.2).

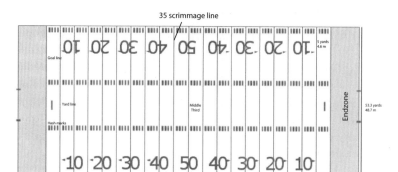

Figure 10.2 Football camera placement.

The first position is the most common. Ideally, photographers stay about 10 to 15 yards ahead of the line of scrimmage as the ball moves toward them. Shooting from the sidelines allows the photographers to obtain better quality close-ups and point-of-view images. Having the players run toward the camera (and sometimes on top of it) gives the viewers a better sense of the action and the emotion of the game. This position also provides richer natural sounds. There is the risk of having the action occur on the other side of the field, but knowing the teams will help anticipate the action and avoid missing the shot.

Shooting from this perspective, though, might be somewhat challenging to beginning sports photographers. The cameraperson constantly has to adjust the focus as the action moves up and down the field. Knowing the camera, especially which way to turn the focus ring to keep the images in focus, is vital to the overall success of the shoot. You should fight the temptation to use the camera's automatic focus. Mastering the equipment will serve you well as a professional.

As stated previously, there are sections of the field that are reserved for the players and coaches (midfield for football). These reserved sections can sometimes obstruct the shooter's field of view. In this case, position 3 becomes your next best location. This position is also a favorite choice for sports photographers as a team nears the end zone. Positioning yourself at the back of the end zone ensures that the action will come toward you (unless there is a turnover). Keep in mind the 180-line rule when setting up in the end zone; you want to stay on the side closest to your sideline position. Beginning photographers can find shooting from the end zone intimidating. One might think that having the action right on top of you would make things easier, but that is not always the case. From that position it is sometimes hard to follow the action and anticipate where the ball will end, because the action also tends to feel as if it is moving at a faster pace than it does from the press box or sideline. According to Cook, "Shooting from the end zone with the athletes moving toward you provides a much clearer

Photo 10.3 This image provides an illustration of professional photographers in action.
Photo courtesy of Chuck Cook

picture with far fewer referees in your way." A cleaner picture simply means the background is not distracting. Cook recommends using a wide-open aperture when shooting from the end zone because it blurs the background so that the action is in focus. Essentially it makes the subject more distinctive.

The second position is from the press box. This position is high above the field of play and removed from high quality natural sound. Although removed from the action, this position does provide some advantages, especially for beginning photographers. This is the one position in which the photographer can actually use a tripod, thus ensuring smooth images. Ideally, the camera should be placed as close to the 50-yard line as possible. From this position, the depth of field will change only slightly if at all, meaning the focus will not have to be adjusted after each shot. From such a high angle, the action is relatively easy to follow. However, shooting from this distance does not provide the chance to obtain quality close-up action shots. Coverage from these vantage points leaves the viewers feeling removed or disengaged from the action when compared with coverage from the sideline or end zone. Most still photographers prefer not to cover the game from the press box for these reasons.

Baseball
Shooting baseball is relatively easy when compared to some other sports because all of the action happens in front of you. With this sport, photographers do not have to run up and down the field to cover the action. As demonstrated in Figure 10.3,

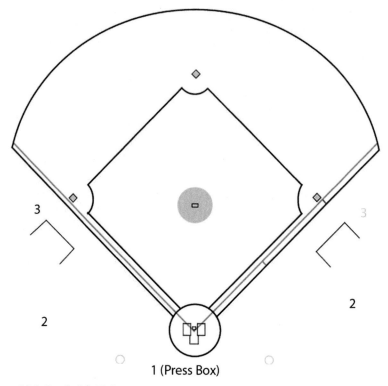

Figure 10.3 Baseball field diagram.
Baseball field diagram illustrates best camera positions.

there are three basic camera positions when covering baseball. Number one is from the press box, two is from an elevated position from one of the baselines and three is field level next to the dugouts.

Do not be deceived by the slow nature of baseball. Although the pace of the game moves slower than other sports, the speed of the ball can top a hundred miles per hour, making it difficult for beginning sports photographers to follow the action. Photographers spend a majority of their time focusing on either the pitcher or the batter. As with any other sport, knowledge of the game and players will help a photographer anticipate the action.

Position one provides a higher angle that allows the photographer to follow the action more easily. From this vantage point it is much easier to follow the ball (or action), but it is important to remain midlevel. If you are at eye level with a fly ball, the depth perception is lost. It is more visually pleasant if you tilt the camera up to follow a fly ball. At higher elevation, it is important to zoom into the action since staying with a wide view makes it harder to follow the action and alienates the viewers from the play.

Position two is from one of the baselines. Although this perspective brings you closer to the action, it also comes with a disadvantage. It is much harder to follow a ball into the outfield at this angle. Beginning sports photographers tend to let the ball leave the frame (or field of view). To avoid this problem, start with a medium shot and widen the view out as the ball is hit and then zoom back in at the end of the play. Also remember that it is critical to use both your eyes. In other words, do not get lost in the viewfinder. Remember to watch the viewfinder while paying close attention to the surroundings at the same time. This tip allows the players as well as the ball to be seen. This is extremely helpful if the ball leaves the frame because the players' movement will indicate where the ball is headed.

The third and final position places the cameraperson adjacent to the dugouts. Depending on the level of competition, the photographer may actually be able to shoot from the field next to the dugouts. According to sports reporter/videographer Jeff Haeger, who works at WXXV Fox 25 (Gulfport, Mississippi), part of covering baseball is shooting from the field. "This angle puts me right into the heart of the action," said Haeger. "My shots are so vivid and engaging from this angle." This location is closest to the action, but it increases the likelihood of being hit by a stray ball, so it is even more important to pay attention to the surroundings as well as to the viewfinder.

When shooting baseball stills from a distance or at a higher elevation it is best to use a wide-angle lens. This type of lens adds perspective and allows people to view the field, umpires, players and fans. Be sure to use a small aperture (f/5.6–f/14) to increase the overall depth of field. Action shots require zooming the camera. In this case the aperture should remain the same, but the shutter should greatly increase (from 1/125 to 1/250), and your ISO should decrease (from 400 to 200). When trying to freeze the action (or trying to take multiple shots of the action) a high shutter speed (1/1250) and ISO speed (1600) is required. Always keep lighting in mind when selecting settings. Typically there is plenty of light during both day games (thanks to the sun) and night games (well-lighted stadiums) to use different shutter speeds. Use slower shutter speeds during overcast days.

Basketball

There are basically two different vantage points to shooting basketball, and determining which one to use will depend on which team is covered. To cover the home team, shoot from position 1, slightly to the left or right of the home-team's basket (the offensive side of the court). Be mindful not to set up directly under the basket. Novice photographers learn the hard way that referees constantly block this position, and thus block them from getting that action shot. Setting up to the left or right of the basket still gives the photographer a unique vantage point. Because the camera is close to the action, even shots using a wide lens will appear to have a deep depth of field resulting in a richer and more inviting feel. Therefore, start medium to wide, but zoom in on the action. In other words, zoom in as the ball heads toward the basket, and then immediately get a reaction shot of the player who just scored. This shot can be challenging, but it is extremely important because it typically displays the emotion of the

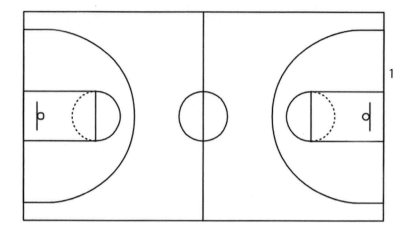

2 (elevated from the stands)

Figure 10.4 Basketball camera placement.

players. It is best to stay medium to wide when the ball is being passed around. Zooming too tight risks the chance of missing a play or creating confusion in the viewers' minds. Basically, the camera should follow the ball until someone makes a shot.

Position 1 can be risky, though. Because the camera is on the floor and very close to the action, there is a risk of players landing on it or running through it or balls hitting it. Always stay alert by keeping one eye on the viewfinder and the other on the surroundings. Furthermore, being on the floor makes it hard to move around. So, be prepared to stay kneeling or sitting on the floor for the length of the game. This is a prime reason why professional sports photographers wear kneepads.

Position 2 is an elevated view from half court. Since camerapersons are above the action, it is a bit easier to follow the flow of the game from this position. Depending on the level of play, however, it may be difficult to find space from this vantage point.

Be sure to get cutaway shots of coaches, fans, the scoreboard and both benches. To help with editing and to keep track of game situations, some photographers will get a shot of the scoreboard after each basket. If this tip is adapted, be sure to also get the highly valued emotional shots after a score. Shooting basketball is similar to football. But the speed of basketball does not allow time to move up and down the field of play the same way you can in covering football. Because the action moves quickly up and down the court, depth of field also changes at a rapid pace. To help keep shots in focus, quickly zoom into the basket where the action is headed, then focus before quickly zooming back out. Having cameras on manual zoom expedites the ability to zoom quickly. Forget using autofocus in the real world.

SPORTS VIDEO

Sports videographers may produce video for sportscasts (packages, VOs, or VO/SOTS), or they may cover live sport events. Videography for television (or online) typically includes covering live sports events or high school or college games. Whether it is football, basketball, baseball, volleyball or any other sport, each one presents its own challenges. Regardless of the final format, camera placement and angles are both vital elements in capturing the essence and emotion of the sport. In live-event coverage, the director will determine camera placement and will guide or direct the camerapersons as to which shot they should get at any particular moment. Experienced camerapersons, however, anticipate which shots the director will call; this ability allows them to obtain these shots quickly, an essential trait in live production. In addition, the production crew meets prior to the event to discuss specific instructions on how to shoot from each vantage point or camera placement. (See Chapter 11 for more details regarding pre-production meetings.) The director, more than any other member of the production crew, must anticipate and stay ahead of the action. If the director is behind on calling the camera shots or calls the wrong camera or angle shot, the viewers miss the action. This position requires an enormous amount of organizational and multitasking skills.

Know Your Camera

It is important to understand film rate and shutter speed before starting to shoot sports. Many television shows and feature films are shot at 24/fps (frames per second), which results in a more filmlike feel. This speed, however, is a bit too slow for sports. A faster rate of 60/fps (NTSC) is far more desirable and will provide you with better images. A faster rate will capture more action since more frames are recorded each second. But more important than frames per second is your shutter speed.

Shutter speed is a measurement of the time the shutter is open when taking a picture (or recording images). It is usually measured in seconds or in fractions of seconds (1/2, 1/200, 1/500, etc.). The faster the shutter speed, the less time the image is exposed to light. Fast shutter speed can suspend time and freeze an action, such as a shot of one stride of a thoroughbred horse in the Kentucky Derby. Slow shutter speeds can result in blurred images. The image blur is a result of both object motion and camera movement (or shake). Slow shutter speeds tend to suggest motion, while high shutter speeds actually record motion. Therefore it is prudent in sports to shoot at higher shutter speeds.

SD or memory card capacity should be high. Most professionals recommend using between a 16 GB to 32 GB SD card with up to 100 Mbs (megabits per second) for both video and still image recording (Gordon, 2014).

Highlights

Make sure to shoot from a variety of points of view, and get cut-away shots (shots removed from the action focusing on the crowd, scoreboard, coaches, cheerleaders, etc.). Shoot extra video for the stories, and do not be afraid to experiment (but be sure to have enough b-roll first). "There's nothing worse than editing your story to find out you do not have enough b-roll or natural sound," said sports anchor/reporter Haeger. Just because you shot the video does not mean you have to use it in the final story.

According to Haeger, "It's all about taking the human eye where it can't go from the stands. There's something about getting the perfect shot, the one you know your competition didn't get, that makes you feel like you caught the touchdown."

Haeger also warns you to "make sure you never take a play off, or you might miss one." "With sports," said sports photography veteran Hartney, "you basically have to roll on everything because you might miss that *big* moment." Shooting an exuberant amount of video, however, could make editing a nightmare. One quick trick Hartney recommends is to "flash color bars after every key moment, so it's easy to find during playback." To help improve your technique, Hartney also says it is important to pay attention to how your competition covered the game. Two excellent sources of professional work include infinitylist.com and mpora.com.

Video Editing

Advancements in digital technology have made things a bit easier when it comes to editing sports video. Basically all nonlinear editing software works on the same premise. It is a matter of importing and then dropping the video into a digital timeline. The trick, however, is placing the video in the correct order that will best tell the story.

Another important element of editing is pacing. In other words, how you edit will determine the overall feel and flow (known as pacing) of your story. We all know that different sports move at different speeds, and this speed can be displayed through the editing process. Rapid edits — showing clips for only a few seconds (:02–:03) at a time — creates a fast pace, while holding shots longer (say :10) dramatically slows the pace.

Time becomes one of the biggest enemies when editing sports stories for traditional newscast or sports shows. The turnaround time from capturing video of the games to airing your stories is usually only a couple of hours and sometimes less.

Photo 10.4 Live sports production editing/switching.

"When I started out I was so scared of the time pressure of the job." Hartney said. "But now, I love the time crunch — it can create a rush and such a sense of satisfaction."

There are several tips that can help speed up the editing process. One of Hartney's favorite tricks is to shoot to edit or edit in the camera. This simply means you sequence your shots (if possible) in the field. For example, you do this by recording six seconds of a wide shot; hit pause reframe and focus then record three seconds of a close-up; then hit pause reframe and focus and finish recording with four seconds of a medium shot. The sequence of framing can vary, but you must pause the recording while you readjust the framing.

In addition to recording color bars after a dramatic play, Hartney also recommends taking a notepad with you on shoots. For each dramatic or emotional video captured, write the time-code down in a notepad. This little trick will also drastically reduce the time spent looking for highlights when you return to the station and begin editing under pressure. It is also critical to keep track of nat pops (natural sound that will be used to help tell the story). Haeger notes, "Know what your nat pops are, and know your best shots. In other words, say it — show it."

When it comes to creating your highlight reel, keep it short. The typical highlight only runs between 10 and 15 seconds (Schultz & Arke, 2015). However, make sure you give yourself enough b-roll to cover the script.

Although there is a multitude of editing software you can choose to use, professionals tend to rely on Adobe Premiere, and most broadcast affiliates use Edius. Both Hartney and Haeger encourage editors to learn the keyboard shortcuts. "Using the keyboard shortcuts will save you so much time in the editing process," said Hartney. Haeger added, "Once you know the shortcuts everything else should fall into place. Overthinking the editing process is just time wasted that you could use to make revisions." The breakout box below provides some of the most useful keyboard shortcuts for both systems.

BASIC SPORT VIDEO TIPS

- Sports uses a faster frame per-second rate, so make sure yours is set at a rate of at least 60/fps.
- Remember the shutter speed measures the time the image is exposed. Faster shutter speeds work to suspend time. Slow shutters speeds, however, can result in blurred images.
- Be sure to record cut-away shots (scoreboard, coaches, fans, etc.).
- Flash record (view seconds) color bars after a big play to help sort video during the editing process and thus save precious time.
- Edit in the camera when possible. Once again, this will help save valuable editing time when you are under pressure.
- Keep track of your natural sound when recording. Natural sound is a critical element in video storytelling.

EDITING KEYBOARD SHORTCUTS

ADOBE PREMIERE	WINDOWS	APPLE
EDIT FUNCTIONS	**SHORTCUTS**	
Undo	Ctrl+Z	Cmd+Z
Redo	Cltrl+Shift+Z	Shift+Cmd+Z
Spacebar	Play/Pause Clip	Play/Pause Clip
Cut	Ctrl+X	Cmd+X
Copy	Ctrl+C	Cmd+C
Paste	Ctrl+V	Cmd+V
Paste Insert	Ctrl+Shift+V	Shift+Cmd+V
Select All	Ctrl+A	Cmd+A
Deselect All	Ctrl+Shift+A	Shift+Cmd+A
Keyboard Shortcuts	Ctrl+Alt+K	Comd+Opt+K
MARKER FUNCTIONS		
Mark In	I	I
Mark Out	O	O
Go to In	Shift+I	Shift+I
Go to Out	Shift+O	Shift+O
Clear In and Out	Ctrl+ Shift+X	Opt+X
Add Marker	M	M
Go to Next Marker	Shift+M	Shift+M
Go to Previous Marker	Ctrl+Shift+M	Shift+Cmd+M
Clear All Markers	Ctrl+Alt+M	Opt+M
TIMELINE FUNCTIONS		
Decrease Audio Tracks Height	Alt+-	Opt+
Decrease Video Tracks Height	Ctrl+-	Cmd+-
Increase Audio Tracks Height	Alt+=	Opt+=
Increase Video Tracks Height	Ctrl+=	Cmd+=
FILE FUNCTION		
Open Project	Ctrl+O	Cmd+O
Close Project	Ctrl+Shift+W	Shift+Cmd+W
Save	Ctrl+S	Cmd+S
Save As	Ctrl+Shift+S	Shift+Cmd+S
Save Copy	Ctrl+Alt+S	Opt+Cmd+S
Import	Ctrl+I	Cmd+I
Export Media	Ctrl+M	Cmd+M

EDIUS	
FUNCTION	
Undo	Z+Ctrl
Redo	Y+Ctrl
Play/Pause Clip	Spacebar
Rewind/Stop/Fast Forward	J/K/L
(left, right) Moves cursor one frame	Arrow Key
10 Frames Left + Right	Shift+Arrow
In Point	I
Out Point	O
Insert Edit	i
Overwrite Edit	J
Fit to Timeline	Ctrl+O
Increase/Decrease Timeline View (zoom)	Ctrl+Mousewheel
Moves video one frame at a time	Mousewheel
Export	F11
Drags all clips right of selected clip	Shift+ALT+Drag
Renders Timeline	Shift+ALT+Q
Selects all clips right of the cursor	Shift+End
Selects all clips left of the cursor	Shift+Home
Speed Adjust	ALT+E
Opens Layouter	F7
Deletes audio only	ALT+A
Deletes video only	ALT-V
Default Transition	Ctrl+P
Create Still Frame	Ctrl+T
Set Group	G
Remove Group	ALT+G

For a full list of Adobe Premiere Keyboard Shortcuts visit: https://helpx.adobe.com/premiere-pro/using/default-keyboard-shortcuts-cc.html

STILL IMAGES

Sports photography, either still or video, has the capability to immortalize sport events. Images of athletes competing are hung on bedroom and office walls for children and adults alike. Although anyone can shoot video or images of sports events, not all can profit from these images. Veteran AP sports photographer Chuck Cook says, "To make money from your photos you need to obtain the commercial license." Getty and AP are the two major organizations that have the rights to commercial professional sports images. Each year the two organizations compete for the rights to commercially distribute sports images from professional sports organizations like the NFL or NBA.

Lens

Having the right lens is extremely important when shooting still sports images. Most photographers use a 35mm camera because of its portability. Cook recommends the following focal lenses: at least a 200mm (millimeter) focal lens, and either a 300mm or 400mm lens. Most professional sports photographers carry two cameras with two different lenses — one for extreme distances and the other for normal or closer range. The number of millimeters your lens has will dramatically impact the quality and coverage length. For every 100mm in lens focal length you get about 10 yards in coverage. To put this in perspective, if you are shooting college football with a 300mm lens from the goal line, you can shoot close-ups (or tight shots) all the way to midfield. If the action moves closer to you, your lens may be too long — thus the need to switch to the shorter lens. Be sure to set your camera to a large file size. This will help when cropping a photo later. Start with as much information as possible before cropping an image to maintain overall professional quality.

Photo 10.5 This image provides an illustration of proper framing and depth of field.
Photo courtesy of Chuck Cook

Frames per Second and Shutter Speed

According to Cook, it's necessary to have a camera that shoots multiple frames per second, with a minimum of five frames a second. Most professionals, however, shoot at least 12 frames per second. When shooting in low light, you need a lens that opens to a F4 or F2.8 aperture in order to let in the maximum amount of light. The camera needs to be set at a high ISO (sensitivity of the sensor), which close to 5,000. "ISO can run as high a 3-million," Cook said. "It's all about better quality images under poor lighting."

Regardless of the sport, your shutter speed should be set at least a 400th of a second. If you're shooting inside, Cook suggests "you shoot wide open at 2.8 (the lens) — at 400th of a second." In this case, Cook said, "the only thing you can really adjust is the ISO — so you may raise it to possibly 5,000."

Still Editing

Professional sports still photographers will shoot about 2,000 photos a game (this is why a large memory card is needed). Cook noted that of the 2,000 photos he takes, he keeps about 100 for stock. During his first round of editing, Cook said he "picks the best action and storytelling images." Cook noted, "The second edit is for stock, such as bench pictures — head shots, helmet off. In other words, the images I could sell later on." Such stock photos help photographers build their portfolios.

It is extremely important to build your portfolio and to add to it as time goes by. The portfolio is your résumé and its quality will determine whether you get hired. According to Cook, "It's never too early to start to build your portfolio. You can shoot local high school or even pee wee — it really doesn't matter." Good tips are to study what others have done that you like and to regularly practice taking similar shots.

STILL PHOTOGRAPHY TIPS

- Most still sports photographers use two cameras with two different focal lenses (shorter lens 200mm and longer 400mm).
- The number of millimeters your lens has dramatically impacts the image quality. (In other words, you will not be able to use a 400mm lens to shoot close-up images.)
- Frames per second and shutter speed matter. Professionals tend to shoot at 12fps. You may use a lower fps, but do not go below 5fps.
- Shooting in low light requires a lens that opens to at least F4 with a high ISO close to 5,000.
- Do not forget to save some photos for your stock file. These could be shots of the bench, headshots of players without helmets, and so on.

FEATURE INTERVIEW

CHUCK COOK AND PATRICK HARTNEY

Photo 10.6   AP photographer Chuck Cook.
Photo courtesy of Chuck Cook

Chuck Cook, a still photographer, has more than 26 years experience as a sports photojournalist and multimedia producer at *The Times-Picayune* in New Orleans. Cook is also a freelance sports photographer for the Associated Press.

Cook began his long career as a sports photographer at the age of 19. "My first NFL game was in 1979. I was still in school and the local newspaper needed a part-time photographer," said Cook. Being a student, Cook's equipment was limited. "I got the job and rented a lens so I could shoot the Saints Game." Cook urges beginning photographers to invest in their equipment. He also emphasizes repetition to beginners. "It doesn't matter if you shoot high school or park-district sports." Cook added, "The point

Photo 10.7   WBBM Sports videographer Patrick Hartney.
Photo courtesy of Patrick Hartney

is to practice. Keep shooting with the goal of improving with each game."

He warns beginners to never overlook the obvious — and this includes making sure you inserted your SD card! "I remember one of my earliest gigs I had forgotten to put film in my camera — luckily I discovered it early enough that I was still able to cover the event," said Cook.

Patrick Hartney, sports videographer, began his sports career in 1999 at station WCIA in Springfield, Illinois. He worked his way up the media ladder, and for the past 10 years he's worked in the highly competitive Chicago market for station WBBM.

Hartney warns beginners that this isn't a 9-to-5 type job. "Starting out in this business you have to be ready to work crazy times, and in all types of weather. But at the end of the day the job is so rewarding." Hartney added, "Be open because it just takes that first job to start moving up the ladder."

The highly competitive nature of the business can cause less experienced photographers and videographers to doubt their ability. Hartney believes this is a natural response, but he warns people to not be afraid of making a mistake, especially those fresh out of school. "Know that you're not perfect and that you'll continue to learn," said Hartney.

CHAPTER WRAP-UP

Advances in photo and video technology have made it somewhat easier to capture sports images at a much lower cost than in previous years. Knowing the equipment and producing quality images, however, are what will help to gain and maintain employment as a sports photographer.

The old expression "it's all about location, location, location" is definitely true when it comes to sports photography and production. In order to capture that highly competitive action/reaction shot, you must be in the right spot. Choosing the right location also impacts depth of field, framing and angles.

Good sports photographers know every element of their cameras. Having the right lens could mean the difference between capturing that pivotal moment in the game or missing it completely. This is why professionals carry two still cameras with two different focal lenses

Whether shooting video or still images, ultimately sports is about people. The beauty of sports video production and sports photo-journalism is the ability to put the viewer in the midst of the action. Fans can live vicariously through the images you provide. Each game is an unpredictable story that plays out in real time. So no matter how you experiment or which equipment you use, it all means little if you do not convey that story.

REVIEW QUESTIONS

1. Describe two ways a photographer can "be there for the action."
2. Describe what the 180-line is and why it is wrong to cross it.
3. Define shutter speed and how using it improves sport images (both for video and for stills).
4. Define what it means to "edit in the camera" and why it is a useful sports editing tool.
5. Why do most professional still sports photographers carry two different cameras?

GROUP ACTIVITIES

1. In class, either show a local sportscaster's package or present a print sports story (newspaper, magazine or online) that is accompanied by still images. Have the students critique the quality of the images and overall storytelling. What makes the images good or look bad? What would you do differently?
2. Have each student capture video images of a sports event, and then exchange SD cards with a classmate. From the raw SD card the student will edit together a highlight reel. The student will turn in a one- to two-page written

critique of the classmate's videography; this will include both positive and negative feedback.

3. Have each student capture still images of a sports event, and then exchange SD cards with a classmate. From the raw SD card the student will edit (or choose) five usable photos to accompany a print story, and 15 for stock. The student will turn in a one- to two-page written critique of the classmate's photography, which includes both positive feedback and addresses weaknesses and areas needing improvement.

CHAPTER 11

Sports Show Production

Ask any sports producer and you will hear that 90 percent of any sports show consists of preproduction, leaving a mere 10 percent for what the audience sees and/or hears. This percentage remains the same whether you're producing a daily or weekly sports show or a live sporting event. Producers will also tell you that a significant amount of preproduction requires organizational skills. You can break broadcast sports production into two basic categories. The first is the daily or weekly sports radio or television show. Within this category are local affiliate daily sportscasts, sports programming (like a coaches' show) and network daily sports shows (ESPN, Fox Sports and college networks such as SEC, Longhorn and Big 10). The second type of coverage is special-event sports coverage or live sports events. No matter which format it is, each sports show equates to an allotment of time that the producer fills with compelling content. In essence, it is the producer who determines the creative look and feel of sportscasts.

PRODUCING FOR A DAILY OR WEEKLY SPORTS SHOW

The Rundown

A producer is the person in charge of the overall feel and flow of the sports show. He or she is largely responsible for the creation and production of sports content. Some job responsibilities include directing staff, creating story ideas and/or content and timing the show. Regardless of the type of format, one of the first things the producer needs to do is to find out how much content time needs to be filled. This amount will vary depending on the format. For example, a television daily local sportscast typically lasts between two to three minutes and a coaches' show a half an hour, while a radio sportscast could last several hours. Next, the producer needs to consider elements of the show such as story selection, story format (package, VO, VO/SOT, live shot etc.), timing and ordering (known as stacking), to name a few.

Once the time element is secure, the producer begins work on elements within the show, such as stories and the order of the show. This is typically accomplished through a rundown. A rundown consists of the following information that both the production team and the anchors/talent need: story slug, format or type of story, story length, position number/identification, graphic/still store information, talent and total run time. The *slug* is simply the name of the story, and is typically one or two words in length. Stories can take several different *forms* and therefore need clarification on the rundown.

In radio, the producer works with similar story formats but the terminology varies, and of course there is no video. The following is a list of radio terminology along with their television counterparts: actuality (TV: Soundbytes); RDR (TV: Reader); RA — announcer/talent reads opening copy followed by an actuality and announcer/talent closes with copy (TV: VO/SOT); Wrap contains an announcer/talent lead into the sound package, which contains the reporter's sound track, actualities and closer (TV: PKG) (see Table 11.1).

Story length refers to the time allocated to the individual story. Readers, VOs and VO/SOTs are usually shorter stories (:20–:45 seconds) that carry less importance in the program. They are also shorter because they are not as visually compelling as the package or live shot. Packages and live shots are given more time because they are used for more important stories. A typical package within a newscast or sportscast can run about 1:30 or so, while a live shot (especially if it includes a package) can last up to five minutes. However, these times are not etched in stone and can vary depending on many variables such as the story, the station and the

TABLE 11.1   Broadcast Sports Story Formats

Medium	Story Form			
TV/Visual	Reader (RDR) Stand alone story/copy/script that the anchor/talent reads live.	Voice-Over (VO) Anchor/talent reads story while video (b-roll) is shown.	Voice-Over Sound on Tape (VO/SOT) Anchor/talent reads script with built-in pauses for sound (sound bite or natural sound that enhances the story) while video (b-roll) is shown.	Package (PKG) Anchor/talent leads into a story that is all inclusive with the reporter's soundtrack, b-roll and sound bites-natural sound.
Audio/Radio	Reader (R) Stand alone story/copy/script that the anchor/talent reads live.	No equivalent	Reader Actuality (RA) Announcer/talent reads copy followed by an actuality. An actuality is actual outside/prerecorded sound (sound bite or natural sound that enhances the story). If the announcer/talent begins with copy, followed by an actuality, and ends with copy, the story is called a DONUT.	Wrap Announcer/talent leads into the sound package, which contains the reporter's soundtrack, actualities-natural sound, and closer.

amount of news covered that day. Timing is a critical element of production and will be discussed in further detail later in this chapter. *Position number/identification* indicates where in the rundown the story appears. Sports shows with commercial breaks contain several blocks of content. The blocks are typically labeled A for the first block, B for the second block and so on. Therefore, a package that runs as the second story in the first block after the first commercial break would be labeled as B2 (B for the second block and 2 for the second story). In a daily sportscast that falls within a newscast you only have one block, so stacking is a bit simpler.

Since television is a visual medium, most stories contain some sort of *graphic element*. If video isn't available, a producer may use a graphic or still store. These can be small pictures that appear in the upper left or right corner on the frame–over the shoulder (OTS) of the sports anchor/talent. It may also refer to a full-screen graphic, which simply indicates computer-generated images and texts that fill the entire screen. The producer provides the graphic information, but the production department creates the graphic. *Talent* in the rundown refers to which anchor will read that particular script/story.

The final category on the rundown is total run time (TRT). TRT refers to actual accumulated time within the show. Each story's time is added to the previous one, thus building the cumulative show time. Time is the master of all in sportscasting and must be strictly adhered to. If your allotted time equates to three minutes, then three minutes is all you have — not a second more or less. Tips on timing will be discussed in greater lengths later in this chapter (see Figure 11.1).

WHLT 10pm - 30 Min [01/15/2016 22:00]

Page	Story Slug	Segment	Anchor*	Type*	Float	Est Duration	Actual	Back	Object Autocreate	MOS Status	Video Notes	DoNotArchive
A1	ANIMTRANS WHLT OPEN	ANIMTRANS		ANIM		0:02	0:00	10:02:22 PM				
A2	10VO1 DISTRICT 79 ELECTION CHALLENGE FOLO	MONITOR	MEL	1SHOTWALL		0:10	0:07	10:02:24 PM		NOT READY	LUCY	
A3	10VO2 JIM HILL REPORTED BODY SLAM	MONITOR	MEL	1SHOTWALL		0:10	0:07	10:02:34 PM		READY	CELL PHONE VIDEO OF BODY SLAM IN VIDEO IMPORTS	
A4	10VO3 MISSISSIPPI RIVER FLOODING VICKSBURG CREST C		MEL	1SHOTWALL		0:10	0:04	10:02:44 PM				
A5	ANIMTRAN WHLT OPEN	ANIMTRA		ANIM		0:02	0:00	10:02:54 PM				
A6	FAST WX	WX LAB	BRAD	WX LAB		0:15	0:00	10:02:56 PM				
A7	ANIM WHLT AT 10	ANIM		ANIM		0:05	0:00	10:03:11 PM				
A8	INTRO DISTRICT 79 ELECTION C	RDR	MEL	MONITOR		0:10	0:11	10:03:16 PM				
A9	PKG DISTRICT 79 ELECTION CHALLENGE FOLO	PKG		PKG		2:00	1:24	10:03:26 PM		READY	LUCY	
A10	TAG DISTRICT 79 ELECTION CH	LIVE	MEL	MONITOR		0:15	0:13	10:05:28 PM				
A11	INTRO JIM HILL REPORTED BODY SLAM	RDR	MELANIE	MONITOR		0:10	0:10	10:05:41 PM				

Printed 1/15/2016 18:06 by Jeffrey Haeger

Page 1

Figure 11.1 WHLT sportscast rundown.
This image provides a typical sports rundown for a sports segment of a local half-hour newscast.
Courtesy of WHLT sportscaster Jeff Heager

Story Ideas

Even before the producer begins work on the rundown, he or she must select which stories will be included in the show. This applies to all platforms. Stories come from a variety of places and sources, and it's up to the producer to select which ones the audience will find most interesting. The sportscaster will sort through an incredible amount of information — public relations releases, Internet stories, social media content and the like — to get story ideas. Sometimes a caller or viewer will suggest a story through a phone call or social media message and these tips can also lead to good stories.

The majority of stories come from editorial meetings. During these meetings, reporters and producers discuss the day's events and pitch viable story ideas. A helpful hint in pitching story ideas is to build contacts within the station's viewing/listening area. These contacts can provide helpful story tips while enabling the producers and reporters to maintain a sense of the community's interest while remaining unbiased. For a producer to succeed, he or she must know the expectation of the audience. (This helps with story selection and the type of coverage.)

Sportscasts aired by network affiliate stations rely heavily on "hyperlocal" stories. To compete with major networks that have the resources and money to cover national and major sports teams (such as ESPN, Fox Sports and the like), affiliate news stations concentrate on local teams. Hyperlocal simply means stories that happen within your market area. These can include stories about local college/university teams, high school teams, junior high school teams or even stories involving local park districts. According to sports radio announcer and director of Seymour Sports (an online television network) Tim Finnigan, in areas where there are no professional sports teams, it's important for sports reporters and producers to not treat high school or college level events "as just kid's play." Rather, Finnigan suggests reporters and producers highlight "the kids that have the potential to be great players."

Sports producers will, however, include a small minority of newsworthy national or state stories in their sportscasts. Producers can obtain these stories from news feeds. As network affiliates (NBC, CBS, ABC, Fox), stations have access to stories from other affiliate stations both within their local areas and nationally, and some pay subscription fees to independent feeds (like CNN or Associated Press). Depending on the story, these feeds may include video and audio, or just the script. Keep in mind that national stories may influence things locally. In other words, national stories can be localized, so that it becomes of greater interest to the audience. For instance, a national story about NFL player concussions can be localized at the junior high, high school or college level. Producers would also need to decide when, where and whether to include live shots within the sportscast.

Also keep in mind that you'll be competing with other stations in your market and you probably will cover the same story. To separate you from the crowd, Finnigan suggests that you look beyond the superstars when suggesting stories. "I found that just because someone isn't the superstar they still know stuff about the sport and what's happening. Interviewing rookies that still have a chip on their shoulder were the best because they were so excited that someone wanted to interview/talk with them that I was able to get great actualities that my competition didn't have."

From this list of possible stories, the producer must choose just a handful to cover for the day's sports segment. Some important elements to consider while choosing stories include audience expectations, editing time, location of the event (which also involves travel time to and from the story), technical requirements (such as a live shot) and number of reporters and photographers assigned to you. A producer must remain realistic when creating the show rundown. If he or she over-assigns a reporter or photographer, the quality of work and show may suffer. Reliance on sport feeds helps supplement a sportscast when a sports producer is short on staff.

These are some of the same elements used to determine the story format. For instance, packages/wraps are usually stories that have the greatest impact on the audience (high audience expectation) and happen within your market. In television stories that lack good visuals or in radio those stories that don't have good natural sound would typically be relegated as a RDR or a RDR with a SOT/Actuality.

Stacking/Building a Rundown

Once the producer has selected which stories to include in the sportscast, he or she begins to build or stack the rundown. *Stacking*, as the name implies, is the process of stacking or placing stories in the order they will appear in the sportscast. As mentioned previously, story relevance or importance to the audience takes precedence. Here is when the hyperlocal aspect of producing a show comes into play. Your lead story (the first story) is the one that has the greatest impact on your audience; typically it pertains to a local team, player, coach or school, but not always. In building your rundown, the stories should have some sort of rational flow. This flow could be based on a variety of topics such as subject matter (type of sport), or a specific location or entity (one particular school, team or district), to list a few. For instance, if your lead story is about the local university football team's chance at becoming bowl eligible, it's logical to follow with a story about the current rankings or a story highlighting the team's key player. Pace your rundown so that you have a mix of all formats.

You should also take into consideration the time when your sportscast airs. Is it in the 5 p.m., 6 p.m. or 10 p.m. slots, or is it the morning show? When a show airs will determine the overall flow, pacing and content. The pace of a morning show typically moves slowly with the majority of the content recapping the previous day's events. Furthermore, the audience differs depending on when the show airs, which influences how a producer stacks the rundown. For television, traditionally the 6:00 p.m. broadcast is the highest rated newscast, and local news trumps national and international news in this show. When stacking the 6:00 p.m. show, producers would begin with the local package or live shot. The same story would then run as a VO or VO/SOT during the 10:00 p.m. show. The 5:00 p.m. (or first sportscast) would serve as a tease for the later shows (in the form of a reader, VO or VO/SOT).

When a show airs is also crucial when producing radio sports shows. In the morning your first broadcast is typically a recap of what happened the day before. "The last thing that happened the night before is typically what I start with to get the listeners up-to-date–it's what the first cast is for," says WBBN Radio news/sports director Tanner Watson. When producing for radio cut-ins (sports segments within music radio shows), your stories will be much shorter than those for television/visual communication. According to Watson, "Short and to the point is the rule in producing for radio cut-ins." Depending on the market size, your first radio show will typically be stacked with readers with one or two actualities. A majority of your wraps will play during peak hours like the 7:30 a.m.–9:00 a.m. and 5:00 p.m.–7:00 p.m. drive time. Each show should also include a local element.

A crucial element of stacking is deciding the story format. In other words, will the story be a RDR, PKG or something else? The flow or feel of the show depends on how it's stacked. You wouldn't want to place four or five readers in a row without giving the talent a break or chance to catch their breath (if you did, you'd have an unhappy anchor). One key element in deciding story format is available resources, both people and equipment. How many reporters/videographers are available? Are you able to go live from a distant location? Is the story important enough to go live? What's included in your newsfeed? As mentioned previously, location is another key element to consider. Where the story is will influence the type of format the story will take. You need to consider travel time along with editing time. For instance, say you're producing for the 5:00 p.m. sportscast and a local college coach schedules a press conference at 3:00 in the afternoon, and the drive time from the station to the location is 30 minutes. You obviously don't have time for a package, but you could edit a VO or a VO/SOT with the ability to include a live shot. Allowing your reporters to make deadline is more important than a perfectly stacked show.

Story strength or importance also influences whether it should be a live shot, package or something shorter. Most stations have a limited number of reporters assigned to sports, so you need to make the best use of that resource. You don't want to waste valuable reporter time on a story that the audience won't find interesting or engaging. Stories the audience finds most interesting will either be a package or a live shot.

Keep in mind that your stacked rundown is really a template and can change at any moment. Producers need to remain flexible and able to handle adversity. Because shows are fluid, it's a smart idea to "over-produce" a show by producing an extra reader and/or package that you can insert into the show in case the time allotment changes. Also be prepared to drop a story or cut its time if the show is running too long.

Communication is critical when producing a show. Although sports is its own segment in a newscast, it's part of a larger show. Keep the lines of communication open between the main news producer and the director (and the production crew), as well as management. If a sports story has a significant impact on the overall audience, you may get help from the news staff, but without communication you could be left short-handed. Within the context of a larger news show, the newscast producer has ultimate authority over the sports segment. That means the sports time can be cut, adjusted or in some extreme cases such as breaking news, eliminated entirely. A good sports producer is in constant contact with the newscast producer.

Sports Rundown Examples

Let's take a more detailed look at how this process works. Say, for example, you are working in a medium-size market in southern Illinois and it's late fall. As the producer, you've looked through the feeds, scanned social media and the newspaper and have had your news meeting. As a result, you've decided on the following list of stories for your sportscasts:

- Local university football team is bowl bound for the first time in five years
- Local high school basketball team ranks in the top three in the state
- Three starters for the L.A. Lakers basketball team were caught taking enhancement drugs
- The Chicago Bears released an update injury report

Remember, since the 5:00 p.m. sportscast has the smallest audience, it typically includes more national news than local. Since the 6:00 p.m. is the highest viewed cast, its focus is more local. In this cast, the producer would stack the show with more locally produced packages and stories. In this case, it's desirable for the story about the local bowl-bound team to become a package.

Don't fall into a bad habit of just recycling your previous stories into the 10:00 p.m. cast or other shows that come later in the day. Remember, faithful viewers will already have seen those stories. Also remember that breaking news information is made available instantly on social media. To compete, a smart producer/reporter will put the information into context. So, the recap story shouldn't be just about the score (see Table 11.2).

TABLE 11.2   Preliminary Rundowns

Story	Slug	Format
5:00 p.m. Show		
A1.	Bowl Bound	SOT
A2.	Local Basketball	VO
A3.	Lakers Scandal	PKG (national)
A4.	Bears	Reader or VO
Story	Slug	Format
6:00 p.m. Show		
A1.	Bowl Bound	PKG
A2.	Fan Reaction	Live Shot (VO/SOT)
A3.	Local Basketball	Reader
A4.	Lakers Scandal	VO/SOT (or a VO)
Story	Slug	Format
10:00 p.m. Show		
A1.	Recap Tonight's Game	VO (or Live Shot)/Graphics
A2.	Bowl Bound	VO/SOT
A3.	Local Basketball	Reader/VO
A4.	Lakers Scandal	VO
A5.	Bears	Reader/VO

Timing

Since most sports segments come toward the end of the local newscasts, sports producers/talent need to prepare for the unexpected. If the newscast is running light (less than the allotted time), then the news producer may allot more time to sports, and the opposite is true if the newscast is running heavy (overtime). Therefore, the sports producer/talent must be agile. A bonus to airing late in the newscast, however, is an extended deadline. Typically, sports producers/talent have until 10 or 15 minutes into the newscast before he or she needs to finish producing. However, there are always exceptions to this routine, and breaking news is one such exception. If the breaking news is sports-related, the news producer will build it into the opening block. In this case, the sports producer/talent has to write and edit the piece for the A block and still produce his or her normal sports segment (usually in the fourth or D block). If the breaking news is nonsports-related then the producer will cut time from the sports segment. In some instances (like election night), the sports segment may be completely cut from the newscast.

BEST PRACTICES FOR PRODUCING DAILY/WEEKLY SPORTS PRODUCTION

- Consider audience expectations, editing time, location of event (including travel time) and the number of reporters/photographers assigned to you when choosing stories to include in your rundown. These same considerations come into play when determining which format your story will take (PKG/wrap stories that have the greatest impact on your audience).
- Building contacts within your viewing/listening area will help in pitching viable story ideas. In other words, know your audience.
- Remember that your stacked rundown is a template and subject to change, so remain flexible. Vary your approach when stacking. In other words, don't stack the segment with three or four readers in a row. This approach is visually/audibly boring and your talent does not have time to breathe.
- Communication is critical when producing, so keep an open line of communication between the director (production crew) and the producer.
- Don't fall into a bad habit of recycling the exact same story into sports shows that air later that day or the following morning. Assume your audience has already seen the original story, so be sure to put the story in the right context.
- Plan for the unexpected, especially the timing of your show. Sports news shows are fluid and subject to change. A good producer will have extra stories ready to air just in case the show is light on time.
- Write compelling stories. Sports fans can easily obtain statistics and scores, so a good producer provides the context.

PRODUCING FOR LIVE SPORT PRODUCTION EVENTS

The production of live sports has grown incredibly in the past few years. Where once only the major networks (CBS, NBC, ABC) produced a game or two a week, the development of technology has drastically increased the number of content providers and thus the number of broadcast events. Today, dozens of outlets are producing hundreds of sports events each week of the year.

Producing live sporting events for outlets like Fox Sports, NBC Golf Channel or the NFL Network takes chaotic control to a whole new height. Depending on the type of event and venue, the production crew can employ more than 80 people for a single broadcast (that number drops to around 10–30 for a regional event such as college basketball or football game). And unlike daily sportscasts, production for live events begins days (sometimes weeks) before the actual broadcast. For example, the NBC Golf Channel coverage of a tour that plays on Saturday begins with what's called "park and power day" on Tuesday. This is the day when the truck with all the production equipment arrives and the truck crew assembles everything from the director's console to the steps leading into each trailer. Included in the set-up that few viewers are even aware of is the running of fiber cables that link every camera positioned at each hole to the director's production console in the live truck/trailer. And in the case of golf coverage, running the fiber cables means actually burying the cables underground and making sure the landscape is pristine in time for the broadcast. This is a job that has to be done each time the crew changes location and at every hole. Most of the set-up work is contracted to companies that specialize in sports production. The producer, however, is responsible for making sure this is done properly.

Live radio play-by-play production requires far less equipment and manpower than visual coverage and is relatively inexpensive. In smaller markets, the talent/announcer would also act as the engineer and the producer. Producers and engineers for larger markets would accompany the announcer, but the crew size is still much smaller than for television. Live coverage is typically transmitted via Tieline, Cellcast or via digital technology. Tieline and Cellcast systems rely on cellular phone technology, allowing the announcer to transmit wherever cellular service is available. Digital technology uses telephone lines but the signal is compressed digitally and sent back to the station for decompression and transmission.

The national television networks have their own production crews and equipment, but they still freelance some jobs within the production team. Usually, the network production crew remains a cohesive group and works together at each assigned event. Familiarity within the crew tends to enhance collaboration and improves the overall production quality. Similar to daily sportscast, it takes a team effort to cover a live sporting event, and it's the producer's job to tie all the elements together.

Producer

In live sports production, the producer is responsible for all aspects of the telecast. It's the producer who controls the overall feel or show flow of the broadcast and oversees its content. More importantly, the producer is the one who keeps

Photo 11.1 This is a medium shot of the graphics and video board inside the main production control room.

the telecast organized and working like a fine oiled machine. He or she makes sure that each individual works with others to produce the best coverage possible. Therefore, this position requires a very detailed-oriented person.

According to sports media production producer Sean Martin, show preparation includes a multitude of things, but can be broken into the following five subcategories: show planning or flow, team facts and relevance, coordination with talent and crew, scouting location (this includes being aware of weather conditions) and attention to detail.

Team facts or knowledge means researching background information beyond simple statistics on the teams you're covering. A good producer doesn't simply focus on the star players, but rather has information on each player, coach and owner, and is always ready for the unexpected. Coordination with talent and crew is discussed later in this chapter, but suffice to say that it is a critical part of production because each production is a team effort that requires communication and leadership. It is the producer who provides these elements. Scouting a location can also be referred to as knowing your surroundings, and has several implications. Live sport coverage means traveling to different locations, and although the coverage may be similar, the venues are not. The producer, therefore, needs to research the location and facility. Producing a game from inside the Superdome is much different than doing one in an outdoor venue like the Rose Bowl.

Weather also plays a factor in knowing one's surroundings, as the crew needs to take precautions and be prepared for rainy or bad weather, especially if the game is played outside. A good tip is to always bring a change of clothing. As mentioned previously, producing is a very detailed-oriented job, and something that initially may seem insignificant could have a very significant impact on the production. Something as simple as making sure food is ordered for the crew and talent may sound trivial, but working with a hungry crew is a disaster waiting to happen. A good producer doesn't leave anything to chance. Show planning is a significant part of being a producer and is discussed in more detail in the following paragraphs.

Show Planning

The producer begins work on a telecast several days (sometimes even weeks) before it airs, and that person can be assigned to more than one game per week. If assigned to multiple games, the producer relies heavily on the production assistant (also known as the field producer) for initial site scouting and set-up. (See the section on production assistant for more information regarding this role on p.203.) Once on site, the producer will meet with the entire crew to review assignments and answer any questions.

As with a daily sportscast, the producer determines which storylines the show will include. To do this, the producer communicates with coaches and/or players, and may conduct pregame interviews. These meetings along with research help the producer determine which stories the audience will find most interesting. Stories may be assigned to feature producers or put together by the head producer; assignments all depend on the size of the crew. Live productions follow a less-structured content rundown compared with daily sportscasts. In a live production, the producer does not stack the show segments with individual stories in a detailed rigid manner; rather, the talent provides extemporaneous analysis and coverage of the game. (Although the dialogue is unscripted, the talent conducts in-depth research in advance to prepare for the show.)

This does not mean that the show lacks structure. In terms of video/audio, when constructing the run-down the producer places preproduced packages or individual stories and video or b-roll in designated segments within the live coverage. So instead of airing at a specific time within the show, they simply will play within a segment. This is one example of the importance of communication between the producer and the entire crew, including talent. If the talent is unaware the story airs within a certain segment he or she may skip over it or, worse, stumble on air. What is structured, however, are the commercial breaks and billboards. ("Billboards" is a trade term for a promotion or prerecorded commercials for a show sponsor; see Table 11.3.)

Billboard placement is determined far in advance of the production by the corporation and the sponsors, and the producer must adhere to this time schedule. The producer will write the billboards or assign it to someone on the crew (such as the production assistant).

There are times when the producer will call for video/audio "flypack," or the replay of video/audio (for example using instant replay to assist the talent describe a play). In order to have the ability to extemporaneously call for a replay of video/audio, the producer must know all aspects of the production. Part of the producer's preparation should include the following questions: Are you recording ISO to camera (meaning, is each camera recorded separately, isolated from the others)? How long are the runs from camera to switcher? How are you recording

TABLE 11.3   Shaw Charity Classic Sunday

BRAD SHAW MESSAGE # 2 TO BREAK BREAK 1 2:00	SCHWAB OWN YOUR TOMORROW - GRAPHIC BREAK 7 2:30
NEXT WEEK ON TOUR OPENING BILLBOARDS TO BREAK BREAK 2 2:05	TICKER BREAK 8 2:30
TICKER BREAK 3 2:30	BREAK 9 2:30
BREAK 4 2:30	BREAK 10 2:30
BREAK 5 2:30	CLOSING BILLBOARDS BREAK 11 2:30
MID BILLBOARDS TO BREAK BREAK 6 2:30	SHAW SHOT OF TOURNAMENT BREAK 12 2:25
	LAST SEGMENT UPDATED SCHWAB STANDINGS OFF AIR: BARRACUDA CHAMP COMING UP NEXT BOEING CLASSIC BEGINS AUG 21

Courtesy of NBC Golf Channel

off the switcher? Are you doing a webcast off the switcher? These questions may seem like information that only the technical director should know, but a professional producer knows the value of being prepared.

Similar to the responsibilities of a daily sports producer, a live event producer is responsible for time elements within the show. Despite the unpredictable nature of when a live sports event may end, producers are still responsible for keeping the show on time. Basically this means timing individual packages and live interviews and coming in and out of commercial breaks. Producers review all show video, including packages, VOs and VO/SOTs, to ensure exact timing and to maintain the overall show quality. Knowing what's on the video helps the producer know when to roll the video during unscripted times throughout the production, such as during a long play stoppage due to player injuries or other unforeseen incidents.

Typically, the producer is the first person on the set or in the production truck. Arriving first is important because in addition to increasing his or her credibility with the crew, it allows extra time to put out fires for mishaps that occur.

Radio producers also begin work on the live show days in advance. For instance, Seymour Sports talent and producer Tim Finnigan begins his prep work for a Friday play-by-play high school football game by downloading the teams' roster from websites or contacting the coaches on Monday. (Two excellent websites that a majority of high school teams use are C2CSchools.org and maxpreps.com.) Although some of the information he gathers won't be used during the broadcast, he can use it for other shows through the week. Finnigan also conducts interviews with the coaches during the week and prepares wraps (radio packages) to use during the show.

According to Finnigan, knowing the players makes production easier and is an essential element to live coverage. The viewers expect announcers to know the players' names, and not knowing results in a lack of credibility. More than this, the audience expects the coverage to provide information, which requires the producer to conduct research. "You're not just supposed to entertain . . . you're supposed to educate," says Finnigan. "If I want to interview a player I wouldn't say, 'Hey 26.' The kid would look at me funny. But if I say his name, I already have an in."

In major sports radio outlets reporters tend to follow a ranking system with the lead reporter acting as team captain who then reports to the producer. According to Tim Finnigan, "prior to becoming a reporter, the positions are typically part-time, so you're looking for any assignment you can get." Finnigan urges you to "be patient and don't give up."

Production Assistant/Field Producer

The role of a production assistant (PA) and/or field producer is both usual and crucial in live/special sport productions, and the role requires a great amount of organizational skills. NBC Golf Channel production assistant Charlotte McLoughlin notes that the PA's responsibility covers a vast number of tasks. While the producer concentrates on the show flow, content and timing, the PA assists the producer by providing detailed content information. Typically, this person makes sure the talent is prepared for the show by providing information on the players, tournament, tour, course or field, and provides stats during the live broadcast. He or she arrives on-site the same day as the production trucks and immediately begins gathering background information for the show. Typically, the trailers are already set up when the PA arrives. So, McLoughlin says she begins her production week by "going around the golf course and getting the list of caddy names and then to the pro shop to get background information on the course." According to McLoughlin, one of the PA's main jobs is researching for the talent. "Basically I'm researching any information that can help the on-air announcers," she says. "I pretty much prep them for the show."

Production assistants/field producers do most of their work in the field and rarely work behind a desk. It's important for PAs to be extremely confident in their communication abilities and to remain flexible. Knowing how to use the equipment is also important. In collecting show content, the PA may have to record interviews without the reporter or videographer being present; a sports reporter will later insert these interviews into packages or a sound bite for live game coverage. (The PA may have to edit the sound bite used for the show.) To maintain credibility, the PA/field producer must not appear timid or unsure, even though he or she is not seen on camera.

Typically, the announcers or talent speaks extemporaneously during live sports production events. So, a critical responsibility of a PA is to gather facts and

Photo 11.2 A producer at work. In this photo, Charlotte McLoughlin is producing a segment for the NBC Golf Channel.
Photo courtesy of Charlotte McLoughlin

stats on all elements of the coverage, and to anticipate any information that is vital to the show's success. Staying with the golf coverage theme, an example would be an up-and-coming player leading the tour and the anchors unfamiliar with him. The PA is then responsible for passing them notes on air with background information on that particular player. If done correctly, the note passing is seamless and it would appear to the viewers/listeners that the anchor/announcer already knew the information.

When members of the production crew (including talent) need information, they turn to the production assistant. The PA can be pulled in a multitude of different directions at once, so this job requires a large amount of organizational skills. McLoughlin says this is the hardest part of her job. "Being pulled 100 different ways — if anyone wants information they come to me — I mean everyone! It can be as small as making a copy of the format because the camera guy lost his or as serious as rescheduling an interview that bailed."

Information can vary from finding a specific piece of video to making sure the graphic person has the right graphics at his or her disposal. This person also assists the producer in scheduling interviews (both live and prerecorded), distributing lineups (rundowns/formats, shot sheets for the camera crew, etc.) and timing special segments. This position requires a juggler of sorts. "I even have to stay ahead of the mail," says McLoughlin. "For example, the golf channel ships production

Photo 11.3 This shows the inside of the main control room of a sports production.

stuff to me to distribute. So if it arrives late, everyone blames me and not the mail. So there is a lot of stuff for me to stay on top of."

Meetings

Before meeting with the entire crew, early in the week of the show the producer typically will have a small meeting with the director, graphics person and the PA to discuss the show's content. Think of this meeting as a brainstorming session to determine the overall show flow. Most live productions have two meetings the day before the show. The producer meets with the production crew in the morning and shares the "show format" or a loose rundown in the first meeting. This meeting is for everyone in the trucks (which includes the graphic person, producer, director, assistant director, replay, audio persons and features producer), as well as for the PA. The producer discusses which local angles the show will focus on, which stories to include, which player to feature, and the look and layout of the graphics. The producer talks with each position and tells them what is expected. If working with a large crew, the producer will typically meet with the PA the night before the game to discuss any changes in the show format and any other items or logistics that may require his or her attention.

The second meeting occurs a couple of hours before the start of the show and includes the talent, producers and key elements of the production team (director, feature producer, audio person and graphics). During this meeting, the producer will discuss camera locations and microphone placements with the director or tech manager. (The type of sport will dictate the number of cameras, microphones and the location of equipment.) Depending on the type of event, tour or game, officials, as well as tournament sponsors, may also attend the meeting. In the golf example, tour officials would provide a statistical breakdown of the course (the projected time of play based on the conditions of the grass and feedback from the players' practice round) while tournament sponsors would include a list of promos (live commercials) and billboards (prerecorded commercials). This meeting is geared toward the talent so the production crew knows who's talking when, and which group they'll be working with.

The producer will also schedule two meetings the day of the show with the same two groups. The production crew meeting is brief, and will typically be inspirational in nature. During this meeting any last-minute changes are discussed, final show formats/rundowns/shot cards are distributed, and any last-minute questions answered. The time of the first meeting depends on the start of the game/show, and can be scheduled as early as 4 a.m. for a noon show. The second meeting is with the talent, director and graphics person. Typically, the producer will review the show graphics and videos for errors sometime during this last meeting. This meeting is also held early in the morning and approximately two hours after the production meeting.

Remember that ultimately, the head producer is responsible for every element in the show. Although things may seem hectic on game day, the producer has already completed a majority of his or her work in the days leading up to the show.

BEST PRACTICES FOR PRODUCING LIVE SPORTS PRODUCTION

- The five basic areas of producing live sport production are show planning, researching team/player/coach/fan facts, coordinating with talent/crew, scouting location (knowing your surroundings) and attention to details.
- Do not simply focus on the star players when researching the teams you will cover. Get the stories behind the stories. Remember, your job is to inform as well as entertain.
- As with daily sports production, communication is a critical element in live production. Never assume your production crew and talent know what you're thinking or planning, so check and double-check.
- Remaining organized and having the ability to overcome adversities are two key elements in being a live producer. Anticipate the unexpected and plan ahead. Remember that 90 percent of production is done before the show or event even begins.
- Because weather plays a factor in covering live sports events, a good tip is to always bring a change of clothing.
- A good producer takes care of his/her crew — so don't overlook what seems to be a little detail like feeding everyone.
- Producers should know how to interview and edit video/audio, so it's important to know the equipment.

FEATURE INTERVIEW

CHARLOTTE MCCLOUGHLIN

Charlotte McCloughlin is a relative newcomer to the world of professional sports media, but she quickly earned the spot as production assistant with NBC's Golf Channel. She's worked for the Golf Channel since she graduated from the University of Southern Mississippi in 2014. Her quick rise to a prestigious position demonstrates that with hard work and the right training, you too can work as a sports media professional.

Photo 11.4   Live producing. This photo captures the producer, along with the assistant producers, during a live broadcast of the NBC Golf Channel programming.
Photo courtesy of Charlotte McLoughlin

McCoughlin suggests that you "gain as much practical experience as you can while in school. Being able to demonstrate that you have the experience could be the one thing that separates you from a hundred other applicants." One way to get that experience is through multiple internships. "Do as many internships as you can, and meet as many people as you can," says McCloughlin. "I got my job through the people I met during my internship — but you must keep in touch with them."

Although sports media might seem like a large professional field, it's not. You will either work with or around the same people through the years. As a result, McCloughlin provides the following advice: "Learn to watch what you say — don't be too vocal on what's in your show," she says. "Remember, even though you make friends with people at other networks, it's a competitive field and you need to put your show first."

Humility and perseverance are key attributes to gaining employment in sports media. "Don't think you know it all and can start at the top. Be willing to start at the bottom and work your way up," says McCloughlin. "I always thought I wanted to be on air, but I took a job completely off air and it was the best move I made." In such a highly competitive field as sports media it's important to have confidence, but if you let it consume you or blind you into thinking all you want to do is "be on air," it can destroy your chance at a professional career. "Although you're confident, be humble," says McCloughlin. "Sport is so much bigger than just the announcers on air."

CHAPTER WRAP-UP

Producing for sports media is an extremely important part of the profession. Producers set the tone and feel of sports shows and live sports coverage. To become a producer, one needs plenty of organizational skills, along with the ability to remain cool under pressure. Although sports anchoring remains extremely popular, there are more opportunities in sports production and producing for those just starting the profession.

Producing also requires excellent writing, editing and people skills. When producing for daily sports shows or live sporting events, producers may have to write and edit stories as well as time the shows. Regardless whether you're producing a live sports event or a local sportscast, communication is a critical element of producing. Producers are leaders. In this role, the producer will work with and have to control a variety of personalities and egos. Therefore, a good producer always takes care of his or her crew.

REVIEW QUESTIONS

1. Describe the role of a daily sports show producer, and how it differs from the role of a live sports event producer.
2. Describe the different rationales used when determining the type of story coverage. For example, why would you package one story and make another a simple VO? Be sure your rationales include radio and television stories.
3. Define "hyperlocal" stories, and list at three that would be relevant to your viewing area.
4. Define the difference between a live sports event producer and a live sports event production assistant.
5. List and define the five subcategories in live sports media production.

GROUP ACTIVITIES

1. Have students pitch story ideas. From these ideas, each student will create a daily sportscast rundown that includes a rationale for the following: story selection, story format and length, and stacking. Be sure to account for the time of the show (example: 5 p.m., 6 p.m. or 10 p.m.).
2. Assign each group a different sports team or athlete, and then have the individual groups research information that could be used during a live sports event by the announcers. For example, the groups' research should provide detailed content information like statistics and background player information (both on and off the field of play).
3. Record a daily sportscast and/or live sports event. Critique the program based on the production and producing value. What would you change or add? What was done well?

Glossary of Key Terms

Note: Please visit the website dedicated for this book at http://www.oup.com/us/kian for more information, including terminology and key terms used in content on various sports.

Access: The ability of sports reporters to be able to cover, interview and report on sports teams and figures. The level of access (e.g., attaining a pressbox pass or field pass) often depends on the individual (player, coach) or organization (school, professional league, etc.) involved.

Advance story: A preview or look-ahead on a game or event published before it happens.

Agenda: As it relates to sports public relations, the unique set of perspectives, goals and attitudes each stakeholder brings to the communication process. As one example, when an athlete gets arrested, the athlete, her/his team and the media often have conflicting agendas in responding to the crisis.

Anchor: The person who delivers sports content to audiences through broadcasting in a live studio or preproduced format.

Aperture: Opening in the lens that light passes through. The amount of light exposed is determined via f/stops (f/2, f/4, etc.).

AP Sports Style: The *Associated Press Stylebook* rules and guidelines for sports writing that are generally followed by most newspapers, magazines and credible online outlets.

Axis Line/180-Line: This is an imaginary line that runs in front of the camera's position. It is used to guide the on-screen spatial relationship between characters.

Beat: The primary team, league, sport, sports or level of sports that a sports reporter covers as part of their job duties (e.g., Los Angeles Lakers beat reporter, Major League Baseball insider, high school sports editor, etc.).

Boosterism (or homerisim): The tendency of sports outlets to give favorable coverage to local athletes and teams, most often done so as not to upset local audiences or advertisers.

Broadcasting: The delivery of events, news and information through television, radio and the Internet with content designed to reach the largest possible audiences.

Call screener: Off-air broadcasting role that is responsible for filtering phone calls being made to a sports talk show.

Citizen journalism: The ability of media audiences to become media content creators and distributors, and thus become more active participants in the media process. This is typically driven by platforms such as YouTube, Facebook and other user-generated sites.

Clip file: A collection of your best writing work, which you send to potential employers along with a résumé and cover letter.

Color commentator: Also called an analyst, the person who works with the play-by-play broadcaster, mainly to offer analysis, perspective and deeper understanding of the game action.

Column: Usually an opinion article/essay published in a newspaper or online source, which also includes the columnist's photo. Most columnists write recurring or regular columns for their print outlets, which ideally become well-known to regular readers.

Comment: A written response to a post on Facebook or on an online site's talk-back forum.

Conflict of interest: Any external or internal relationship that threatens the integrity or objectivity of the sports reporting. An example of internal conflict would be a news manager requesting a sports reporter to give favorable coverage to an event. External conflict could be an advertiser threatening to remove ads for the same reason.

Cover letter: A short introductory letter or email, generally not more than one page, which introduces you to a potential employer, indicates the job you are applying for, and describes the qualifications and experience that make you an ideal candidate for that job.

Crisis communication: A sports public relations strategy in which the stakeholders are responding to potentially damaging news or information. Many outlets have crisis communication plans that are developed in advance and that attempt to anticipate potential problems.

Crisis strategies: Specific responses to crisis public relations situations. These can vary greatly and include such responses as denial, shifting blame, stonewalling and accepting responsibility.

Cut-aways: These are typically short nonaction shots used to help tell the story, and to fill time between edited plays. These can include shots of fans, cheerleaders, scoreboard, coaches, etc.

Deadlines: Set times (e.g., 10:30 p.m.) or time period (e.g., 15 minutes after the game ends) when sports reporters must file or submit their content to editors and producers.

Demo reel: A collection of your best broadcasting work, generally organized with the most impressive material at the front. The demo reel is normally curated online, and is sent digitally to potential employers.

Depth-of-field: Refers to the range of focus between the closest object and farthest object within the image. It is determined by aperture size, distance from lens and the focal length of the lens.

Digital manipulation: The ability of technologies (such as Photoshop) to alter the content of visual images in order to change their fundamental meaning or give a false impression of reality.

Digital sports media: Sports media content that can be created, modified, viewed and distributed through digital, electronic platforms (e.g., Internet, social media).

Direct message: A private message on Twitter between two or more accounts.

Edit in the camera: This means that you sequence your shots in the field in a pre-edited fashion. For example, you would record on :06 of a wide shot then hit the pause button and refocus on a close/up shot–hit record for :03 then hit the pause button and refocus on a medium shot–hit record for :04.

Enterprise reporting: In-depth and deeper examinations on complex, historical and/or culturally relevant topics that often result in a series of articles, broadcasts or a full multimedia package (e.g., an enterprise package consisting of a main story, sidebar and video feature).

Facebook: A data-rich social network that focuses on the interaction of profiles created as digital proxies for individuals.

Facebook Live: A streaming video service natively hosted by Facebook, allowing for users to interact with audiences on the network while streaming live video.

Facebook page: A business or nonpersonal account on Facebook. Pages allow users to "like" the business without sharing intimate details of their own personal profiles.

Facebook profile: A personal account on Facebook belonging to a private individual. The profile is self-populated with information by the user.

Features: Usually human interest, in-depth profiles on an athlete(s), coach, team or event.

Focal length/lens: In basic terms, this refers to the zoom capability of your camera. It is measured in millimeters. For every 100mm in lens focal length you get about 10 yards of coverage.

FOIA (Freedom of Information Act): A federal law that grants public access to most information possessed by the federal government. Most states have similar laws, although the type and amount of information available to the public varies by states.

Gamers: A print sports article that focuses on a sports game or event. This is the most common type of article appearing in newspaper sports sections.

Graphic element: These can be pictures that appear in the upper left or right corner of the frame (over the shoulder — OTS — of the talent). It may also be a full screen image (e.g., a map or statistics).

Hashtag: A searchable word or phrase primarily used in Twitter, but also available in Instagram and Facebook, used primarily as a grouping mechanism for particular tweet topics.

Insider reporter: A sports reporter who specializes in providing exclusive information, usually from inside sources. Jay Glazer (NFL) and Ken Rosenthal (MLB) of Fox Sports are examples of league-specific information reporters. ESPN actually dubs such reporters as "insiders."

Instagram: A social network where users share images with each other.

Inverted pyramid style: The most basic and common method for AP-style sports print reporting, which emphasizes putting the most important information in a print story toward the beginning because content is often cut from the bottom by editors, and readers often stop reading after a few paragraphs. The 5 Ws (who, what, where, when and how) generally should appear within the first five paragraphs of most sports articles.

ISO (International Standards Organization): This determines the camera's sensitivity and ability to capture light. Lower numbers mean the less your camera is sensitive to light. ISO along with shutter speed and aperture determine light exposure in your camera. It begins with 100 and doubles from there (100, 200, 400, 800, etc.).

Lead (or lede): Usually the first paragraph of a print sports article, although it can be the first two to five paragraphs if they flow together. Usually a feature-style or human-interest in nature if writing for the independent press, or a straight AP-style sports lead that includes the 5 Ws (who, what, where, when, why).

Lead story: The story that has the greatest impact on your audience, and thus should lead or begin a show (if on radio or television) or be placed at or near the top of a print or online article.

Libel: The publication of false information about someone that injures or damages that individual in some way. It usually refers to written defamation, but has also come to include slander, which is spoken.

Like: An action on Facebook indicating a positive reaction toward a story, a page or a profile on the network.

Mass media convergence: Used to describe the trend toward corporate consolidation of mass media outlets and partnerships across media.

Media convergence: From a skills and practitioner standpoint, this means the mixing of multimedia content produced and disseminated across multiple platforms (e.g., broadcast, print article, social media, podcast, video, etc.) and potentially through different media (e.g., Internet sites, magazines, newspapers, social media, television, radio).

Multimedia reporting: The reporting of a single sports story across multiple platforms — any or all combinations of broadcast, print, Web and social media — so as to reach diverse audiences.

Narrowcasting: The evolution of broadcasting, thanks to new technologies, into a system where content is designed for smaller, targeted niche audiences.

News cycle: The length of time it takes new information to cycle through to audiences. Thanks to technology, the news cycle is constantly decreasing, from days (newspapers and magazines) to hours (television and radio) to seconds (Internet and social media).

News feed: The core information feed for all Facebook users. This information feed uses an algorithm to personalize the news displayed for each user, based on their prior actions and preferences.

Online host: A Web site or service that houses sports podcasts.

Online portfolios: A website, usually with your own domain name, to house your résumé, contact info, links and sample multimedia works.

Package: Broadcast stories in a complete "package" that includes video, sound and reporter narration.

Periscope: A live video streaming service operated by Twitter.

Personal brand: The ability of the sports anchor or reporter to create audience attachment to himself or herself rather than the media outlet. Bill Simmons is an example of someone with a strong personal brand. Such a brand is particularly important to develop in the digital era of social media and broad audiences.

Personalization: Incorporating the personal side of the sports story — such as feelings and emotions — rather than just giving a description of the story's basic events. Also called "humanizing" a story.

Play-by-play: The broadcast description of a sporting event that primarily focuses on telling the live unfolding of events.

Podcast: A sports talk format that is entirely prerecorded, and generally contains longer and more in-depth periods of discussion than sports talk radio shows.

Producer: Person responsible for the show's content, timing and flow. Basically this person is responsible for all elements of the show.

Production assistant (PA) (also called a field producer): This person assists the producer by providing detailed content information. He or she makes sure the talent is prepared by providing information on players, tournament, course or field, statistics, etc.

Quotes: Comments put into sports media content from those involved in the action (e.g., players, coaches, front office staff, etc.) or with expertise.

Résumé: A one or two sheet summarization of your career, including job experiences, skills and educational background.

Retweet: The Twitter version of a "share"; this allows a user to either directly copy a tweet into their own timeline, or provide commentary on a tweet that they have quoted in their timeline.

RSS: A syndication feed that allows podcasts to be found by special software programs.

Rundown: Table that lists the show's content in the order of appearance and contains items such as story slug, format or type of story, story length, position number, graphic or still store information, talent name and total run time of the show.

Share: An action taken on both Facebook and Instagram, allowing for a user to copy a story or post from another timeline and insert it into their own timeline.

Shutter Speed: This is a measurement of time the shutter is open when taking pictures. It is the time the digital sensor/film is exposed to light. It is usually measured in seconds or fraction of seconds (1/2, 1/200, 1/500, etc.). The faster the shutter speed, the less time the image is exposed to light.

Sidebar: An article that appears in a print or online source usually to accompany a primary story on a game or event. Sidebars generally focus on a key player, a moment during a contest, a trend, etc., and are generally not as long as the primary story.

Sideline: A broadcast position where the reporter is stationed on or near the playing surface, providing occasional updates throughout the game.

Sideline reporter: The person of the broadcast team of a live sporting event who watches and reports from the sidelines or field level. Typically, this person reports information that is not directly obvious by watching the game, such as injury updates.

Skills: Job-related abilities, which are not necessarily related to a single past employer. For instance, working at a television station would not be a skill, but being able to effectively edit video in *Final Cut* is a skill.

Snapchat: A private messaging application that sends messages filled with images and/or video to selected lists of users. Utilized by brands to deliver directed messages to younger audiences.

Social media: Digital media that has interactivity with other users as a core element of its functionality.

Soundcloud: A branded online hosting service for audio files, including podcasts.

Sources: Individuals with insight and/or expertise who provide information for stories. They are generally quoted on the record, but — depending on the type of story and rules or norms of your media outlet — can occasionally be cited anonymously.

Sports information director: The person at a school or organization in charge of handling the relationship between the organization/athletes/coaches/teams and the media.

The SID is typically in charge of creating and distributing content for media, regulating media access to players/coaches, supporting the organization's institutional goals, and dealing with the media in crisis situations. People in this profession are now often called athletics communications directors or sports communications directors at the intercollegiate level, and media relations directors or communications managers at the professional level of sport.

Spotting board: A two-sided sheet of paper that contains roster notes, statistical information and storylines about the players and teams in a broadcast. Used by broadcasters as an informational aid during the broadcast.

Stacking: The process of placing stories in the order they will appear in the sportscast.

Stakeholders: The various constituencies related to a particular story that the sports reporter will incorporate into the story. If a high-profile athlete is arrested on drug charges, the stakeholders could include the athlete, her or his coach/teammates and police.

Story slug: This simply is the name of the story. It is typically one or two words that identifies the main theme of the story.

Storytelling: The delivery of sports content that usually includes a main story theme or idea and the support of that theme, presented in an interesting and compelling way.

Theme: Also called the hook or angle, it is the point of the story the sports reporter is trying to tell. All stories should develop and support a simple, basic theme that the audience can understand.

Timeline: A feature of both Facebook and Twitter. A Facebook user's timeline is filled with posts that they have made, while a Twitter timeline is filled with posts from accounts that they have followed. Both timelines display messages in reverse chronological order.

TRT (total run time): The actual accumulated time within the show. Each story's time is added to the previous thus building the cumulated show time.

Tweet: An individual, publicly viewable message on Twitter. Currently tweets are limited to 140 characters, including spaces.

Twitter: A social network that emphasizes short messages and instantaneous communication between online users.

Web 2.0: The high-speed, interconnected, interactive and easily accessible Internet and social media platforms that are prevalent today, which evolved from the static screens and limited features of Web 1.0 (i.e., the Internet of the 1990s and early 2000s).

References

Adgate, B. (2013, April 4). Can sports help radio fight disruption the way they help TV? *Ad Age*. Retrieved from http://adage.com/article/media/sports-save-radio-pandora-spotify/240697/

Ahead of the curve. (2010, August 5). Panel presentation at the national convention for the Association of Education in Journalism and Mass Communication, Denver, Colo.

Allen, Jason. (2013). Disappearing diversity? FCC deregulation and the effect on minority station ownership. *Indiana Journal of Law and Social Equality (2)*1: 230–247.

Almasy, Steve. (2015, August 26). Curt Schilling suspended by ESPN after controversial tweet. *CNN*. Retrieved from http://www.cnn.com/2015/08/25/us/curt-schilling-insensitive-tweet/

Alonso, M. (2014, September 10). Ray Rice: A social media case study. *Social Media Today*. Retrieved from http://www.socialmediatoday.com/content/ray-rice-social-media-case-study

Anderson, D. A. (1994). *Contemporary sports reporting* (2nd ed.). Chicago: Nelson- Hall.

Badenhausen, Kurt. (2015, July 15). The world's 50 most valuable sports teams 2015. *Forbes*. Retrieved from http://www.forbes.com/sites/kurtbadenhausen/2015/07/15/the-worlds-50-most-valuable-sports-teams-2015/

Barrett Sports Media (2015, August 31). Are you willing to break the rules? *Barrett Sports Media*. Retrieved from http://sportsradiopd.com/2015/08/are-you-willing-to-break-the-rules-to-be-great/

Barrett Sports Media (2016, February 4). America's top 20 national sports talk shows of 2015 are. . . . *Barrett Sports Media*. Retrieved from http://sportsradiopd.com/2016/02/americas-top-20-national-sports-talk-shows-are/

Barthel, M. (2016, June 15). 5 key takeaways about the state of the news media in 2016. *Pew Research Center*. Retrieved from http://www.pewresearch.org/fact-tank/2016/06/15/state-of-the-news-media-2016-key-takeaways/

Baughman, J. L. (1993, March). Television comes to America 1947–57. *Illinois History*. Retrieved from http://www.lib.niu.edu/1993/ihy930341.html

Beaujon, Andrew. (2014, June 19). Here's a list of outlets and journalists who won't use the name "Redskins." *Poynter Institute*. Retrieved from http://www.poynter.org/news/mediawire/256258/heres-a-list-of-outlets-and-journalists-who-wont-use-the-name-redskins/

Begley, Ian. (2009, January 6). Jets' Jenn Sterger does the impossible: She makes Gang Green look good. New York *Daily News*. Retrieved from http://www.nydailynews.com/sports/football/jets/jets-jenn-sterger-impossible-gang-green-good-article-1.421020

Belson, K. & Isaac, M. (2016, April 5). Twitter gains rights to stream Thursday NFL games. *New York Times*. Retrieved from http://www.nytimes.com/2016/04/06/sports/football/nfl-will-stream-thursday-games-on-twitter.html

Benoit, W. (1995). *Accounts, excuses, and apologies: A theory of image restoration strategies*. Albany: State University of New York Press.

Berg, Ted. (2015, August 31). Jessica Mendoza draws rave reviews in historic Sunday Night Baseball debut. Retrieved from http://ftw.usatoday.com/2015/08/jessica-mendoza-espn-sunday-night-baseball-mlb

Berr, J. (2014, October 6). Disney and TNT go all in on a new NBA TV deal. *CBS Money Watch*. Retrieved from http://www.cbsnews.com/news/espn-and-tnt-go-all-in-on-a-new-nba-tv-deal/

Bien, L. (2014, November 28). A complete timeline of the Ray Rice assault case. *SB Nation*. Retrieved from http://www.sbnation.com/nfl/2014/5/23/5744964/ray-rice-arrest-assault-statement-apology-ravens

Billings, A .C., Butterworth, M. L., & Turman, P. D. (2015). *Communication and sport: Surveying the field* (2nd ed.). Los Angeles: Sage.

Bishop, R. (2003). Missing in action: Feature coverage of women's sports in *Sports Illustrated*. *Journal of Sport and Social Issues, 27*(2), 184–194.

Blum, R. (2004, January 6). Rose details betting. *Associated Press*. Retrieved from http://archive/boston.com/sports/baseball/articles/2004/01/06/rose_details_betting/

Bouton, Jim. (1981). *Ball four plus ball five*. New York: Stein & Day.

Boyd, Jimmy. (2015, January 26). Super Bowl commercial prices. *Boyds Bets*. Retrieved from http://www.boydsbets.com/super-bowl-commercial-prices/

Bryant, J., & Holt, A. M. (2006). A historical overview of sports and media in the United States. In A. A. Raney & J. Bryant (Eds.), *Handbook of Sports and Media* (pp. 21–43). Mahwah, N.J.: Lawrence Erlbaum Associates.

Butler, B., Zimmerman, M. H., & Hutton, S. (2013). Turning the page with newspapers: Influence of the Internet on sports coverage. In P. M. Pedersen (Ed.), *Handbook of sport communication* (pp. 219–227). London: Routledge.

Cantor, George. (1997). *The Tigers of '68: Baseball's last real champions*. Lanham, Md.: Taylor Trade.

Careers in sports: Play-by-play announcer. (1999, September 7). *ESPN*. Retrieved from http://www.espn.go.com/special/s/careers/anno.html

Carmody, Deirdre. (1994, June 25). Time responds to criticism over Simpson cover. *New York Times*. Retrieved from http://www.nytimes.com/1994/06/25/us/time-responds-to-criticism-over-simpson-cover.html

Chandler, R. (2008, September 16). The National Anthem? Josh Howard "doesn't celebrate that s***." *Deadspin*. Retrieved from http://deadspin.com/5050396/the-national-anthem-josh-howard-doesnt-celebrate-that-s

Chase, C. (2014, February 16). Bode Miller broke down in NBC interview talking about his late brother. *USA Today*. Retrieved from http://ftw.usatoday.com/2014/02/bode-miller-brother-nbc-interview

Chase, Chris. (2014, September 4). Fox's Pam Oliver was "humiliated" at being replaced by Erin Andrews. *USA Today*. Retrieved from http://ftw.usatoday.com/2014/09/pam-oliver-fox-erin-andrews-demotion-humiliated-essence

Chatelain, D. (2015, September 1). New Husker PA announcer Jon Schuetz loses job over Facebook post criticizing Nebraska chancellor. *Omaha World-Herald*. Retrieved from http://www.omaha.com/huskers/new-husker-p-a-announcer-jon-schuetz-loses-job-over/article_07e6db14-50ef-11e5-8a50-63b3ceb0ae69.html

Clapp, Brian. (June 29, 2015). A day in the life of producing live sports. Workinsports.com. Retrieved December 10, 2015 from http://www.workinsports.com/blog/live-sports-production-day-in-the-life/#sthash.P7qK2Cmi.dpuf

Constine, J. (2013, August 13). Facebook reveals 78% of US users are mobile as it starts sharing user counts by country. *TechCrunch.com*. Retrieved from http://techcrunch.com/2013/08/13/facebook-mobile-user-count/

Cooky, C., Messner, M. A., & Hextrum, R. H. (2013). Women play sport, but not on TV: A longitudinal study of televised news media. *Communication & Sport 1*(3): 203–230.

Culpepper, C. (2016, April 4). Kris Jenkins hits buzzer-beating three-pointer to lift Villanova past North Carolina for NCAA title. *The Washington Post* online. Retrieved from https://www.washingtonpost.com/sports/colleges/kris-jenkins-hits-buzzer-beating-three-pointer-to-lift-villanova-past-north-carolina-for-ncaa-championship/2016/04/04/d9a0a136-fa99-11e5-886f-a037dba38301_story.html

Dalrymple, Jim II. (2014, December 10). Fox suspends sports reporter over "I Can't Breathe" comments. *Buzz Feed News*. Retrieved from http://www.buzzfeed.com/jimdalrympleii/fox-suspends-sports-reporter-over-i-cant-breathe-comments#.nm3epGMNr

Deitsch, R. (2015, May 3). An in-depth look at ESPN Audio and the future of sports talk radio. *SI.com*. Retrieved from http://www.si.com/more-sports/2015/03/02/espn-audio-sports-radio-qa-noise-report

Deitsch, R. (2016, June 26). Should sports media members discuss politics publicly? *SI.com*. Retrieved from http://www.si.com/tech-media/2016/06/26/media-circus-sports-media-politics-michele-tafoya-adam-schefter-jemele-hill

DiCaro, J. (2015, September 28). Threats. Vitriol. Hate. Ugly truth about women in sports and social media. *Sports Illustrated*. Retrieved from http://www.si.com/cauldron/2015/09/27/twitter-threats-vile-remarks-women-sports-journalists

D'Onfro, J. (2015, July 29). Facebook beats earnings expectations, but the stock sinks. *Business Insider*. Retrieved from http//www.businessinsider.com/facebook-q2-earnings-2015-7.

Facebook. (2015, September 23). Facebook reports second quarter 2015 results. Facebook.com. Retrieved from http://investor.fb.com/releasedetail.cfm?ReleaseID=924562

Fainaru-Wada's statement to the court. (2006, September 22). *San Francisco Chronicle*, A14.

Fang, Ken. (2014, May 7). U.S. Olympic broadcast rights fees since 1960. *Fang's bites*. Retrieved from http://fangsbites.com/abc-sports/u-s-olympics-broadcast-rights-fees-since-1960.html

Fisher, E. (2015, March 13). ESPN leads ComScore rankings for 12th-straight month with 74.7 unique visitors. *Street&Smith's SportsBusiness Daily*. Retrieved from http://www.sportsbusinessdaily.com/Daily/Issues/2015/03/13/Media/ComScore.aspx

Flint, J. (2016, April 12). CBS, Turner strike $8.8 billion deal to televise NCAA's March Madness through 2032. *The Wall Street Journal*. Retrieved from http://www.wsj.com/articles/cbs-turner-strike-8-8-billion-deal-to-keep-ncaa-mens-basketball-tournament-through-2032-1460484096

Fry, J. (2010, May 15). ESPN wins the courtship of Bill Simmons. *Deadspin*. Retrieved from http://deadspin.com/5539777/espn-wins-the-courtship-of-bill-simmons

Gardner, Eriq. (2015, May 8). HBO beats defamation lawsuit at trial. *Hollywood Reporter.* Retrieved from http://www.hollywoodreporter.com/thr-esq/hbo-beats-defamation-lawsuit-at-794471

Garrison, B., & Sabljak, M. (1993). *Sports reporting* (2nd ed.). Ames: Iowa State University Press.

Garrubbo, G. (2016, May 24). NPR tops Podtrac's new podcast audience ranker. *WPSU. org.* Retrieved from http://radio.wpsu.org/post/npr-tops-podtracs-new-podcast-audience-ranker

Gisondi, J. (2011). *Field guide to covering sports.* Washington, D.C.: CQ Press.

Glasspiegel, R. (2016, May 31). Bill Simmons is trying something ambitious, but he's not an underdog. *The Big Lead.* Retrieved from http://thebiglead.com/2016/05/31/bill-simmons-is-trying-something-ambitious-but-hes-not-an-underdog/

Gordon, A. (2014, May 14). Lights, action, action! Shooting live sports. Retrieved from http://videoandfilmmaker.com/wp/index.php/features/lights-action-action-shooting-live-sports/

Greenfield, K. T. (2012). ESPN everywhere sports profit network. *Bloomberg.* Retrieved from http://www.bloomberg.com/news/articles/2012-08-30/espn-everywhere-sports-profit-network

Groden, Claire. (2015, August 6). This is how much a 2016 Super Bowl ad costs. *Fortune.* Retrieved from http://fortune.com/2015/08/06/super-bowl-ad-cost/

Halberstam, David. (1989). *Summer of '49.* New York: Avon Books.

Hardin, M., & Whiteside, E. (2006). Fewer women, minorities work in sports departments. *Newspaper Research Journal 27*(2): 38–51.

Hardin, M., & Zhong, B. (2010). Sports reporters' attitudes about ethics vary based on beat. *Newspaper Research Journal 31*(2): 6–19.

Hardy, R. (2015, June 21). Every keyboard shortcut that you will ever need for premiere pro & after effects. Retrieved from http://nofilmschool.com/2015/06/every-keyboard-shortcut-you-will-ever-need-premiere-pro-and-after-effects

Heisler, Y. (2015, December, 2011). Cable providers still have no answer for Netflix as cord-cutting accelerates. BGR.com. Retrieved from http://bgr.com/2015/10/08/cable-tv-vs-netflix-cord-cutting/

Hinckley, D. (2010, February 19). Tiger Woods apology: Golfer's mouth said "I'm sorry," demeanor said "I don't want to be here." New York *Daily News.* Retrieved from http://www.nydailynews.com/entertainment/tv-movies/tiger-woods-apology-golfer-mouth-demeanor-don-article-1.195608

Hottie topic. (2000, December 25–January 1). *Sports Illustrated.*

Hurley, M. (2015, February 5). Hurley: Failed deflategate accusations mean it's time for Irsay, Pagano to be banned from NFL. *WBZ-TV.* Retrieved from http://boston.cbslocal.com/2015/02/05/hurley-failed-deflategate-accusations-means-its-time-for-irsay-pagano-to-be-banned-from-nfl/

Inabinett, Mark. (1994). *Grantland Rice and his heroes: The sportswriter as mythmaker in the 1920s.* Knoxville: University of Tennessee Press.

Jenn Sterger weighs in on Ines Sainz: "She accomplished exactly what she set out to do." (2010, September 16). *Deadspin.* Retrieved from http://deadspin.com/5639946/jenn-sterger-weighs-in-on-ines-sainz-she-accomplished-exactly-what-she-set-out-to-do

Jocks & Jill: CBS' Arrington featured in photo spread in FHM. (2002, August 14). *Sports Business Daily.* Retrieved from http://www.sportsbusinessdaily.com/Daily/Issues/2002/08/Issue-226/Sports-Media/Jocks-Jill-CBS-Arrington-Featured-In-Photo-Spread-In-FHM.aspx

Jurgensen, J. (2015, August 27). Men in blazers: Soccer's outlier sportscasters. *Wall Street Journal*. Retrieved from http://www.wsj.com/articles/men-in-blazers-soccers-outlier-sportscasters-1440687946

Kain, Meredith. (September 14, 2014). 10 tips for shooting live sporting events with a small crew. Crews Control. Retrieved December 17, 2015 from http://crewscontrol.com/blog-central/10-tips-for-shooting-live-sporting-events-with-a-small-crew/

Ketchum, Geoff. (2006, October 25). "Is that my son?" Yes, and a hero to boot. *Austin American-Statesman*. Retrieved from http://www.statesman.com/sports/content/sports/stories/longhorns/10/25/25bailey.html

Ketterer, S., McGuire, J., & Murray, R. (2014). Contrasting desired sports journalism skills in a convergent media environment. *Communication & Sport 2*(3): 282–298.

Key events in the Ray Rice story. (2014, September 14). *CNN*. Retrieved from http://www.cnn.com/2014/09/09/us/ray-rice-timeline/

Kian, E. M., Ketterer, S., Nichols, C., & Poling, J. (2014). Watchdogs of the Fourth Estate or homer journalists? Small and mid-sized newspaper coverage of local BCS college football programs. *The Sport Journal, 17*. Retrieved from http://thesportjournal.org/article /watchdogs-of-the-fourth-estate-or-homer-journalists-newspaper-coverage-of-local-bcs-college-football-programs/.

Kian, E. M., & Murray, R. (2014). Curmudgeons but yet adapters: Impact of Web 2.0 and Twitter on newspaper sports journalists' jobs, responsibilities, and routines. *#ISOJ, 4*(1): 61–77.

Kian, E. M., & Zimmerman, M. H. (2012). The medium of the future: Top sports writers discuss transitioning from newspapers to online journalism. *International Journal of Sport Communication, 5*: 285–304.

Kurtz, Howard. (1993). *Media circus*. New York: Times Books.

Kurtz, Howard. (2010, August 31). Post sportswriter Mike Wise suspended for Roethlisberger hoax on Twitter. *Washington Post*. Retrieved from http://www. washingtonpost.com/wp-dyn/content/article/2010/08/31/ AR2010083104105.html

Lamb, C. (2012). *Conspiracy of silence: Sportswriters and the long campaign to desegregate baseball*. Lincoln: University of Nebraska Press.

Lapchick, R. (2015, June 10). *The 2014 Associated Press sports editors racial and gender report card*. Retrieved from http://nebula.wsimg.com/038bb0ccc9436494ebee1430174c13a0?AccessKeyId=DAC3A56D8FB782449D2A&disposition=0&alloworigin=1

Laucella, P. C. (2014). From print to online sports journalism. In A. Billings & M. Hardin (Eds.), *The Routledge Handbook of Sport and New Media* (pp. 89–100). London: Routledge.

Lieberman, Trudy. (2015, June 18). Questions about Mayo Clinic deal with Minneapolis TV station. *Health News Review*. Retrieved from http://www. healthnewsreview.org/2015/06/questions-about-mayo-clinic-deal-with-minneapolis-tv-station/

Lombardi, T. (2015, March 3). Ray Rice didn't deserve another cent! *Russell Street Report*. Retrieved from http://russellstreetreport.com/2015/03/03/word-on-the-street/ray-rice-didnt-deserve-another-cent/

Lutz, A. (2012, June 14). These 6 corporations control 90% of the Media in America. *BusinessInsider.com*. Retrieved from http://www.businessinsider.com/these-6-corporations-control-90-of-the-media-in-america-2012-6

Maese, R. (2014, September 2). Adam Schefter is NFL reporting machine. *The Washington Post online*. Retrieved from https://www.washingtonpost.com/sports/redskins/adam-schefter-is-nfl-reporting-machine/2014/09/02/93e009f2-32cc-11e4-9f4d-24103cb8b742_story.html

Manahan, Kevin. (2015, July 24). ESPN's Colin Cowherd makes another silly racist comment. *New Jersey Advance Media.* Retrieved from http://www.nj.com/sports/index. ssf/2015/07/is_colin_cowherd_a_racist_recent_comments_seem_to. html

McChesney, R. W. (1989). Media made sport: A history of sports coverage in the United States. In L. A. Wenner (Ed.), *Media, sports & society* (pp. 49–69). Newbury Park, Calif.: Sage.

McGuire, J. P., & Murray, R. (2013). Attitudes of sport print journalists developing electronic media skills: Study of two major newspapers. *International Journal of Sport Communication* 6(4): 464–477.

McManus, Jane. (2013, September 11). Sainz incident helped Jets grow up. *ESPN.* Retrieved from http://espn.go.com/newyork/columns/nfl/story/_/id/9658974/new-york-jets-ines-sainz-incident-helped-spark-change-jets-locker-room

Miller, Monica R. (2013). *Religion and hip hop.* New York: Routledge.

Mink, P. (2014, March 24). Steve Bisciotti shows compassion for Ray Rice. *Baltimoreravens. com.* Retrieved from http://www.baltimoreravens.com/news/article-1/Steve-Bisciotti-Shows-Compassion-For-Ray-Rice/7ae432d7-bebb-4d41-981d-3166b525981c

Miracle, R. (2007, January). Sports photography. Retrieved from http://photo.net/learn/ sports/overview

Myers, Gary. (2014, January 28). Seahawks' Marshawn Lynch not doing himself any favors with Super Bowl Media Day silence. New York *Daily News.* Retrieved from http://www.nydailynews.com/sports/football/myers-super-bowl-confidential-silence-not-golden-lynch-article-1.1594861

New York *Daily News* to stop use of term "Redskins." (2014, September 3). *Sports Illustrated.* Retrieved from http://www.si.com/nfl/2014/09/03/redskins-new-york-daily-news-stop-term-nfl-controversial

Nielsen Research. (2014, March 10). Sports fans amplify the action across screens. Retrieved from http://www.nielsen.com/us/en/insights/news/2014/sports-fans-amplify-the-action-across-screens.html

Nine for IX: Let Them Wear Towels. (2013). [Producers: Annie Sundberg and Ricki Stern]. *ESPN Films.*

Official Adobe Premiere Keyboard Shortcuts. Retrieved from https://helpx.adobe.com/ premiere-pro/using/default-keyboard-shortcuts-cc.html

O'Keefe, Michael. (2014, September 19). Jenn Sterger, TV personality allegedly harassed by Brett Favre, blasts NFL's handling of violence. New York *Daily News.* Retrieved from http://www.nydailynews.com/sports/football/jets/exclusive-tv-star-harassed-brett-favre-blasts-nfl-handling-violence-article-1.1945121

Ortiz, M. (2011, June 27). Amy Jo Martin blazes trials with Shaq. *ESPN.* Retrieved from http:// sports.espn.go.com/espn/page2/story?page=burnsortiz-110627_amy_jo_martin

Ourand, J. (2009, June 22). ESPN sends strong signal on role of podcasts. *Street&Smith's SportsBusiness Daily.* Retrieved from http://www.sportsbusinessdaily.com/Journal/ Issues/2009/06/20090622/This-Weeks-News/ESPN-Sends-Strong-Signal-On-Role-Of-Podcasts.aspx

Papper, B. (2012). *RTNDA-Ball State University Annual Survey.* Washington, D.C.: Radio-Television Digital News Association.

Papper, Bob. (2013, July 29). Little change for women, minorities in TV/radio. *Radio-Television Digital News Association.* Retrieved from http://www.rtdna.org/ article/ little_change_for_women_minorities_in_tv_radio#.VCCTGfldV20

Pedersen, P.M. (2014). The changing role of sports media producers. In A. C. Billings & M. Hardin (Eds.), *Routledge handbook of sport and new media* (pp. 101–109). London: Routledge.

Pedersen, P.M., Laucella, P., Kian, E.M., & Geurin, A. (2016). *Strategic sport communication* (2nd ed.). Champaign, Ill.: Human Kinetics.

Pennsylvania State University. (2012). *Schools across country increase focus on sports communication.* Retrieved from http://news.psu.edu/story/152329/2012/01/23/schools-across-country-increase-focus-sports-communication

Plaschke, Bill. (2000, January–February). The reporter. *Columbia Journalism Review*, 43–44.

Raptopolous, Lilah. (2014, June 17). The OJ Simpson case 20 years later: Making "trials into television." *The Guardian.* Retrieved from http://www.theguardian.com/ world/2014/jun/17/oj-simpson-trial-cameras-court-justice-culture.

Reinardy, S., & Wanta, W. (2015). *The essentials of sports reporting and writing* (2nd ed.). New York: Routledge.

Rhoden, William. (1992, April 9). An emotional Ashe says that he has AIDS. *New York Times.* Retrieved from http://www.nytimes.com/1992/04/09/sports/an-emotional-ashe-says-that-he-has-aids.html?pagewanted=all

Rovell, D. (2014, October 6). NBA in unique position with TV deal. *ESPN.com.* Retrieved from http://espn.go.com/nba/story/_/id/11653435/new-tv-deal-shows-league-unique-position

Ryan, S. (2016, June 20). Why aren't more women working in sports radio? *Chicago Tribune.* Retrieved from http://www.chicagotribune.com/sports/ct-women-sports-radio-spt-0621-20160620-story.html

Rydberg, M. (2015, August). 8 top tips: How to make an action sports video edit. Retrieved from http://www.boardseekermag.com/longform/8-top-tips-how-to-make-an-action-sports-video-edit/#m31wejWrwZ2QYZs6.97

Sandomir, Richard. (2004, June 17). Honesty, not salary, cost Albert his job.*New York Times.* Retrieved from http://www.nytimes.com/2004/06/17/sports/tv-sports-honesty-not-salary-cost-albert-his-job.html?_r=0

Sandomir, Richard. (2014, February 17). NBC pushes too far in bringing Bode Miller to tears. *New York Times.* Retrieved from http://www.nytimes.com/2014/02/17/sports/olympics/nbc-pushes-too-far-in-bringing-bode-miller-to-tears.html?_r=0

Sandomir, R. (2014, May 7). NBC extends Olympic deal into unknown. *New York Times.* Retrieved from http://www.nytimes.com/2014/05/08/sports/olympics/nbc-extends-olympic-tv-deal-through-2032.html?_r=0

Schultz, B., & Arke, E. (2015). *Sports media: Reporting, producing, and planning* (3rd ed.). New York: Routledge.

Schultz, B., Caskey, P. H., & Esherick, C. (2014). *Media relations in sport* (4th ed.). Morgantown, W.Va.: Fitness Information Technology.

Schultz, Brad & Sheffer, Mary Lou (2007). Sports journalists who blog cling to traditional values. *Newspaper Research Journal, 28*(4), 62–76.

Schultz, B., & Wei, W. (2013). Sports broadcasting: History, technology, and implications. In P. M. Pedersen (Ed.) *Routledge Handbook of Sport Communication.* New York: Routledge.

Seeger, M.W. (2006). Best practices in crisis communication: An expert panel process. *Journal of Applied Communication Research 34*(3): 232–244.

Sessler, M. (2014, September 9). Bisciotti: "Decision to let Ray Rice go was unanimous." *nfl.com.* Retrieved from http://www.nfl.com/news/story/0ap3000000392323/article/bisciotti-decision-to-let-ray-rice-go-was-unanimous

Settimi, C. (2014, March 26). MLB's most valuable television deals. *Forbes.* Retrieved from http://www.forbes.com/sites/christinasettimi/2014/03/26/mlbs-most-valuable-television-deals/#20a161563491

Shapiro, Michael. (2000, January–February). The fan. *Columbia Journalism Review*: 50–51.

Smith, C. (2015, January 16). Could a Super Bowl commercial really be worth $10 million? Surprisingly, yes. *Forbes*. Retrieved from http://www.forbes.com/sites/chrissmith/2015/01/16/could-a-super-bowl-commercial-really-be-worth-10-million/

Smithson, J., & Venette, S. (2013). Stonewalling as an image-defense strategy: A critical examination of BP's response to the Deepwater Horizon explosion. *Communication Studies, 64,* 393–410.

Soltys, M. (2011). Social Networking. *ESPN Front Row.com*. Retrieved from http://www.espnfrontrow.com/2011/08/social-networking/

Sowell, M. (2008). The birth of national sports coverage: An examination of the *New York Herald's* use of the telegraph to report America's first "championship" boxing match in 1849. *Journal of Sports Media 3*(1): 51–75.

Sports-talk radio host. (1999, September 7). *ESPN*. Retrieved from http://espn.go.com/special/s/careers/sptalk.html

Stofer, K. T., Schaffer, J. R., & Rosenthal, B. A. (2010). *Sports journalism: An introduction to reporting and writing.* Lanham, Md.: Rowman & Littlefield.

Stoldt, C., Noble, J., Ross, M., Richardson, T., & Bonsall, J. (2013, March). Advantages and disadvantages of social media use: Perceptions of college athletics communicators. *College Sports Information Directors of America CoSIDA Strategic Communicators for College Athletics E-Digest.* Retrieved from http://www.cosida.com/media/documents/2013/3/March_2013_EDigest.pdf

Stoldt, G.C., Dittmore, S.W., & Branvold, S.E. (2012). *Sport public relations* (2nd ed.). Champaign, Ill.: Human Kinetics.

Tannenbaum, R. (2014, April 29). 18 things Rolling Stone couldn't fit into its Bill Simmons profile. *Deadspin*. Retrieved from http://deadspin.com/18-things-rolling-stone-couldnt-fit-into-its-bill-simmo-1569216946

The sportscasters: Behind the mike. (2000). *The History Channel*. (George Veras, Director).

Thornton, Patrick. (2009, March 30). Leaderboard for week of 3-30-09: Sports reporter edition. *beatblogging.org*. Retrieved from http://beatblogging.org/tag/ derrickgoold/

Tiberii, J. (2014, January 31). Whistleblower calls for reform in educating athletes at UNC. *WUNC*. Retrieved from http://wunc.org/post/whistleblower-calls-reform-educating-athletes-unc#stream/0

Time Inc. settles suit filed by former Alabama coach. (2005, October 15). *ESPN*. Retrieved from http://sports.espn.go.com/ncf/news/story?id=2186402

Top 25 U.S. consumer magazines for June 2014. (2014, August 7). *Alliance for Audited Media*. Retrieved from http://auditedmedia.com/news/blog/2014/august/top-25-us-consumer-magazines-for-june-2014.aspx

Tuchman, G. (1978). Introduction: The symbolic annihilation of women by the mass media. In G. Tuchman, A.K. Daniels, & J. Benét (Eds.), *Hearth and home: Images of women in the mass media* (pp. 3–29). New York: Oxford University Press.

Turner, April. (2012, September 19). NABJ Releases 2012 television newsroom management and network diversity census. *National Association of Black Journalists*. Retrieved from http://www.nabj.org/ news/103235/NABJ-Releases-2012-Television-Newsroom-Management-and-Network-Diversity-Census.htm

Turner, K. (2014, September 25). Ray Rice case shows perils of justice by social media. *Fansided*. Retrieved from http://thebaltimorewire.com/2014/09/25/made-example-social-media/

Twombly, Wells. (1970, November 7). Cosell will never disappoint you. *Sporting News,* 14.

University of Notre Dame Archives (n.d.). The "Four Horsemen" by Grantland Rice. *New York Herald Tribune* from October 18, 1924. Retrieved from http://archives. nd.edu/research/texts/rice.htm

Van Bibber, R. (2015, April 7). Ray Rice feels guilty about "collateral damage" he caused the NFL and Roger Godell. *SB Nation.* Retrieved from http://www.sbnation.com/ nfl/2015/4/7/8360989/ray-rice-interview-nfl-roger-goodell

Vogan, T. (2014). *Keepers of the flame: NFL Films and the rise of sports media.* Champaign, Ill.: University of Illinois Press.

Volin, B. (2015, January 22). Bill Belichick throws Tom Brady under the bus. *Boston Globe.* Retrieved from http://www.bostonglobe.com/sports/2015/01/22/ bill-belichick-message-don-blame-for-deflategate/JjltLRRkse07jqkpQK4E9I/story.html

Wagner, K. (2016, April 12). Facebook wants you streaming live video from whatever device you choose. *ReCode.* Retrieved from http://recode.net/2016/04/12/ facebook-live-video-api-launch-f8/

Wanta, W. (2006). The coverage of sports in print media. In A. A. Raney & J. Bryant (Eds.), *Handbook of Sports and Media* (pp. 105–115). Mahwah, N.J.: Lawrence Erlbaum Associates.

Wasko, Janet. (Ed.) (2010). *A companion to television.* New York: John Wiley & Sons.

Wenner, L.A. (2015). Communication and sport, where are thou? Epistemological reflections on the moment and field(s) of play. *Communication & Sport 3*(3): 247–260.

Willis, Jim. (2010). *The mind of a journalist: How reporters view themselves, their world, and their craft.* Thousand Oaks, Calif.: Sage.

Wilner, J. (2015, May 16). A dad's legacy: Warriors' Kerr guided by father's example. *The San Jose Mercury News Online.* Retrieved from http://www.mercurynews.com/warriors/ ci_28131254/dads-legacy-warriors-kerr-guided-by-fathers-example

Wilstein, S. (2001). *Associated Press Sports Writing Handbook.* New York: McGraw- Hill.

Winslow, Donald. (2012, November 29). Sports Illustrated changes color of Baylor jerseys. *National Press Photographers Association.* Retrieved from https://nppa.org/

Yen, H. (2013, January 13). Census: White majority in U.S. gone by 2043. *NBC News* online. Retrieved from http://usnews.nbcnews.com/_news/2013/06/13/18934111-census-white-majority-in-us-gone-by-2043.

Zhou, J. (2010, November 29). Where anonymity breeds contempt. *New York Times.* Retrieved from http://www.nytimes.com/2010/11/30/opinion/30zhuo.html

Zinser, L. (2011, November 9). Memo to Penn State: Ignoring a scandal doesn't make it go away. *New York Times.* Retrieved from http://www.nytimes.com/2011/11/10/sports/ penn-state-fails-a-public-relations-test-leading-off.html

Credits

PHOTOGRAPHS

Chapter 1
Photo 1.1, 1.2 Michael Peters
Photo 1.3 Courtney Bey
Photo 1.4 J. J. Cooper

Chapter 2
Photo 2.1 Robert Sutton Photography

Chapter 3
Photo 3.2 Courtney Bey
Photo 3.3 John Read

Chapter 4
Photo 4.1 Twitter
Photo 4.2 Derrick Goold
Photo 4.4 Howard Schlossberg

Chapter 5
Photo 5.1 Ray Murray
Photo 5.2 Jenni Carlson/*The Oklahoman*
Photo 5.3 Dr. Kathleen McElroy
Photo 5.4 Berry Tramel
Photo 5.5 Mark Schlabach

Chapter 6
Photo 6.6 Josh Baird

Chapter 7
Photo 7.1 Northern Illinois University
Photo 7.2 William Cohan/Joy Harris Literary Agency

Chapter 8
Photo 8.2 Carrie Anderson/WMC
Photo 8.6 Norman Seawright III

Chapter 9
Photo 9.1, 9.2 Edward Koton
Photo 9.5 Tom Ackerman

Chapter 10
Photo 10.1 a,b, 10.2, 10.3, 10.5, 10.6 Chuck Cook
Photo 10.7 Patrick Hartney

Chapter 11
Photo 11.2, 11.4 Charlotte McLoughlin

FIGURES

Chapter 2
Figure 2.1 Golf.com

Chapter 7
Figure 7.3 Memphis Redbirds
Figure 7.4 Georgia Southern University/AJ Henderson

Chapter 11
Figure 11.1 WHLT sportscaster Jeff Heager

Index